Advanced Spreadsheet Modelling with Lotus 1-2-3™

Advanced Spreadsheet Modelling with Lotus 1-2-3™

Mary Jackson
London Business School

232710

JOHN WILEY & SONS
Chichester · New York · Brisbane · Toronto · Singapore

Library of Congress Cataloging-in-Publication Data:

Jackson, Mary, 1936–
  Advanced spreadsheet modelling with Lotus 1-2-3.

  1. Lotus 1-2-3 (Computer program)   2. Electronic
spreadsheets.   3. Business—Data processing.   I. Title.
HF5548.4.L67J327   1988   005.36′9   88-5598
ISBN 0 471 91989 6 (pbk.)

British Library Cataloguing in Publication Data:

Jackson, Mary, 1936–
  Advanced spreadsheet modelling with Lotus 1-2-3.
  1. Microcomputer systems. Spreadsheet packages : Lotus 123
  I. Title
  005.36′9

  ISBN 0 471 91989 6

Printed and bound in Great Britain at the Anchor Press, Tiptree, Essex

Acknowledgements

My thanks go to participants on various LBS courses for sharing my enthusiasm for Lotus 1-2-3 and for trying out much of the material in the book. I am grateful to Angela Aubertin, Chris Beaumont, Jim James, Mike Staunton and many other people for their help and advice.

Once again, my family have borne the brunt of the book-writing and I owe them a big thank you.

1-2-3 and Lotus are registered trademarks of Lotus Development Corporation.

Contents

CHAPTER 1

Introduction

1.1 Spreadsheet modelling as a stepping stone

Managers have been quick to seize on electronic spreadsheets as useful tools for exploring accounting and financial relationships. Many managers and analysts are now aware and have used spreadsheets: indeed, spreadsheet modelling can be regarded as part of the set of basic business skills required by the younger aspiring managers of tomorrow. Now that a basic level of awareness and experience has been built up, there is increasingly more demand for what could be called advanced spreadsheet models. There seems to be considerable interest in what can be developed once you have mastered the rudiments of elementary spreadsheeting. Hence the motivation for this book.

Lotus 1-2-3 is the best known of the advanced spreadsheet programs which followed on from the original Visicalc. The first spreadsheets were mainly used as planning tools for financial analysis and budgeting. Their successors include extra features such as database management and graphics. These additions are integrated with the spreadsheet into one program. Because of the new facilities, the scope for spreadsheet modelling is now much wider than the earlier accounting applications.

Many users merely scratch the surface of their chosen software package using only a fraction of its features. They often remain unaware of its powerful capability. Certain of the commands and facilities are used extensively: for example the copying command for replicating formulae and the rapid recalculation ability which forms the backbone of much sensitivity analysis (or 'what-if'-ing). Often, the spreadsheet is used essentially as a giant calculator. However, the more recent offerings, such as Lotus 1-2-3 Release 2, provide managers with powerful general purpose modelling languages. Knowledgeable users can program their models deploying an ever-growing range of commands and special calculation routines. In fact, 1-2-3 is now widely available, easy to learn and hence an excellent tool for decision support applications.

The Personal Computer has released the present generation of youthful managers and analysts from the daunting complexity of the mainframe computing world and the spreadsheets have put powerful tools for analysis at their disposal. Now, if ever, the time must be ripe for getting across some of the ideas of quantitative analysis to the generalist audience, particularly to the newly computer literate. This requires some of the ideas to be revised and restructured to fit into the spreadsheet idiom. It may help to explain with a minimum of jargon what the quantitative techniques do and show how they can be implemented in spreadsheets.

1.2   Who the book is written for

Broadly speaking, this book is intended for people who know some of the basics of Lotus 1-2-3 (or Symphony), have had some exposure to quantitative analysis and are concerned with decision-making in a business context. This includes managers who have some working knowledge of 1-2-3, business analysts and other professionals with an MBA, accounting or similar background. The definition includes current students on MBA and similar business administration and business studies courses. It should also be of use to management consultants, corporate planners, some accountants, operational researchers and engineers working in business.

Newcomers to 1-2-3 may need to learn the rudiments before tackling the material in this text. Luckily, beginners are well provided with introductory material. Tutorial material forms part of the Lotus package and the excellent, comprehensive Instruction Manual systematically works its way through the different parts of the program describing how to use each command group in turn.

The author's earlier book, *Creative Modelling with Lotus 1-2-3* (Wiley, 1985), provides a basic grounding for those learning 1-2-3 from scratch. The present book starts where *Creative Modelling* stopped: when the fundamentals have been grasped and the modelling is becoming useful. At this stage, there is a lot to be learnt from tackling some real-life business applications. Although 1-2-3 is the spreadsheet software chosen in this text, the modelling methods should apply for other spreadsheet software.

1.3   The range of example applications

The Contents List illustrates the variety of modelling applications covered in the text. Since the term 'model' is widely used in the following Chapters, perhaps a definition is in order at this point.

The word model is used to describe a worksheet which has been set up to solve a particular problem. Essentially, a model is a calculating framework superimposed on the empty worksheet by putting data or mathematical formulae into cells in selected columns and rows, and perhaps in addition specifying settings for graphs and other procedures. Thus when the spreadsheet program is first accessed, all the cells of the 1-2-3 worksheet are empty. In contrast, when a spreadsheet model is first retrieved, some of those cells have entries. When a model is saved to disc, a record of the cell entries and settings is made. It can then be retrieved and 'slotted' back into the worksheet. (Elsewhere in the literature, 'template' is sometimes used instead of model.)

The examples of applications in the book come from many different fields. There are examples from accounting and finance, and also from sales and marketing. The models developed should be regarded as illustrations rather than ready-made, definitive solutions and they may need some tailoring to meet particular requirements.

The first example in Chapter 2 acts as an introduction to simple model building. Kilroy Kitchens require a quotation model for estimating costs and hence providing customers with quotations for renovating kitchens. This simple cost-estimating model is made the focus of an examination of the step-by-step process of model-building for decision-making. There are questions of layout and design. The model uses some of Lotus 1-2-3's special calculation procedures (known as @ functions). Above all, it attempts to provide Kilroy Kitchens with a decision-making program that is an improvement on 'back-of-the-envelope' figuring. The discussion introduces Lookup Tables which may be unfamiliar and are important in later chapters.

The next chapter on graphs in modelling describes the range of graphs available in 1-2-3 and shows how graphical presentation of data can form a springboard for analysis. The context is the forthcoming presentation by the Qwiksales Sales Manager on the performance of his sales team.

Chapters 4 and 5 concentrate on the many uses of spreadsheet modelling in financial planning and budgeting. Chapter 4 attempts to describe a variety of approaches to carrying out sensitivity analysis. Chapter 5 concentrates on the budgeting model of Ash Electronics which produces proforma financial statements.

The following Chapter on forecasting includes examples of explanatory modelling and uses the regression facilities in 1-2-3 to build a simple sales forecasting model. Fitting trend curves to sales data is also discussed together with the calculation of seasonal indices.

Decision trees can be implemented in spreadsheets and a general method of structuring such spreadsheet implementations is described in Chapter 7 on decision models. Since the inputs for decision analysis may often be contained in spreadsheets, it is useful to be able to carry out the necessary analyses in this environment.

Perhaps the most original and useful innovation in 1-2-3 is the macro. This is a means of combining several single key commands into a sequence which can then be brought into action by pressing a single key. The role of a macro is to 'automate' repetitive procedures which would otherwise be too tedious or too error prone to be a practicable proposition. Chapter 8 introduces macros and illustrates how some simple macros can relieve the user of much repetitive typing. The chapter explains how special 'menus' can be constructed, so that an automated model can include menus of its own commands. Other features include the automatic loading and execution of models for use by those not familiar with 1-2-3 terminology.

Macros are used in Chapter 9 on Simulation Models. Here the sequences of repeated sampling in the simulations are driven by macros. Thus it is true to say that macros extend the scope of the spreadsheet modelling. They can be incorporated wherever they improve the performance and practicability of a model. The simulations for Alexsville and Novaduct in Chapter 9 could not be handled realistically in 1-2-3 without the addition of macros. Perhaps it should be added that more sophisticated macros could be written for these applications. However, the emphasis in this text is on developing macro writing ability in those readers who are relatively new to this area.

Finally, at the end of the book, a short appendix summarizes the most frequently used 1-2-3 commands for use as a quick reference source.

1.4   How to use the book

Each chapter is written round one or more business examples of a practical problem where a model can be developed to get some answers. Many sections of the text are written for hands-on use with Lotus 1-2-3 and a Personal Computer.

Like *Creative Modelling*, the book comes with a disc (referred to as the ASM disc) containing the 1-2-3 datafiles for the models described. This approach seems to be an effective way of learning how to model-build with 1-2-3. To reduce the keying-in burden, the datafiles on disc provide data for an exercise or the starting model. This allows the use of a range of more developed models than would be the case if each application were to be developed from scratch. The structure and formulae are always documented and the logic in each of the models is explained in detail. However, since some familiarity with 1-2-3 is assumed, it is considered unnecessary to describe every keystroke.

As far as possible, 'generic' models have been developed in the context of the different types of problem. The objective is to build spreadsheet models capable of generalization to fit a wider range of problems. If the process of model-building is grasped, it should be possible to extend or modify models for other similar-seeming types of problem. Happily, one of the great advantages of the spreadsheet format is that modification and amendment are extremely easy. The aim of the book is to encourage the use of spreadsheet modelling as a personal modelling language, rather than to present the user with solutions on disc.

1.5 Spreadsheet techniques

The documentation that comes with Lotus 1-2-3 is extremely clear and comprehensive and removes the need for a text such as this to duplicate its admirable effort. Although called 'spreadsheet techniques', the focus in this section is rather different. The objective is to attempt to outline some of the particular techniques and facilities that characterize the more advanced use of 1-2-3. It is of course assumed that the familiar 1-2-3 user has no particular difficulty in entering information into the spreadsheet and has a clear grasp of the command structure of 1-2-3.

Firstly, some thought must be given to layout when developing a spreadsheet model. In many of the models developed in the following chapters, there are assumptions, for example the discount rate, and then calculations that follow from the assumed values, for example the net present value of an investment with the specified discount rate. One of the important principles of spreadsheet layout is to separate the assumptions from the calculations. The assumptions (called planning values) should be grouped together in one area of the worksheet. All cell entries that use the assumptions should contain formulae that use the assumptions by referencing the appropriate planning value cells. In this way all uses of the assumptions will be linked to the planning value cells. Any changes to the planning values will radiate out to all linked cells and an entirely accurate recalculation of the worksheet will result.

Thus the practice of separating planning values and computed values ensures that valid 'what-if' analysis can be carried out. It also enables the powerful Move command to be employed to restructure the spreadsheet layout without too many unforeseen complications to the spreadsheet logic. The Move command enables the worksheet layout to be drastically rejigged, leaving 1-2-3 the task of adjusting all the formulae to reflect new cell addresses. Thus the Move command coupled with the Worksheet Insert/Delete sequence for inserting/deleting rows and columns give great flexiblity when it comes to changing the layout of an emerging worksheet. (These points are illustrated more fully in the next chapter.)

Another facility that makes later restructuring of layout easy is the range-naming facility. If a range is 'named', thereafter it can be referred to in formulae and commands by its name. In addition, the use of range names in macro routines facilitates later editing problems. Also, since range names can be used as suggestive variable names, writing macros becomes much more akin to conventional programming. The importance of progressing from using cell addresses to range names cannot be stressed too highly for advanced spreadsheet work.

Last but not least, there is the use of the cell pointer. Access to cells in the worksheet involves use of the cell pointer. This is controlled by the arrow keys (or pointer movement keys). One of the important skills in spreadsheet modelling is to master 'pointing', that is the use of the pointer, particularly in keying in formulae and using 1-2-3 commands.

For example, it is often necessary to specify ranges and formulae in the text in terms of cell addresses, such as R4..S7. Wherever possible, these cell addresses should be entered into 1-2-3 using pointing rather than typing; that is the user should attempt to point to cell R4, then 'anchor' by pressing the fullstop key, then move the pointer to cell S7. It is clearly very long-winded to describe this pointing procedure and much more concise to specify the range as R4..S7. Nevertheless, the evidence is that fewer mistakes occur with pointing than with typing. Another allied skill is that of using the 'Page Up', 'Page Down', the 'Tab' and 'End' keys to speed up pointer movement around a large spreadsheet by 'jumping' in 'pages' and moving rapidly in a single operation to the end of an active area of the worksheet. These are skills that are difficult to write about in a text but should be encouraged in practical work.

1.6 Software and hardware considerations

There are some differences between the earlier and later versions of 1-2-3. This book is based on the IBM PC implementation of 1-2-3, Release 2. This later version of 1-2-3 has a much improved and extended macro writing language, and also enhanced facilities for data analyses such as regression. Although the material in the book, particularly on macros and regression, depends on features in Release 2, users of the earlier version of 1-2-3 should be able to implement many of the models. The absence of Release 2 features may cause minor differences but this should not get in the way of their understanding of the text.

With reference to hardware, there are very few differences between the versions of 1-2-3 sold for the different types of Personal Computer. Each version of the program has its own Reference Manual, so any differences are properly documented.

In general a printer is not required to cope with the material in this book. Only one of the examples in the book (AUTOMAIL) is intended to generate printed output. However, it is handy to be able to print out interesting results and graphs. The most flexible arrangement with graphs is to be able to print them directly from screen, using the PrintScreen key. The *1-2-3 Getting Started (Installation) Manual* describes the printer interfacing arrangements provided by the program and also refers the reader to his own printer User's Manual.

CHAPTER 2

Estimation Models

2.1 Introduction

Estimation and pricing models implemented in spreadsheets can be used to considerable effect not only to reduce calculation labour but also to improve accuracy, control and speed of response. In this chapter, we look at one particular quotation model. The discussion follows the model through various stages of its development and demonstrates how a simple working model can be incrementally improved.

In fact, this type of estimation and pricing is an excellent application for spreadsheet modelling. The context is producing a quotation (or job estimate) for modernizing a kitchen. It is convenient to store all the factual information on rates of pay, discount structures, proposed margins, etc., in the worksheet. This information can be updated easily as and when necessary. The formulae for the various costs are straightforward— 'back-of-the-envelope' standard—and a working quotation model can easily be improved and embellished as more information about the accuracy of the estimates becomes available.

2.2 Example: quotation model for Kilroy Kitchens

Andrew Kilroy runs a small firm in the kitchen refurbishment business. Kilroy Kitchens (KK for short) supply customers with modernized kitchens, installing all the new kitchen appliances and equipment for an inclusive price. The nature of the business is such that the conversion rate of quotations to orders is very low and as a consequence KK need a slick estimating procedure. The procedure must also be very reliable because there is little opportunity to change the price once a quotation has been made.

The quotation for a kitchen job depends on making reasonably accurate estimates of the various costs involved: the cost of appliances and other building materials used, the cost of labour, travelling costs and the times involved. In particular, the man-hours required for carpentry, electrical and plumbing work and the redecoration costs must be estimated. It may also be possible to take advantage of discounts available on some of the appliances chosen.

Previously, estimating and quoting for jobs has been done on an *ad hoc* 'back-of-the-envelope' basis. However, in several cases recently, the quoted price turned out to be on the low side and, in consequence, produced little profit for Kilroy. In another case, KK's representative who made the quotation forgot to include an allowance for travelling costs and the use of a vehicle. For a variety of reasons, Andrew Kilroy has recently invested in a spreadsheet package and a Personal Computer. One of his plans is to improve the quality of the estimating process by building a simple quotation model for himself. If successful, this model will form the basis of future quotations made by KK representatives.

The objective of the exercise in the following sections is therefore to help Andrew develop a flexible model. This is done in stages to illustrate the incremental approach to model-building. One of the pleasures of working with 1-2-3 is this facility for 'proto-typing', that is building simple working models, which can go through many stages of improvement as they are used.

2.3 Model layout

One approach is to lay out the estimating model as shown in Figure 2.1, so that there are separate areas in the spreadsheet for data input, for the assumptions (often referred to as 'planning values') and for the cost-estimation calculations. The 'input' part of the model will contain the details of the job. These can only be filled in after a representative from KK has visited the customer and gauged his requirements. The 'assumptions' part will contain all the known facts about labour rates, travelling costs and proposed margins for ensuring that the job pays for itself and contributes to profit. These values remain the same from job to job, but will need to be updated from time to time. The 'cost-estimation' part will consist of all the intermediate calculations of costs that lead to the pricing of the job, together with some estimate of its profit contribution. Figure 2.1 shows a further area of the worksheet where the resulting quotation is displayed. This area could form a useful summary of the actual quotation details and could possibly be detached from the rest of the model to send to the customer.

The customer information required by the model is provided by the KK representative on his return from a customer visit. He records details of the job, such as the types and makes of appliances the customer requires and their retail prices. He estimates the labour content of the job, in particular the total man-hours required, the number of men needed for the job, together with the total duration. He also notes down the distance of the house from Kilroy's premises. This information is entered into the appropriate cells of the 'input' area of the spreadsheet.

To cost the job, estimates must be made of the main cost elements, namely:

Cost of the Appliances
Cost of other Materials
Labour Costs
Travel Costs—both Vehicle and Travel Time Costs

To complete the quotation, mark-ups are added to the costs of the Appliances, Labour and other Materials. Finally, a Profit Margin is added for the overall job.

```
KILROY KITCHENS:           |
------------               |
                           |
Details of Job:            |    Quotation:
------------------         |    ---------
Appliances(Retail)         |    Client No:
Discount rate              |    Date:
Labour (hours)             |
Job Duration(days)         |    Price:
Men                        |      + VAT
Distance (miles)           |                    ------------
                           |    Total Price:
                           |
___ ___ ___ ___ ___ ___ ___|___ ___ ___ ___ ___ ___ ___
                           |
Assumptions:               |    Cost Estimate:
---------------------------|    ---------------------------
Labour rate:               |    Appliances at Cost
 Paid/Hr                   |    Total Labour Cost
 Factor Gross              |    Materials Cost
Materials:                 |    Travel Costs
 Factor Matls.             |       vehicle
Transport:                 |       travel time
 Rate/mile                 |
 Hours/mile                |    Total Direct Cost
                           |
Margins:                   |    Full Cost
------------               |
Mark up (Appl.)            |    Profit
Mark up (Lab.)             |    V A T
Mark up (Matls.)           |
Profit                     |    Price
                           |
V A T rate                 |
```

Figure 2.1   Worksheet layout for the Kilroy quotation model

2.4   Estimating costs

Figure 2.2 shows a first shot at a quotation model for Kilroy. A quotation is given for a kitchen job with appliances costing £1000 and an estimated labour content of 60 man-hours. The total price for the job with VAT is quoted as £2329.

As discussed in the previous section, there are separate areas for the input and assumptions, etc. The range A4..C11 headed Details of Job is the 'input' area, and the 'quotation' area is adjacent in cells E4..G11. The assumptions are set out below the job details in the cell range A16..C34, and the cost estimates are in the adjacent area, namely cell range E16..G38. For completeness, the datafile called KILROY1, of which Figure 2.2 is a printout, is given on your ASM disc. You may wish to retrieve this file and explore it as you read through the following description of its structure and content. To do this, use the command sequence:

/ File Retrieve KILROY1

Details of job

Referring to Figure 2.2, the details of the job as reported by the KK salesperson are entered in the cell range C6..C11. For the initial model, these are restricted to the retail price of the appliances and any discount, the labour content of the job and the distance of the customer from Kilroy's premises.

Assumptions

The range A16..C34 contains the assumptions used in estimating the costs. The labour rate in cell C19 is the rate paid per hour to the men. This has to be multiplied by the 'grossing-up' factor of 1.5, shown as 150 per cent in cell C20, to cover National Insurance, holiday pay and other employment costs. The resulting product is the gross rate of pay.

The Materials Factor summarizes Kilroy's experience in costing the other materials used on a job. Usually, they amount to about 80 per cent of the labour cost. The Materials Factor is therefore stored as an assumption in cell C22.

To work out the travelling costs for the job it is necessary to know the cost of using a Kilroy van on the job. Thus the Rate per mile and the Hours per mile figures for the vehicle are entered as assumptions in cells C24 and C25.

Cost estimates

The calculations to produce the cost estimate for the job are set out in the range E18..G38. Prime cost estimates for each job element appear at the top and, moving down column G, these are progressively converted into full costs and eventually a price.

Appliances at cost The retail price for the appliances chosen by the customer together with the discount determine this term. The appliance cost is: Retail Price (in C6) less the discount (in C7) given by the maker. Hence, the formula in cell G18 is therefore:

+C6*(1-C7)

Total labour cost Labour costs depend on the rates of pay and the man-hours for the job. From the estimated labour content in hours in cell C8 and the pay rate per hour (in cell C19), grossed up by the factor of 1.5 (in cell C20), the formula is:

+C8*C19*C20

```
              A        B     C      D       E          F      G
 1 KILROY KITCHENS:
 2 ------------
 3
 4 Details of Job:                        Quotation:
 5 ------------------                     ---------
 6 Appliances(Retail)      £1,000         Client No:
 7 Discount rate               35%        Date:                07-Dec
 8 Labour (hours)           60
 9 Job Duration(days)        3            Price:               £2,025
10 Men                       3             + VAT                £304
11 Distance (miles)         20                                ------------
                                          Total Price:         £2,329


15 KILROY KITCHENS:
16 Assumptions:                           Cost Estimate:              16
17 ----------- --------------------       ---------------------------- 17
18 Labour rate:                           Appliances at Cost    £650   18
19  Paid/Hr                £3.50          Total Labour Cost     £315   19
20  Factor Gross            150%          Materials Cost        £252   20
21 Materials:                             Travel Costs
22  Factor Matls.           80%             vehicle             £72   22
23 Transport:                               travel time         £95   23
24  Rate/mile              £0.60
25  Hours/mile              0.05          Total Direct Cost   £1,384   25

27 Margins:                               Mark up (Appl.)       £163   27
28 ------------                           Mark up (Lab.)         £79   28
29 Mark up (Appl.)         25.00%         Mark up (Matls.)       £63   29
30 Mark up (Lab.)          25.00%
31 Mark up (Matls.)        25.00%         Total Mark up         £304   31
32 Profit                  20.00%
                                          Full Cost           £1,688   33
34 V A T rate              15.00%
35                                        Profit                £338   35
36                                        V A T                 £304   36
37                                                                     37
38                                        Price               £2,329   38
```

Figure 2.2   First try at quotation model (KILROY1 on disc)

Materials cost Experience suggests that these vary directly with labour costs (in G19). KK estimate materials usage as 80 per cent (in C22) of labour costs, giving the formula:

+G19*C22

Travel Costs There are two costs, one concerned with the cost of running the KK vehicle and one to do with the time spent travelling to the job, which has to be paid for at the labour rate. Dealing first with the Vehicle costs, there will be two journeys each day, and there are estimates of the distance of the job from base (in cell C11) and the duration of the job in days (in C9). The cost per mile (£0.60 per mile) is set out as an assumption (in C24). Hence, the expression for the Vehicle cost in cell G22 is:

2*C11*C9*C24

The cost of Travelling time depends on the number of men travelling (in C10) and the journey time. In turn, the journey time depends on the assumed speed of the vehicle, which is an assumption stored in cell C25 in terms of Hours per mile (in fact, 0.05 hours per mile). The formula for Travel time is thus:

2*C11*C9*C25*C10

and the cost in cell G23 is therefore:

2*C11*C9*C25*C10*C19*C20

Total direct costs These are obtained by summing the appliances at cost, the labour cost, the materials cost and the travel costs, so the formula in cell G25 is:

@SUM(G18...G23)

(*Note*: This is one of the many special calculation routines in 1-2-3, called @functions. The @SUM routine computes the sum of all the entries in the range specified in the brackets—here the range G18..G23).

Mark-ups These come directly from the margins assumptions in cells C29 to C31. Mark-up is defined as follows: if goods are bought for £100 and sold for £155, the mark-up is 55 per cent. Hence, the Mark-up for appliances in cell G27 is given by:

+G18*C29

Full cost The full cost for the job is the Total Direct Costs plus the Mark-ups; that is the formula in cell G33 is:

+G25+G31

Profit and VAT The profit margin is an assumption (in cell C32) and the current VAT rate is another (in cell C34). Hence the formula for Profit is:

+C32*G33

and for VAT it is:

+C34*(G33+G35)

Price The price for the job is the Full Cost together with the Profit and the computed VAT; hence in cell C38 the formula is:

+G33+G35+G36

The quotation area of the model shows the price before and after VAT quoted. This part of the worksheet could be used when sending the quotation to the customer.

This then represents a first pass at a quotation model for Kilroy. If you have not yet loaded and explored the model KILROY1, you should do so at this stage, before moving on to the next section. As a KK salesperson, you can try out different values for the appliances cost, labour content and distance that is the entries in cells C6 to C11 under the heading Details of the Job. Like Andrew Kilroy, you can gauge the effect of changing more important assumptions such as the various margins.

2.5   Improving the quotation model

Having built the model, it is possible to modify and improve it in various ways. Since our first model has a modular structure, it is easy to change the blocks around with the Move command. When blocks of the worksheet are 'moved', 1-2-3 takes care of changing all the cell addresses in the formulae. This enables us to restructure the worksheet to 'hide' the model logic from view and to restrict the user to enter data only in the 'input' area of the worksheet. The objective is to provide protection against inadvertently overwriting the model logic.

In practice, KK deal with appliances from several manufacturers and the discounts available differ. This information can be included in the model by using a Lookup Table which holds the discount information for the different manufacturers. For example, suppose there are four different manufacturers. Figure 2.3 shows the information on discounts stored in tabular form. The table range has been named APP. Suppose the manufacturer's identification number is stored in cell K7 (with the Details of the Job) and suppose the entry is 2. Then 1-2-3 works horizontally across the Lookup Table until the value 2 is encountered. In subsequent use of the function:

	A	B	C	D	E
2 6 Lookup Table:			Range of cells named APP		
2 7 Appliance Discount (APP)					
2 8 -------			-------------		
2 9 Make -->		1	2	3	4
3 0 Discount		0.3	0.35	0.4	0.55
3 1 -------					

Figure 2.3   Lookup Table for appliance manufacturers' discounts

@HLOOKUP(K7,APP,1)

the entry in the cell below (that is one row below) will be returned as the value. (If you have not used Lookup Tables before, you may wish to study the section on this topic at the end of the Chapter.)

The changes suggested in the previous paragraphs will now be made to the model KILROY1. It is worth following through these moves within 1-2-3 on your PC if the Move command is new to you and also the use of Lookup Tables. The detailed steps to modify the KILROY1 model are:

1. Point to cell A1 and move the 'input' and 'quotation' areas A1..G14 to the next page across; that is choose:

   / Move A1..G14   to I1

2. Similarly, point to cell A15 and choose:

   / Move A15..H38   to A1

   to relocate the 'assumptions' and 'cost estimates' areas to the top left-hand corner of the worksheet.

Note how the formulae in the worksheet adjust; for example the formula for Appliance Cost in cell G4 becomes:

+K6*(1-K7)

3. Add the Lookup Table shown in Figure 2.3 to the cells A26..E31 positioning the make and discount figures in the cells B29..E30.
4. Use / Range Name Create to attach the name APP to the cell range B29..E30.
5. Alter the label in cell I7 to Manufacturer; enter the value 2 in cell K7. Reset the Range Format to remove the percentage format.
6. Adjust the formula for Appliances at Cost in cell G4 to become:

   +K6*(1-@HLOOKUP(K7,APP,1))

The model should now tie up with Figure 2.4. The quotation has not changed but will do so if different manufacturers' identification numbers (in the range 1 to 4) are tried.

Once the model is built, it is sensible to keep the assumptions and model logic safely guarded so that it is not inadvertently overwritten when data is input. Two 1-2-3 facilities help in this process—the Worksheet Titles command which allows formulae to be tucked out of sight and the Protection facility that limits the cells into which a user can enter data.

The steps are:

1. Move the pointer so that cell H1 is in the top left-hand position on the screen. Then point to the adjacent cell I1 and choose:

	A	B	C	D	E	F	G	H	I	J	K	L	M	N	O
1	KILROY KITCHENS:								KILROY KITCHENS:						
2	Assumptions:				Cost Estimate:							Quotation:			
3		------							---------			---------			
4	Labour rate:				Appliances at Cost		£650		Details of Job:						
5	Paid/Hr		£3.50		Total Labour Cost		£315		-----------						
6	Factor Gross		150%		Materials Cost		£252		Appliances(Retail)		£1,000	Client No:			
7	Materials:				Travel Costs				Manufacturer		2				
8	Factor Matls.		80%			vehicle	£72		Labour (hours)		60	Date:			07-Dec
9	Transport:					travel time	£95		Job Duration(days)		3				
10	Rate/mile		£0.60						Men		3				
11	Hours/mile		0.05		Total Direct Cost		£1,384		Distance (miles)		20				
12															
13	Margins:				Mark up (Appl.)		£163					Price:			£2,025
14		-------			Mark up (Lab.)		£79						+ VAT		£304
15	Mark up (Appl.)		25.00%		Mark up (Matls.)		£63								
16	Mark up (Lab.)		25.00%												
17	Mark up (Matls.)		25.00%		Total Mark up		£304					Total Price:			£2,329
18	Profit		20.00%												
19					Full Cost		£1,688								
20	V A T		15.00%												
21					Profit		£338								
22					V A T		£304								
23															
24					Price		£2,329								
25															
26	Lookup Table:														
27	Appliance Discount (APP)														
28		-------													
29	Make -->	1	2	3	4										
30	Discount	0.3	0.35	0.4	0.55										
31		-------													

Figure 2.4   Second try at quotation model (KILROY2 on disk)

/ Worksheet Titles Vertical

to hide the columns A to G to the left.
2. First Unprotect cells K6 to K11 with:

/ Range Unprotect K6..K11

3. Then switch on the protection with:

/ Worksheet Global Protection Enable

These three steps ensure that the user can enter values into the Unprotected cells in range K6 to K11 but nowhere else. Try it out and notice 1-2-3's response. (Get out of the error message by pressing the Escape key).

At this stage, the quotation model should tie up with datafile KILROY2 on your ASM disc. To explore how the model KILROY2 works in detail, you will need to 'unfreeze' the titles with:

/ Worksheet Titles Clear

and remove the global protection with:

/ Worksheet Global Protection Disable

2.6 Further refinements

Further reflection on the quotation model suggests that since labour costs directly and indirectly have a sizeable effect on the final quotation, more accurate representation would improve the model. It might be worth while to attempt to estimate the labour content of the job more precisely. First of all, different grades of labourer are required on the job, for example carpenters, gas fitters, electricians, painters, etc., and their rates of pay may differ. Secondly, the number of labour hours may depend on the type of house in which the kitchen refurbishment is taking place. For example, the modernization of a Victorian kitchen could require more labour than for a post-war house. Thirdly, the decorative condition of the house may also affect the labour content. It is usually the case that the house type and age have most effect on the work of carpenters, gas fitters and electricians, whereas obviously it is the decorative condition that most affects the painters.

It is easy to include this type of information in the quotation model. Firstly, rather than fix a single figure for labour, the KK representative can estimate the job in terms of 'standard times' for the work to be undertaken by carpenters, gas fitters, electricians, painters, etc. Secondly, he records details of the type of house and its decorative condition when he visits the property. A simple scale from 1 to 5, say, can be devised to measure the degree to which the house is difficult or easy to work on. The scale can then be converted to a cost 'uplift' factor to reflect the effect on costs of type and decorative condition. These scales are best handled (like the discounts on appliances) via Lookup Tables.

Figure 2.5 shows how these suggestions can be implemented in a third (and final!) quotation model for Kilroy. In addition, there is more 'managerial' information for Andrew Kilroy in this model concerning the contribution that each job is making to profits. The accompanying datafile KILROY3 is on your ASM disc and should be retrieved at this point.

The main changes are the inclusion of standard time estimates for the different types of labourer in cells M10 to M13 and their associated labour rates in cells C6 to C10.

The inputs for Type of House and Decorative Condition in cells M8 and M9 respectively are used with Lookup Tables called TYPE in rows 42 and 43 and COND in rows 47 and 48. (The Lookup Tables at the bottom of Figure 2.5 show how this information may be laid out in the worksheet.)

Cost estimates

The data on type of house and decorative condition affects the estimated hours put in by the carpenters, gas fitters, etc. This has been set out in a new column (H) under the 'cost estimates' heading. Thus for carpenters, the estimated time in hours (in cell H6) is obtained by scaling up the standard time (in cell M10) by the factor:

@HLOOKUP(M8,TYPE,1)

where M8 contains the 'score' on the house-type scale from 1 to 5.

Similarly, the entry in cell H9 for estimated hours for the painters is obtained by scaling up the standard time (in cell M13) by the factor:

@HLOOKUP(M9,COND,1)

where M9 contains the 'score' on the decorative-condition scale from 1 to 5.

In this model, the amount of labourer time (in cell H10) is estimated as half the total tradesman-hours (@SUM(H6..H9)/2).

Cost of Travel time   The only difference is that the time is costed using an average rate obtained by dividing the Total Labour Cost (in G11) by the total hours (in H11).

Contribution   A calculation of the Contribution is included. This is Price for the job (in G30) less VAT (in G28), less Full Cost (in G17) plus the VAT recovered on the purchase of the appliances (C25*G4). The Contribution is also expressed as a percentage of the Price for the job (in cell G33).

KILROY3 contains the quotation (in cell Q12) for the 'easiest' type of house (Postwar scaled as 5) and one in the best decorative condition (scaled as 5). The quotation is not very different from the figures given by the two previous models. Try altering these scores from 5 to 1 and watch the effect on the price for the job. In particular, look at the effect on the man-hours shown in column H.

As with the previous model, KILROY2, the model logic can now be hidden by using the Worksheet Titles Vertical sequence. Further, after specifying that only cells M6 to M16 and Q6 are to be unprotected, the protection can be 'enabled'. Then when a

```
           A      B     C      D      E         F     G    H  I      J       K      L     M         O       P      Q
        KILROY KITCHENS:                                         |KILROY KITCHENS:
        Assumptions:                     Cost Estimate:          |
        ---------                        --------------          |
 4 Labour rate:                          Appliances at Cost  £650|Details of Job:              Quotation:
 5 Paid/Hr                                                 (Hrs) |---------------              ---------
 6 Carpenter      £3.50                     Carpenter      £53  10|Appliances (Retail) £1,000  Client No:
 7 Gas Fitter     £3.80                     Gas Fitter     £57  10|Manufacturer            2   Date:           07-Dec
 8 Electrician    £3.80                     Electrician    £57  10|Type of House           5
 9 Painter        £3.30                     Painter        £50  10|Decorative Condition    5   Price:          £1,979
10 Labourer       £2.80                     Labourer       £84  20|Carpenter Hrs.         10     + VAT           £297
11 Factor Gross   150%                   Total Labour Cost £300  60|Gas Fitter Hrs.       10                  ---------
12 Materials:                            Materials Cost   £240   |Electrician Hrs.       10   Total Price:    £2,276
13 Factor Matls.  80%                    Travel Costs           |Painter Hrs.           10
14 Transport:                               vehicle       £72   |Job Duration (days)     3
15 Rate/mile      £0.60                      travel time   £90   |Men (average per day)   3
16 Hours/mile     0.05                                          |Distance (Miles)       20
                                         Total Direct Cost £1,352|
18 Margins:                              Mark up (Appl.)  £163   |
   ---------                             Mark up (Lab.)    £75   |
20 Mark up (Appl.)  25.00%               Mark up (Matls)   £60   |
21 Mark up (Lab.)   25.00%                                      |
22 Mark up (Matls.) 25.00%               Total Mark up    £298   |
23 Profit           20.00%                                      |
                                                                |
25 V A T rate       15.00%               Full Cost       £1,650  |
                                                                |
27                                       Profit           £330   |
28                                       V A T            £297   |
                                                                |
30                                       Price          £2,276   |
                                                                |
32                                       Contribution     £725
33 Lookup Tables:                        Contn. (%)      31.85%
34 a) Appliance Discount (APP)
   ------------------------------------------------------
36 Make -->     1      2      3      4
37 Discount    0.3   0.35    0.4    0.55
   ------------------------------------------------------
39 b) Type of House (TYPE)
   ------------------------------------------------------
              Vict.  Edw.   20's   30's  Post war
42 Score -->    1      2      3      4      5
43 Factor      1.4    1.3    1.2    1.1     1
   ------------------------------------------------------
   c) Decorative Condition (COND)
   ------------------------------------------------------
47 Score -->    1      2      3      4      5
48 Factor      1.8    1.6    1.4    1.2     1
49 ------------------------------------------------------
```

Figure 2.5   Third try at quotation model (KILROY3 on disk)

Kilroy representative uses the model, he merely enters the Details of Job section and gets the required quotation. There is no danger of accidentally changing the spreadsheet formulae.

It would be relatively easy to extend this model so it actually printed out a quotation for the customer. The full name and address would be added to the Details of Job section and a suitable standard letter would be placed at some convenient location in the spreadsheet. A Macro could be written to copy the name and address together with selected data from columns G and H onto the standard letter. (The 'automated letter writer', AUTOMAIL, developed in Chapter 8 on macro models works in much the same way.) KK should of course check over the letter before final printing and despatch.

The main emphasis in the forgoing discussion of Kilroy's quotation model has been building a suitable model in 1-2-3. Naturally, whatever the modelling language chosen, the quotations will be useless if the assumptions are wrong. Therefore, it is critical that any quotation made by the model should be checked out against the results that are actually achieved. It is not sufficient to check just the total cost since there may be offsetting errors that cause the model to appear to be better than it really is. The right approach is to compare actuals versus estimates for each type of cost. For example, the estimated travel costs should be checked by collecting actual figures for vehicle use and cost, and travel time and cost. Similarly, data should be collected to verify the scaling-up factors used to reflect the type of house and decorative condition.

2.7   Note on Lookup Tables

The Kilroy model makes use of several horizontal Lookup Tables, using the special function @HLOOKUP. 1-2-3 also has a Vertical Lookup function @VLOOKUP. Since these functions are useful in many contexts, they are explained more fully in this section. The special functions @HLOOKUP and @VLOOKUP enable you to extract an entry (by interpolation if necessary) from a table of data by specifying its row or column reference.

To illustrate how this works look first at the table in rows 3 to 5 of Figure 2.6, which shows the price per item achieved by buying different quantities from two different manufacturers. Thus, if we buy 50 items the price will be 15 for manufacturer 1 and 14 for manufacturer 2. The prices will pertain as the quantity increases until it gets to 100, when the lower price of 12 starts.

	A	B	C	D	E	F	G	H	
1	Quantity	53							
2					Price	per	item		
3	Index row	Quantity		10	20	50	100	500	Table range
4		Manufacturer	1	20	18	15	12	10	D3..H5 also
5			2	18	16	14	12	10	named PRICE
6									

Figure 2.6   Lookup Table for unit price when buying in quantity

The @HLOOKUP function is the mechanism for extracting the price from this type of table. If the quantity to be bought is in cell B1, then the expression:

@HLOOKUP(B1,D3..H5,1)

will select the price per item for the first manufacturer. Notice that @HLOOKUP has three 'arguments': the 'entry' cell (here the quantity in cell B1), the table range D3..H5 and the number of rows down (here one row down).

Similarly, if the table range is named PRICE (that is the sequence / Range Name Create is used to attach the 'name' PRICE to cell range D3..H5), the expression:

@HLOOKUP(B1,PRICE,2)

will select the price per item for the second manufacturer.

The horizontal Lookup Table compares the value in B1 to each cell in the top (or index) row in the table called PRICE. When it finds a cell that matches the contents of B1, it stops moving horizontally and moves down the column the number of rows specified in the Lookup function (1 or 2 in our case).

In the illustration in Figure 2.6, there is no cell in the index row that exactly matches the quantity in B1 (53). @HLOOKUP searches the index row until it finds a value that is larger than 53 (namely the entry 100 in cell F3). It then moves back to cell E3 (which in effect contains the largest number that is less than or equal to the entry in cell B1). It moves down column E the number of rows specified in the third argument of the function. (Notice that for @HLOOKUP to work properly, the cells in the index row must contain entries of increasing value.)

The vertical Lookup @VLOOKUP is exactly comparable working down the columns to find the row whose index column entry is the highest value less than or equal to the entry in the function. The syntax is therefore:

@VLOOKUP(entry cell address, range of table, number of columns across)

The @VLOOKUP function is used extensively in Chapter 9 on simulation models.

CHAPTER 3

Graphs for Data Presentation and Modelling

3.1 Introduction

In this chapter, we shall be examining the contribution 1-2-3 can make to the problem of presenting sales statistics. It is relatively simple to set up individual graphs with 1-2-3. By keeping vital sales information in a spreadsheet file, this can form the basis of a graphical presentation for a variety of purposes. The discussion that follows is intended also to act as a thorough review of the graphics facilities in 1-2-3.

The main advantages of holding vital sales statistics in a 1-2-3 spreadsheet file, as compared to holding them solely within conventional computer programs, are as follows:

1. Prior to detailed analysis, different sets of data can be examined and compared visually. This is best done by putting the sets of data in adjacent columns or rows.
2. A wide range of statistical functions are available so sophisticated techniques normally only found in specialist programs can be brought to bear on the analysis.
3. The different ways of formatting the worksheet display together with the very extensive graphics capability enable really professional presentation material to be produced.

As well as data presentation, graphs can be used for detecting relationships. The last two sections of the chapter illustrate how visual inspection of data can often be a springboard for hypothesizing about relationships and trying out different models.

3.2 Example: Qwiksales plc presentation

Joe Rowton, Sales Director at Qwiksales, is preparing to make his annual presentation to his managers. He plans to explain what went on last year, hand out bouquets and black marks and then announce next year's targets. This year he wants the presentation to be rather more pointed and specific than in previous years when there was a tendency for people to be overwhelmed by masses of figures. These, if anything, obscured rather than emphasized the points he was making. Therefore, this year, Joe plans to analyse the basic data and produce the visual aids using 1-2-3.

Figure 3.1 contains the data on which the presentation is to be based. This shows actual sales and targets for the previous twelve months, divided into the four UK and three export territories into which the firm is organised. Monthly sales figures run from column C to column O: rows 8 to 11 contain sales for the four UK territories and rows

	A	B	C	D	E	F	G	H
1	SALES ANALYSIS: for QWIKSALES plc							
2	===============================							
3			a) Sales versus Target for 1987:					
5	1987			ACTUAL MONTHLY SALES in 1987		ACTUAL MONTHLY SALES in 1987		
6	ANNUAL TOTALS	1987	TERRITORY	SALES	SALES	SALES	SALES	SALES
7	--------------		(U.K.)	Jan-87	Feb-87	Oct-87	Nov-87	Dec-87
8	£313,290		1	£31,145	£30,353	£24,354	£26,195	£25,443
9	£317,125		2	£24,325	£24,500	£28,365	£26,810	£27,310
10	£627,645		3	£51,605	£59,500	£52,360	£49,560	£52,595
11	£610,340		4	£23,555	£25,610	£61,555	£69,210	£64,210
12	£1,868,400		TOTAL (U.K.)	£130,630	£139,963	£166,634	£171,775	£169,558
			(EXPORT)					
15	£354,365		10	£14,325	£19,500	£38,365	£46,810	£47,310
16	£208,025		11	£4,325	£24,500	£22,365	£16,810	£12,310
17	£410,018		12	£34,325	£44,500	£12,346	£22,810	£27,310
18	£972,408		TOTAL (EXP.)	£52,975	£88,500	£73,076	£86,430	£86,930
20	£2,840,808		GRAND TOTAL	£183,605	£228,463	£239,710	£258,205	£256,488
22	TARGET TOTALS	1987	TERRITORY	TARGET	TARGET	TARGET	TARGET	TARGET
23	--------------		(U.K.)	Jan-87	Feb-87	Oct-87	Nov-87	Dec-87
24	£367,500		1	£32,500	£32,500	£30,000	£30,000	£30,000
25	£302,500		2	£24,000	£24,000	£26,000	£26,000	£26,000
26	£660,000		3	£50,000	£50,000	£55,000	£55,000	£55,000
27	£675,000		4	£45,000	£45,000	£55,000	£55,000	£55,000
28	£2,005,000		TOTAL (U.K.)	£151,500	£151,500	£166,000	£166,000	£166,000
			(EXPORT)					
31	£300,000		10	£10,000	£10,000	£40,000	£40,000	£40,000
32	£276,000		11	£18,000	£18,000	£25,000	£25,000	£25,000
33	£480,000		12	£40,000	£40,000	£40,000	£40,000	£40,000
34	£1,056,000		TOTAL (EXP.)	£68,000	£68,000	£105,000	£105,000	£105,000
36	£3,061,000		GRAND TOTAL	£219,500	£219,500	£271,000	£271,000	£271,000

Figure 3.1   Qwiksales monthly sales and targets in datafile QWIK1

15 to 17 for the Export territories. Annual sales totals for each of the seven territories are given in column A. (These have been calculated using the special function @SUM to sum the appropriate row entries.) The upper section of spreadsheet (rows 5 to 20) contains actual sales results: the lower section (rows 22 to 36) contains the Targets for sales, which were set at the start of the year.

The aim of the exercise is therefore to help Joe get his sales data into suitable shape for the presentation. This divides up into two main stages: data analysis and setting up the graphs for the presentation. Section 3.3 describes a few simple analyses that Joe might wish to perform and Sections 3.4 to 3.6 outline how the graphs would be set up and the presentation organized.

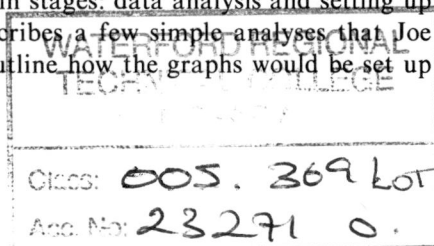

3.3   Data analysis for Qwiksales

Suppose Joe is anxious to show his managers how their performance has matched up to target. Graphing actual sales against targets month by month would be appropriate. If the actual sales figures were expressed as percentages of target sales, this would provide a measure of 'percentage achieved' for each sales territory. He might also want to compare the different export territories one with another and similarly the UK territories. Finally, a comparison of quarterly sales this year as opposed to last year might be informative.

These are simple examples of the kind of analysis that can be done to extract some meaning from raw sales statistics. Many other lines of attack can be used. For example:

1. Trends can be examined using a moving average to emphasize the underlying patterns.
2. The degree to which sales vary from month to month can be analysed by comparing Actual Sales with Average Sales.
3. Export Sales can be adjusted for the effect of currency fluctuations.
4. Sales can be adjusted for inflation.
5. Territories can be grouped as 'Good', 'Average' and 'Bad'. It is then possible to estimate how much better results would have been if the 'Bad' had achieved the same results as the 'Average'.

Having decided the graphs needed for his presentation, Joe then determines the data manipulation and analysis required.

The data shown in Figure 3.1 is saved in datafile QWIK1 on the disc, so first Retrieve this File using the command sequence:

/ File Retrieve QWIK

As well as the data shown in Figure 3.1, QWIK1 contains some empty table areas with text labels, to reduce the amount of keying-in required. The worksheet has a 'global currency format'; that is any numerical value keyed into the worksheet will be displayed as a currency (to the nearest £). Certain areas have been formatted to display entries as percentages. However, if a value is displayed inappropriately, the format can be altered for individual groups of cells using the Range Format sequence and choosing the appropriate format.

Percent of Target Achieved

First calculate the Percent of Target Achieved for each Sales Territory in each month. Arithmetically, each entry is the Actual Sales divided by the Target Sales displayed in percentage format. By maintaining the same positioning on each table, the formula only has to be entered once. So, for example, in cell D42, key in the formula:

+D8/D24

which should be displayed as 96 per cent.

Thereafter, other entries can be entered using the Copy command. For example, with the pointer on D42, from the main command menu, choose:

Copy From:D42   To:D43..D54   to Copy down column D

Then use / Range Erase to remove the formula from all the cells showing the error message ERR. This leaves column D containing the formulae on the rows corresponding to sales territories. Next, with the pointer on D42 again, choose:

Copy From:D42..D54   To:E42..O42   to Copy across for all months

Lastly, copy the formulae in range D42..D54 to A42 to get the percentages on an annual basis.

Notice that the entries in this area of the worksheet are displayed as percentages—see the symbols (P0) at the top of the control panel on the entry contents line. The cells have been formatted in advance to display their contents as percentages to the nearest whole per cent (Using/Range Format Percentage, etc.).

The percentages resulting from entering the formulae should tie up with those shown in Figure 3.2. The annual figures reveal that, overall, actual sales reached about 93 per cent of the target level. There was, however, considerable variation from month to month and across territories. This is well worth displaying graphically.

	A	B	C	D	E	F	G	H
38		b) Percent of 1987 Target		Achieved:				
40 ANNUAL % ACHVT				% ACHVT	% ACHVT	% ACHVT	% ACHVT	% ACHVT
			(U.K.)	Jan-87	Feb-87	Oct-87	Nov-87	Dec-87
42	85%		1	96%	93%	81%	87%	85%
43	105%		2	101%	102%	109%	103%	105%
44	95%		3	103%	119%	95%	90%	96%
45	90%		4	52%	57%	112%	126%	117%
46	93%		TOTAL (U.K.)	86%	92%	100%	103%	102%
			(EXPORT)					
49	118%		10	143%	195%	96%	117%	118%
50	75%		11	24%	136%	89%	67%	49%
51	85%		12	86%	111%	31%	57%	68%
52	92%		TOTAL (EXP.)	78%	130%	70%	82%	83%
54	93%		GRAND TOTAL	84%	104%	88%	95%	95%

Figure 3.2   Achievement against target

Quarterly Sales Totals

Headings and labels have been prepared for the table of quarterly sales totals in columns R to V. From the A1 position, jumping across to 'page four' using the Tab key reveals the Quarterly Sales area.

The Quarter 1 Sales Total for Territory 1 comes from adding together the sales in January (D8), February (E8) and March (F8). Therefore, point to cell S8 and enter the special function:

@SUM(D8.F8)

which should display as £89 937.

Similarly, enter the appropriate sum expressions for Quarters 2, 3 and 4 for Territory 1. Once the formulae are complete in cells S8 to V8, they can be copied down for the other territories and 'totals' rows.

The expected numerical results are shown in Figure 3.3.

	Q	R	S	T	U	V
3		(c) Quarterly Sales for 1987				
5			QUARTERLY SALES in 1987			
6	1987	TERRITORY	Quarter 1	Quarter 2	Quarter 3	Quarter 4
7		(U.K.)	SALES	SALES	SALES	SALES
8		1	£89,937	£75,438	£71,924	£75,992
9		2	£74,660	£79,110	£80,870	£82,485
10		3	£156,810	£151,280	£165,040	£154,515
11		4	£82,780	£141,435	£191,150	£194,975
12		TOTAL (U.K.)	£404,187	£447,263	£508,984	£507,967
14		(EXPORT)				
15		10	£55,660	£73,110	£93,110	£132,485
16		11	£54,660	£46,010	£55,870	£51,485
17		12	£101,660	£79,110	£166,782	£62,466
18		TOTAL (EXP.)	£211,980	£198,230	£315,762	£246,436
20		GRAND TOTAL	£616,167	£645,493	£824,746	£754,403

Figure 3.3   Quarterly sales

When the data analysis is complete, save the enlarged spreadsheet with the commands:

/ File Save MYDATA

calling your file MYDATA or whatever. Incidentally, it is good prectice to position the pointer somewhere sensible (such as over the A1 or title cell) before saving the worksheet. If this is done, the first screen displayed when the worksheet is retrieved again is likely to be more meaningful to the user.

The next stage is to create the graphical displays from which the visual aids will be made.

3.4 Setting up the first graph

Graphs are set up by specifying ranges of cells to be plotted and issuing commands from
the Graph menu. Many of the graphs for the presentation are to be plots of sales or
percentages against time, so the range of cells containing the dates (D6..06) is specified
as the *X* (horizontal) axis. The various sales series are assigned to the *Y* axis. Up to
six data-sets can be plotted on the same graph—they are given the letters A through
to F. Once the A range of cells has been specified (for example suppose it is specified
as range D20..O20 which contains the monthly sales totals), the graph is displayed on
screen by choosing to View. A simple line graph appears. The type can be changed to a
bar or stacked bar. Once the graph type is settled, the last step is to arrange the titles,
legends (labels) and scales so as to convey the graphical message in the most effective
manner.

To illustrate, the five graphs shown in Figures 3.4 to 3.8 will be set up using the
QWIK1 worksheet in its present form.

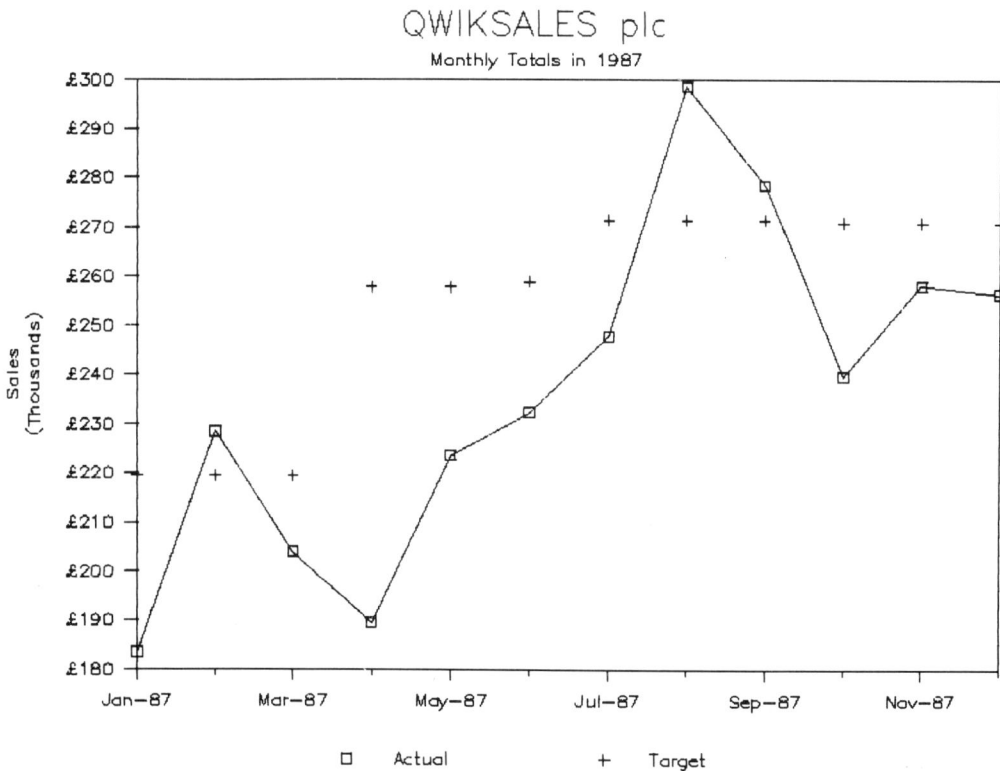

Figure 3.4   Actual monthly sales and target sales (graph 1)

When setting up a graph, always start from READY mode with the pointer on one
of the cells used in defining a cell range to be plotted. For example, in this case, put the
pointer on cell D6, the first date. Then, choose the Graph menu, using:

QWIKSALES plc

% of Target Achieved

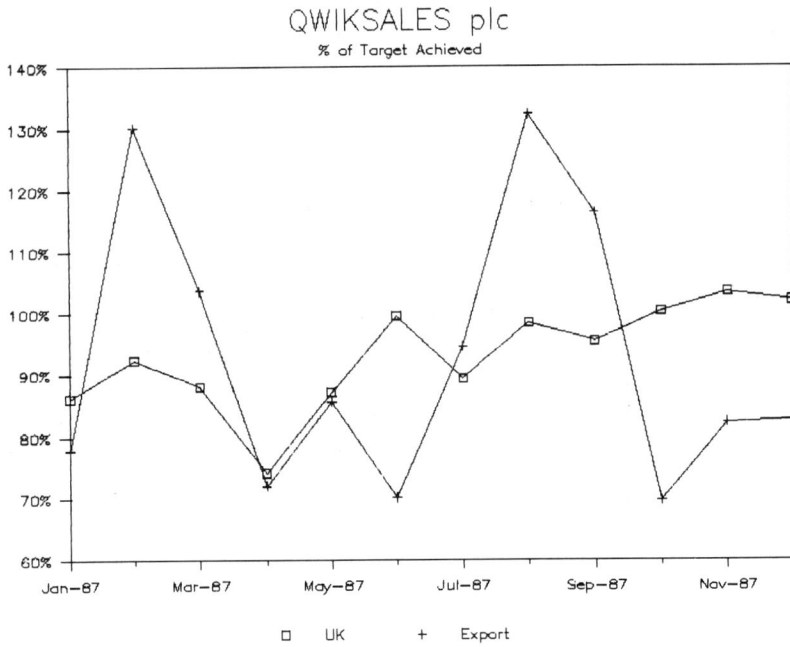

□   UK   +   Export

Figure 3.5   Percentage of target achieved (graph 2)

QWIKSALES plc

% Achieved in UK Territories

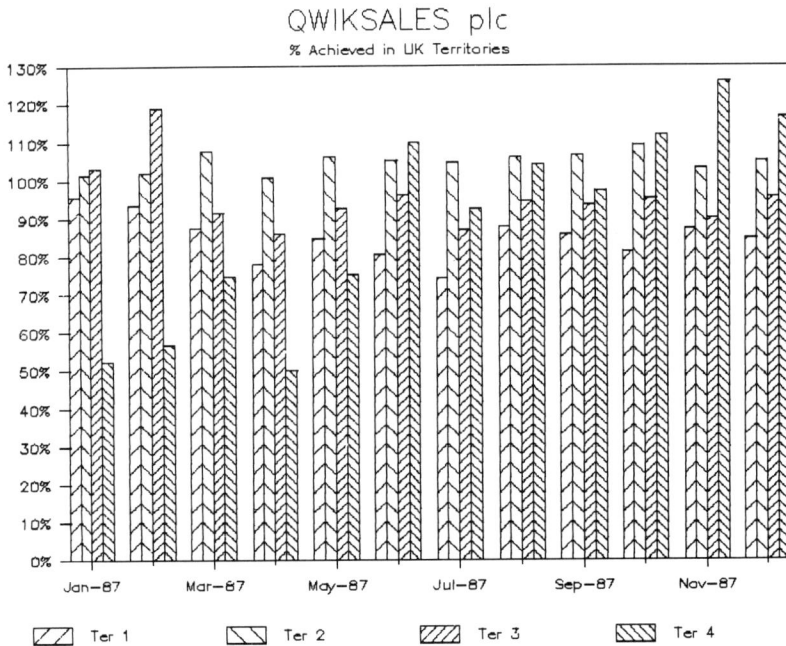

Ter 1   Ter 2   Ter 3   Ter 4

Figure 3.6   Home sales by territory (graph 3)

QWIKSALES plc
Sales in Export Territories

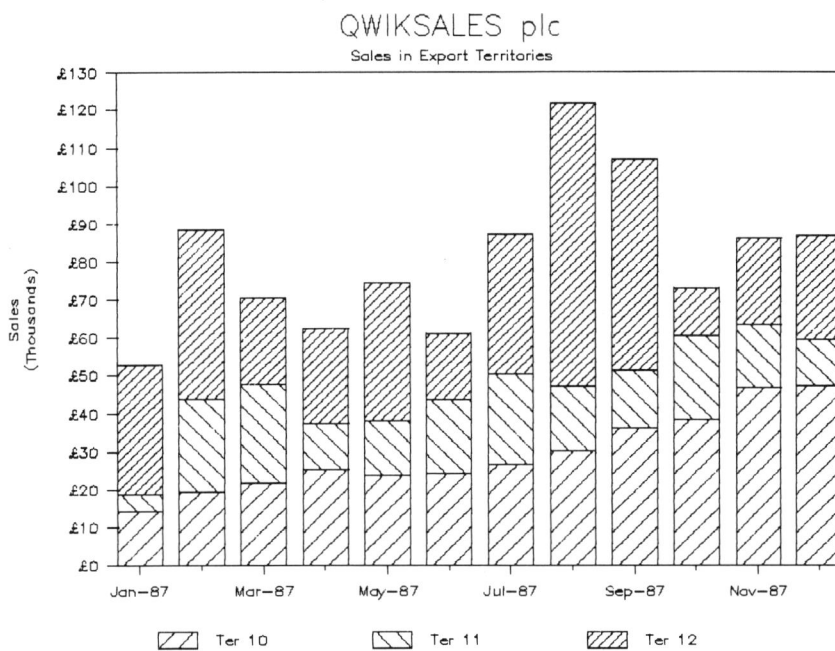

Figure 3.7   Export sales by territory (graph 4)

QWIKSALES plc
Total Annual Sales by UK Territory

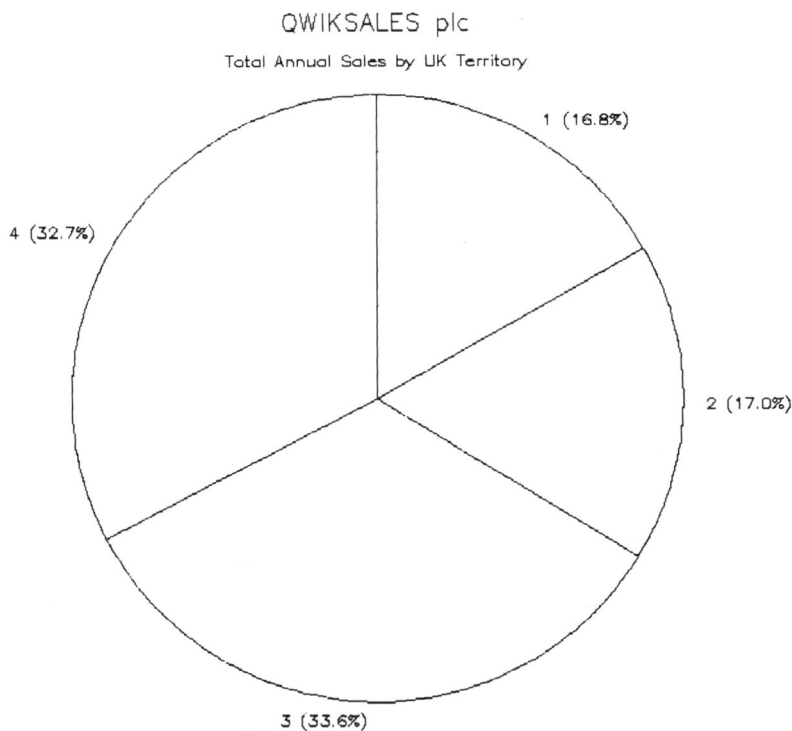

1 (16.8%)
2 (17.0%)
3 (33.6%)
4 (32.7%)

Figure 3.8   Annual sales by UK territory (graph 5)

/ Graph

Graph 1. Monthly Total Sales 1987

The Grand Totals of monthly Sales for all territories are in row 20: Target Sales Totals for the whole firm are in row 36. To set up a graph of Actuals and Targets, specify X, A and B ranges and possibly graph Type as follows:

X	D7..O7	to specify the *X* axis to consist of dates
A	D20..O20	to specify the A range as the monthly sales Totals
B	D36..O36	to specify the B range as monthly sales Targets
View		to display the graph on screen

If graph type is not specified, a line graph is obtained. If some other type, say a bar-chart, is required, choose:

Type   Bar   View   to change the Type to a Bar-chart and then View it

Assuming a line graph is best, the next stage is to add Titles and Legends and to decide the best display Format. From the Graph menu, choose Options to move down to another menu of choices. To add headings at the top of the graph, choose from the Options menu:

Titles First

and specify the heading at the top of the graph to be:

QWIKSALES plc

Choose Titles again and this time set up the subtitle by choosing:

Second

and specify this to be:

Monthly Totals in 1987

You may also like to give the *Y* axis a 'title' such as Sales Levels.

Next set up the key to the different graphs displayed, by choosing:

Legend

and specifying A- and B-range legends (labels) as follows:

A Actual
B Target

Note: These legends need to be short if there are several legends. Also they can be cell addresses (rather than text), provided that the backslash keystroke precedes the cell address. For example, the entry D22 would result in the legend TARGET (the current contents of cell D22).

The current graph would have more impact if Target Sales were represented in a different style from Actual Sales. One possibility is to choose color from the Options menu, which results in colour differentiation. Alternatively, instead of two line graphs, it might be preferable to display the Target Sales using symbols only. This is achieved by selecting Format from the Options menu; therefore:

Format   B   Symbols   to display the Target Sales by their + symbols

and leave Actual Sales as a line graph. Finally, Quit from the Format menu and Quit again from the Options menu and View the enhanced graph. The two formats are shown in Figure 3.4.

Finally, from the Options menu, choose Scale to improve the labelling of the horizontal axis. At present, the date labels crowd each other because there are too many characters on screen. Also, the Y-axis labelling should be in currency units. From the Scale menu, choose:

Skip 2   to eliminate every other date label along the X axis

Then from the Scale menu, choose:

Y-axis Format Currency 0   to display the labels on the vertical axis as pounds

Escape back to the Graph menu to View the result of these changes. The resultant graph is shown in Figure 3.4.

When the graph is considered satisfactory, it should be 'named'. This ensures that it can be displayed again and printed if required. The command sequence Graph Name Create allows names to be associated with different graph settings. The worksheet containing one or more named graphs is then saved to disc, using File Save in the normal way. Several different graphs (in effect different graph settings) can be named in this way and saved with the worksheet. The graphs can be recalled to the screen with the sequence Graph Name Use.

To name the current graph of actual and target sales, from the Graph menu choose:

Name Create G1   to attach the Name G1 to the first graph.

From time to time, remember to save your worksheet, so, for example, escape back to READY mode, and then:

/ File Save MYDATA Replace etc.

to save the spreadsheet plus graph settings to disc. The graph settings for graph G1 are now an integral part of worksheet MYDATA saved in its latest version on disc.

There is another choice in keeping a record of a graph: the special Save command on the Graph menu which saves the graph in a separate file of its own in the form of a binary 'screen dump'. This file contains pixel by pixel information from which the graph can be reconstituted, but only for printing purposes.

When a graph is saved in this way, it is not possible to make any alterations or amendments to the picture. If you use the Graph Save alternative, you will not be able to make any further alterations to the graph. Use the Graph Save sequence only if and when the graph is ready for printing.

3.5   Setting up further graphs

Graph 2. Percentage of Target Achieved

The data comes from rows 46 (TOTAL (UK)) and 52 (TOTAL (EXPORT)) and the monthly percentages are plotted against time. The second graph can be constructed from Graph 1 by modifying the settings where necessary. Start with the pointer on cell D46 where the percentages Achieved in the UK territories in January is entered.

From the Graph menu, with G1 as the current graph, the sequence of steps starts by specifying the data to be plotted as:

A   D46..O46   to set the A range to the UK Totals in row 46
B   D52..O52   to set the B range to the Export Totals in row 52

If you want to 'point' to the ranges, the Backspace key 'frees' the pointer from any previous setting. If the graph is Viewed at this stage, incorrect titles, legends and scaling will be seen. The next step is to adjust these, so choose:

Options Titles Second

and erase the current subtitle with Backspace and type:

% of Target Achieved   as the Second Title

Choose Titles again and erase the current title on the *Y* axis.

Next, choose Legend from the Options menu and using the Backspace as an 'eraser', specify the legends to be:

A UK
B Export

Finally select Format and display the Graph as Both (that is Lines and Symbols) and Scale to display the *Y* axis in Percentage Format. The resulting graph is shown in Figure 3.5.

Once again from the Graph menu, use Name Create to call this graph G2 so that it can be Used again.

Graph 3. Sales Percentages Achieved in UK territories

The percentage achieved data for the UK Territories aggregated together is shown in Figure 3.2. To set up the new graph by modifying graph 2, from the Graph menu, carry out the following steps:

Type Bar		to choose a Bar graph

A	D42..O42	to specify territory 1 data as the A range
B	D43..O43	similarly for the B to D range
C	D44..O44	
D	D45..O45	

Options Titles Second	and use Backspace to amend the text to:

% Achieved in UK Territories

Legends

and use Backspace to replace previous entries as necessary so that the legends become:

A	Ter 1
B	Ter 2
C	Ter 3
D	Ter 4

The graph now appears as shown in Figure 3.6. Its most noticeable feature is the improving performance of territory 4 over the year. Again, give the graph a Name (say G3) for future use.

Graph 4. Sales in Export Territories

In contrast, Export sales data will be displayed using a stacked bar-graph. This will show the contribution made to Total Sales by each of the Export Territories. The data for the graph is in rows 15 to 17, so start by pointing to D15. To alter graph 3, from the Graph menu, choose:

Type Stacked-Bar

to change the graph Type and then:

Reset D	to cancel the D-range setting

For the other data ranges, specify these as:

A	D15..O15	for Sales in Territory 10
B	D16..O16	for Sales in Territory 11
C	D17..O17	for Sales in Territory 12

and amend the Legends to be, for example, Ter 10, Ter 11 and Ter 12. Cancel out the Legend for the D range using Backspace.

Revise the Second Title to be Sales in Export Territories
Revise the Y axis Title to be Sales
Revise the Scale Format on the Y axis to be Currency with 0 decimal places

At this point, the graph should be similar to that shown in Figure 3.7. Give the graph a name, say G4, as previously.

Graph 5. Total Sales by UK Territory

A pie-chart is used to show the breakdown of Total UK Sales by Sales Territory in 1987. If a pie-chart is chosen, only one set of data (the A range) is displayed. If in addition the X range is specified, the segments of the pie will be labelled.

Therefore to construct the new graph, choose Reset from the Graph menu to clear the old graph settings before entering the following:

Type	Pie		to choose a pie-chart
X	C8..C11		to label the Territories
A	A8..A11		to specify the Total annual sales data for the pie

As before, choose Options then Titles. Enter the First and Second titles as follows:

First	QWIKSALES plc
Second	Total Annual Sales by UK Territory

The result should be similar to Figure 3.8. Name it as before.

Having Named all five graphs, the file MYDATA should be saved to disc.

For reference, the datafile QWIK2 on your ASM disc shows the worksheet at this stage and it contains the five named graphs.

3.6 Presenting the graphs

For the presentation, Retrieve the file MYDATA and from the Graph menu use the sequence Name Use to recover the set of named graphs. Choose each graph in turn by pointing to its name on the control panel. To change to the next graph in the sequence, choose Name and Use again, etc. Alternatively, write a short macro to produce the menu of graph names in one keystroke. (Macros are described later in Chapter 8 on macro models.)

If you want to print the graphs, you may be able to do this directly from the screen if your printer and software is configured correctly. To do this, turn the printer on, get the graph on screen and press the PrintScreen key. If this does not work, the picture must be saved in pixel form using Graph Save. In this case, using the Graph menu, get each of the named graphs on screen one at a time and then choose Save, giving each picture file so saved a different graph name. Notice that these picture files are saved separately from the spreadsheet and have the file extension PIC added to them. They are not worksheet files. They consist of pixel by pixel information which enables the graphs to be reconstituted with suitable software when the files are transferred to a printer.

1-2-3 contains a separate program called PrintGraph which arranges the transfer of the pixel data to the printer. The PrintGraph program contains interfaces for different types of printer. Therefore, you set up PrintGraph to suit your particular printer using the Configure option. Depending on the printer design, you can select a variety of different print options arranged under the headings Page Size, Colour, Font and Eject (this one determines how the paper is fed through the printer). For details refer to your printer manual and read the PrintGraph section of the 1-2-3 Manual.

It will be evident that 1-2-3 graphics and the PrintGraph program offers a wide range of permutations from which to choose how best to present your particular data.

3.7   Graphs for detecting relationships

The graphs displaying Qwiksales' performance over the last year and the differences between the Sales Territories are likely to have raised several questions in Joe's mind about his salesmen's efforts. Often, such visual presentations form the starting point for further analyses.

For example, after viewing the previous graphs, Joe may now wish to explore whether sales performance is related to the other measures of performance that he also collects routinely. As it happens, Joe holds annual statistics on the number of accounts sold to in each sales territory and also the number of calls each salesman made in 1987. Could it be that sales are high in territories where many calls are made and there are many accounts? Can we pick performance measures that appear to 'explain' variation in sales across the sales territories?

In the first instance, plotting sales against accounts sold to would reveal whether any simple relationship between these two variables exists or not. To explore relationships between variables, the graph types used earlier in the chapter are of limited use. The appropriate graph type is a 'scatter' plot which in 1-2-3 terms is the XY graph. This graph type has both horizontal and vertical axes numerically scaled (in contrast with the Line graph for which the X axis is merely a labelling device). Thus accounts sold (the explanatory variable) can be represented numerically on the horizontal (X) axis and sales on the vertical (Y) axis.

Some summary data on Accounts Sold to and Calls Made has been entered in a worksheet file called QWIKEXT, also on your disc. The name denotes that the datafile forms an 'extension' to the original Qwiksales file QWIK1. The layout and contents of this file are shown in Figure 3.9. Annual totals of Accounts Sold and Calls Made are lined up adjacent to the Annual Sales for each Territory. Similar data is available for the previous year, 1986, as is shown. Using 1986 and 1987 data, it is therefore possible to calculate the percentage change in each variable. For example, the percentage increase in sales is calculated from:

(1987 Sales–1986 Sales)/(1986 Sales)

and the result displayed as a percentage. In most cases, the percentage change is positive and hence represents an increase in the normal sense of the word.

The QWIKEXT worksheet can be treated separately, that is as a 'stand-alone-spreadsheet', or alternatively, it can be 'combined' with the existing Qwiksales spread-sheet. In the description that follows it will be treated as part of the larger worksheet.

	X	Y	Z	AA	AB
	QWIKSALES plc				
3	(e) Calls Made & Accounts Sold for 1987 & 1986				
6	1987	TERRITORY	Statistics for 1987		
7			Ann Sales	Accounts Sol	Calls Made
8	(U.K.)	1	£313,290	139	1423
9		2	£317,125	200	1322
10		3	£627,645	376	1051
11		4	£610,340	320	1111
12	(EXPORT)	10	£354,365	180	1661
13		11	£208,025	89	1752
14		12	£410,018	264	1220
16	GRAND TOTAL		£2,840,808	1568	9540
18	1986	TERRITORY	Statistics for 1986		
19			Ann Sales	Accounts Sol	Calls Made
20	(U.K.)	1	£278,005	134	1252
21		2	£297,433	190	1057
22		3	£547,680	353	914
23		4	£550,760	304	1044
24	(EXPORT)	10	£300,107	169	1827
25		11	£176,821	86	1839
26		12	£348,622	237	1305
28	GRAND TOTAL		£2,499,428	1473	9238
30	1987 v 86				
31		TERRITORY	% Increase 1987 over 1986		
32			Sales Incr	Accounts Inc	Calls Inc
33	(U.K.)	1	13%	4%	14%
34		2	7%	5%	25%
35		3	15%	7%	15%
36		4	11%	5%	6%
37	(EXPORT)	10	18%	7%	-9%
38		11	18%	3%	-5%
39		12	18%	11%	-7%
41	GRAND TOTAL		14%	6%	3%

Figure 3.9 Sales performance statistics

This allows us to try out some of the file handling features in 1-2-3. With the current Qwiksales worksheet in memory, QWIKEXT, the 'extension' file will be incorporated into the existing Qwiksales spreadsheet. (If you are starting from this point in the chapter, you can retrieve the file you last saved to disc under the name MYDATA.)

The current Qwiksales file has entries in columns up to column V. Put the pointer over into column X which is currently empty. The second set of Qwiksales data will be entered in the area bounded by columns X and AC.

Crucial to the success of the File Combine operation is the starting position of the cell pointer, because the incoming file is copied into the cells to the right and below the current pointer position. Therefore, with the pointer on cell X1, choose:

/ File Combine	to incorporate the extension File
Copy Entire-File QWIKEXT	by Copying the Entire-File QWIKEXT

Thus the command sequences File Combine (and File Xtract) can be used to merge separate spreadsheets (and to extract parts of worksheets to form separate spreadsheets). The data shown in Figure 3.9 should now be included in the current worksheet, four 'pages' across, spanning columns X to AB.

3.8   Setting up XY graphs

Graph 6. Annual Sales versus Accounts Sold

First explore the relationship between Annual Sales (in column Z) with Accounts Sold (in column AA). From the Graph menu, choose Reset to remove all the previous graph settings. Specify the X range and the A range as follows:

X	AA8..AA14
A	Z8..Z14

If you view the graph at this stage, an incorrect line graph appears. In particular, notice that the X axis (horizontal) is not scaled. The different values for Accounts Sold are attached like labels, but their relative magnitudes are not represented as positions along a scaled axis. For this application, the Type should be the XY scatter plot. So from the Graph menu, choose:

Type   XY View   to see if there is any relationship

At this stage, the plot resembles a tangle of lines and needs to be displayed by individual points with a different format. To change the format, choose Options from the Graph menu, then:

Format Graph Symbols Quit   to get a display of points only and to return to the Options menu

The next stage is to add Titles, say:

QWIKSALES plc   for the First

and

Annual Sales v Accounts Sold   for the Second

Next Scale the Y axis to display the Format known as Currency (0 decimal places) then escape back to the Graph menu and View the graph. The scatter of points suggests that sales tend to be highest where account numbers are highest and possibly the underlying relationship is linear (that is a straight line could be fitted to approximate to the trend). A rough and ready way of estimating the relationship is described below, but a fuller coverage of the main fitting technique, regression, is contained in Chapter 6.

Figure 3.10 shows a similar graph, but after further modification to the scaling. The vertical scale ranges from 0 to £700,000. 1-2-3's automatic scaling on the vertical axis has been replaced by manual scaling with selected upper and lower limits. Similarly, the X axis starts from 0 and extends to 500. This has been achieved by choosing Scale on the Options menu. From the Scale menu, the Y axis is specified, then Manual scaling with Upper and Lower limits specified as 700,000 and 0 respectively. A similar process using the Scale option on the X axis should make the graph correspond with that shown in Figure 3.10.

The inclusion of the origin in the graph of a possible relationship assists us in estimating the equation of the best fitting straight line, if this is to be done visually. To fit a line to some data, its slope and intercept need to be measured. This is a matter of simple geometry. A printout of the graph and a pencil and ruler assist the process. Working in a rough and ready manner, a line fitted to the data in Figure 3.10 would intersect the Y-axis at roughly £70,000 and have a slope of roughly £1,400 per Account Sold. (Draw

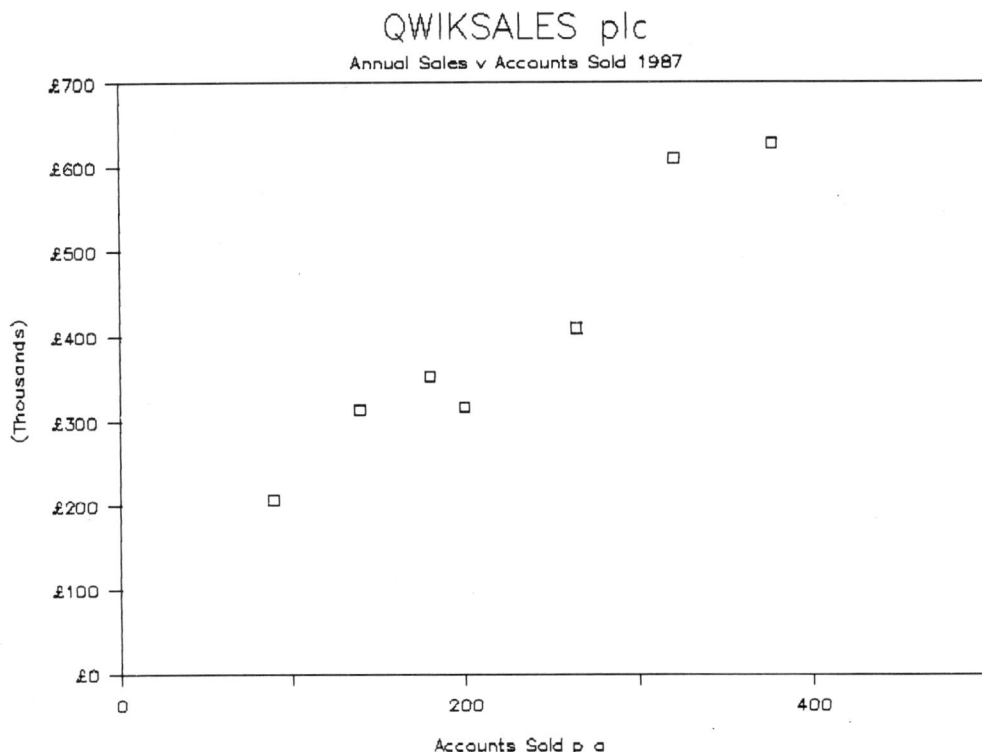

Figure 3.10   XY graph of annual sales versus accounts sold

a 'best-fitting' line and read off the intercept on the vertical axis; work out the slope by calculating the ratio of the 'Y-step' to the 'X-step'). Combining the estimated slope and intercept in an equation, this says:

Sales = £70,000 + £1,400 * (Accounts Sold)

A more accurate estimation of the line can be made using regression. The procedure using 1-2-3's regression facilities is described in Chapter 6 on business forecasting.

Before moving on to the next graph, Name the graph (say G6) and save the worksheet file in its new extended form.

Graph 7. Annual Sales versus Calls Made

Now investigate whether sales are related to the number of Calls Made (in column AB). To modify the last graph, from the Graph menu, respecify the X range to be:

X AB8..AB14

and change the second title to be more appropriate. Also change the scaling on the X axis making the Upper limit 2000 (or, alternatively, return to Automatic scaling). The result should be similar to that shown in Figure 3.11. It appears that Sales are lower in Territories with a high call rate but this result needs further probing. There are marked differences between UK and Export Territories. Again Name the graph (G7).

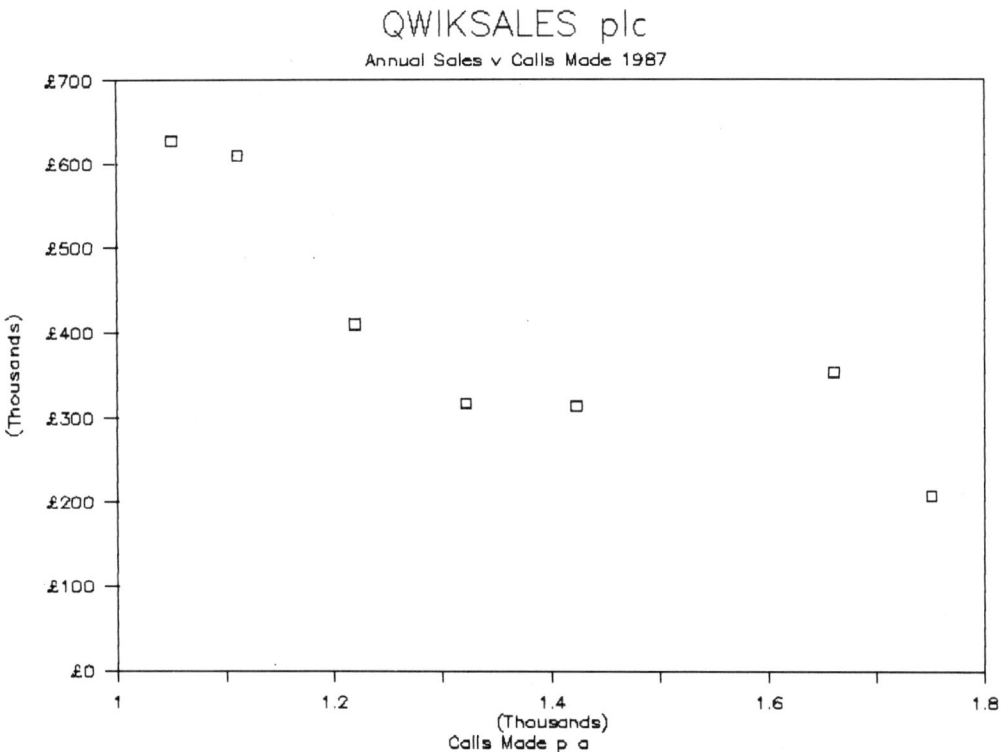

Figure 3.11   XY graph of annual sales versus calls made

38

Graph 8. 1987 Improvement on 1986

The final graph explores the percentage Increase in Sales in 1987 as compared with 1986. Can the increases across territories be linked to changes in Accounts Sold to and changes in Calls Made? The data for further graphs are in rows 33 to 39.

From the Graph menu, first Reset the graph, then specify the data ranges as follows:

X Y33..Y39
A Z33..Z39
B AA33..AA39
C AB33..AB39

Choose a Bar type of graph. From the Options menu, add the Titles and the Legends. Also Scale the *Y* axis in Percentage Format.

The final graph should correspond with that shown in Figure 3.12. The graph suggests differences between the UK and Export sales territories. Further steps are to explore the Increase in Sales against the Increase in Calls Made, etc., using XY graphs. These further analyses are left to the reader for consolidation purposes.

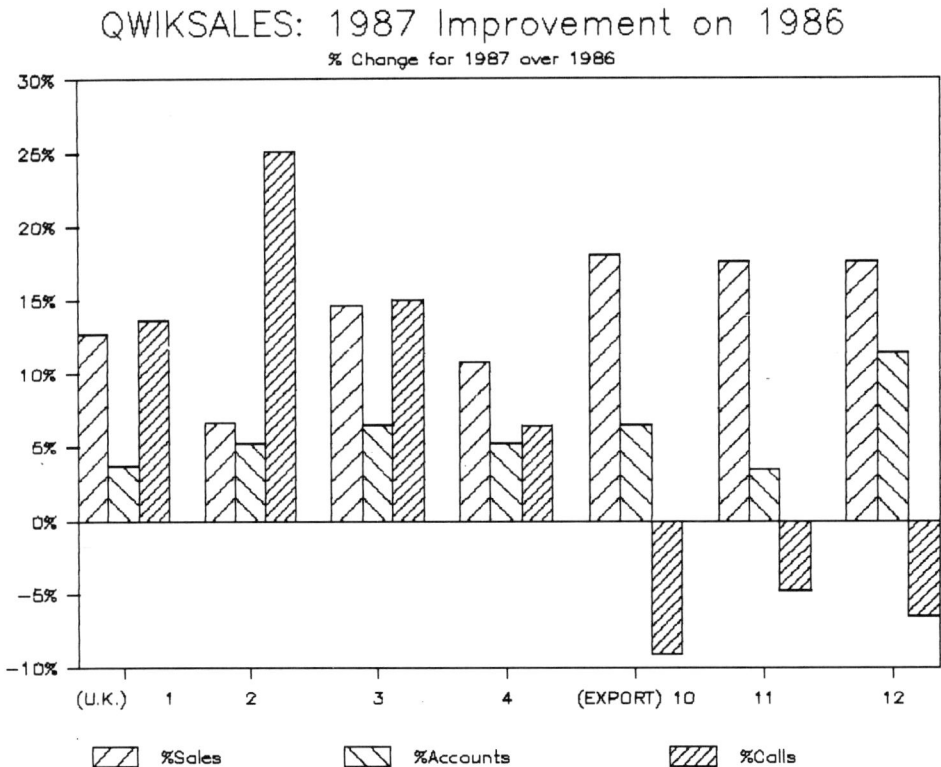

Figure 3.12 Sales performance in 1987 compared to 1986 by territory

Before proceeding, however, remember to Name the previous graph (G8) and then Save the File MYDATA.

Again for reference purposes, a datafile QWIK3 is included on disc. It contains the extended worksheet and the eight named graphs, representing the stage reached in the analysis at the end of this chapter.

CHAPTER 4

Financial Modelling — Planning

4.1 Introduction

Lotus 1-2-3 has been most widely used for financial modelling and planning work. Much of this type of application depends on estimates and predictions. However skilfully produced, estimates are rarely exactly on target. It is here that sensitivity analysis has a major part to play. You can examine the impact that errors in estimates will have on results.

1-2-3 has been praised for its extensive facilities for 'what-if' sensitivity analyses. At a basic level, automatic recalculation in response to any changed inputs allows as much 'what-if'ing as many users require. However, if depth questions are to be properly and systematically answered, more thought needs to go into the conduct of sensitivity analyses.

This chapter attempts a systematic development of sensitivity analysis in the context of planning. As in other chapters, the procedures are explained in the context of examples.

Skywalker Video illustrates a wide range of sensitivity procedures—data tables, windows, what-if graphs, scenarios. Glowworm Lamps shows how what-if graphs and change factors can be used to extend the usefulness of a planning model. The chapter attempts to summarize in one place some different approaches to building financial planning models.

4.2 Example: Skywalker Video

Skywalker Video sell advice on how to set up a video cassette rental business. Their promotional literature claims that if you pay them £2,000 and follow their advice, you should be able to make £50,000 a year. They advise on the type and relative number of videos to stock, where to get them and how often to replace them. They also give suggestions on the type of shop you need and show how you can expect to make £50,000 in the first year.

The basic facts are that to set up a video rental business you need to buy an initial stock of 1000 videos and, to keep up with new releases, a further 50 videos a month. Skywalker will advise on the appropriate titles and supply them at £30 each. Their videos are described as 'first rate'. However, they do not last forever because Skywalker suggest that you can only expect about 30 plays per tape.

The price at which tapes are rented out is left up to the individual operator, but Skywalker suggest charging £2.50 per day. At that price they expect all the stock, on average, to be rented out once a week. However, in their opinion, a lower price coupled with a faster turnover makes sense in some situations but is unlikely to make very much difference to the total rental income.

Suppose it is possible to rent a suitable shop for £6,000 per annum and get money from the bank at 10 per cent per annum. Also after paying Skywalker for their advice, the opening cash position is £3,000. What are the implications for cashflow through the first year of trading? And what kind of overdraft facilities will be required at the bank? For simplicity, assume that any tax and VAT payments can be ignored.

4.3 Problem formulation for Skywalker

Before tackling Skywalker's cashflow in 1-2-3, some assumptions help the task of modelling. The main assumptions concern the pattern of tape usage and replacement. These can be made more realistic (and hence more elaborate) at a later stage. The numerical values used come directly from the problem description in Section 4.2 above: these values can be varied later in sensitivity analysis.

Plays per month

Once a week is taken to mean 52/12 or about 4.33 plays per month. The simplest model would assume a steady usage for each tape of about 4.33 plays per month from the start.

Replacements

On average each tape is assumed to last for 30/4.33 or approximately 7 months. Therefore, assuming a mixed stock of tapes (some used, some semi-used and some new), roughly one-seventh of the current stock of tapes would need replacing in any month.

Purchases

As well as replacements for worn-out tapes, sufficient tapes are to be bought each month to increment the overall stock level of tapes by 50.

Interest

The same rate of interest is assumed to apply for loans from banks and for deposits. This simplifies the calculation of the interest term, but could be lower for deposits and higher for loans.

Rental on shop

This is assumed to be paid quarterly in January, April, etc.

4.4   Modelling Skywalker in 1-2-3

This section contains some hints for modelling Skywalker's cashflow using 1-2-3. The
initial layout for the model is described first. Then the formulae for the various items
of cashflow are described and the process of expanding the spreadsheet across twelve
months is outlined.

Layout of spreadsheet

Figure 4.1 shows the suggested layout for the Skywalker Video cashflow model. Only the
first six months are shown in the figure, although the layout extends across to December
in column M. This spreadsheet is in datafile SKY1 and can be loaded from disc using:

/ File Retrieve SKY1

The upper thirteen lines when completed will show the cash-in and cash-out figures, all
computed from the assumptions ('planning values') and initial values (such as Opening
Cash). The 'planning values', such as Plays per Month and Rent per Day, are separated
out from the 'computed values'. They are positioned in a separate area of the worksheet,

	A	B	C	D	E	F	G
1	Skywalker Video						
2		Jan	Feb	Mar	Apr	May	Jun
3	Average Stock	1000					
4	--------------						
5	Opening Cash	3000					
6	Rental recpts						
7	Purchases						
8	Replacements						
9	Rent qtrly						
10	--------------						
11	Total						
12	Interest						
13	Closing Cash						
14							
15	Planning Values						
16	MonthlyPurchase	50					
17	Tape Price	30					
18	Tape Life	30					
19	Plays per Mth	4.33					
20	Rent per Day	2.50					
21	Shop Rent p a	6000					
22	Interest p a	10					

Figure 4.1   Initial spreadsheet layout for Skywalker cashflow model

which can be below the cashflow as here or on a separate 'page' at the top of the worksheet. This layout is advantageous when sensitivity analysis is carried out. It also helps when formulae have to be copied. Generally speaking, when keying in formulae for subsequent copying, entries taken from the 'planning value area' of the worksheet need to be addressed absolutely whereas entries from cells that are computed values do not (see below).

Formulae for January

Figure 4.2 shows the numerical results for January. The underlying formulae in column B are set out in Figure 4.3 and explained more fully below.

Rental receipts in B6   This is given by:

Plays per Month $\times$ Rent per Day $\times$ Jan Stock level

Therefore the formula in cell B6 is:

+$B$19*$B$20*B3

```
           A           B      C      D      E      F      G
  1 Skywalker Video
  2                    Jan    Feb    Mar    Apr    May    Jun
  3 Average Stock     1000
  4 ----------------------------------------------------------------
  5 Opening Cash      3000
  6 Rental recpts    10825
  7 Purchases       -30000
  8 Replacements     -4330
  9 Rent qtrly       -1500
 10 ----------------------------------------------------------------
 11 Total           -22005
 12 Interest          -183
 13 Closing Cash    -22188
 14
 15 Planning Values
 16 MonthlyPurchase     50
 17 Tape Price          30
 18 Tape Life           30
 19 Plays per Mth     4.33
 20 Rent per Day      2.50
 21 Shop Rent p a     6000
 22 Interest p a        10
```

Figure 4.2   Values for January

```
               A                    B              C        D        E
  1 Skywalker Video
  2                                 Jan            Feb      Mar      Apr
  3 Average Stock              1000
  4 ---------------------------------------------------------------------
  5 Opening Cash               3000
  6 Rental recpts     +$B$19*$B$20*B3
  7 Purchases         -B3*$B$17
  8 Replacements      -($B$19/$B$18)*$B$17*B3
  9 Rent qtrly        -0.25*$B$21
 10 ---------------------------------------------------------------------
 11 Total             @SUM(B5..B9)
 12 Interest          +B11*$B$22/1200
 13 Closing Cash      @SUM(B11..B12)
 14
 15 Planning Values
 16 MonthlyPurchase            50
 17 Tape Price                 30
 18 Tape Life                  30
 19 Plays per Mth            4.33
 20 Rent per Day             2.5
 21 Shop Rent p a           6000
 22 Interest p a             10
```

Figure 4.3   Formulae for January

As noted above, where formulae involving planning values are to be copied across the rows of the spreadsheet, 'absolute addressing' is used. Therefore, in the formula for Rentals, the contents of cells B19 and B20 are referenced as $B$19 and $B$20 since the formula will subsequently be copied. The values must always be obtained from column B, whereas the stock (B3) changes relative to the position of the formula. (Strictly speaking, it is permissible to use 'mixed addressing', for example $B19, since formulae are copied across rows and *not* down columns). If formulae are input by 'pointing' (in POINT mode), an address can be made 'absolute' by pointing to the cell address required and pressing the Abs key (f4). Otherwise, when keying in formulae (in EDIT mode), remember to include the $ signs for planning values.

Purchases in B7   Purchases involves a cash outflow given by:

— Jan Stock × Tape Price

Therefore the formula in cell B7 is:

— B3*$B$17

Replacements in B8 Another cash outflow given by:

$$- \quad \frac{\text{Proportion of Stock}}{\text{wearing out this month}} \times \text{Tape Price} \times \text{Jan Stock}$$

Therefore the formula in cell B8 is:

– ($B$19/$B$18)*$B$17*B3

Rent in B9 This is an outflow, so the formula in cell B9 is

-0.25*$B$21 (that is a quarter of the annual rent stored in B21).

Total in B11 The sum of the cash inflows and outflows in the cell range B5 to B9 is:

@SUM(B5.B9)

Interest in B12 The annual interest percentage is stored in cell B22 as 10 per cent. Monthly interest is therefore one-twelfth of this. A month's interest on the total cash at the end of January (in cell B11) is given by:

+B11*$B$22/1200

which is the formula in cell B12.

Closing Cash in B13 The final cash position in cell B13 after allowing for interest is:

+B11+B12 or @SUM(B11.B12).

Extending the spreadsheet

Figure 4.4 shows the values for January together with the formulae for February where they differ in kind from those of January.

Stock This consists of January stock incremented by the monthly purchase of 50 tapes (in cell B16). Therefore the formula in cell C3 is:

+B3+$B$16

In general the Stock in any month will be obtained by adding the contents of cell B16 to Stock in the previous month. Hence, the Stock formula in cell C3 is general and can be copied for the other months up to December.

Opening Cash February's Opening Cash is equal to January's Closing Cash, and this will hold generally. Therefore the entry in cell C5:

+B13

```
            A          B          C          D        E
 1 Skywalker Video
 2                     Jan        Feb        Mar      Apr
 3 Average Stock       1000    +B3+$B$16
 4 -----------------------------------------------------------
 5 Opening Cash        3000    +13
 6 Rental recpts      10825
 7 Purchases         -30000   -$B$16*$B$17
 8 Replacements       -4330
 9 Rent qtrly         -1500
10 -----------------------------------------------------------
11 Total             -22005
12 Interest            -183
13 Closing Cash      -22188
14
15 Planning Values
16 MonthlyPurchase       50
17 Tape Price            30
18 Tape Life             30
19 Plays per Mth       4.33
20 Rent per Day        2.50
21 Shop Rent p a       6000
22 Interest p a          10
```

Figure 4.4   Formulae for February (where different from January)

can be copied across the cells of row 5 as far as column M (December).

Rental receipts   The formula for February's Rental Receipts has the same structure as that for January's Receipts in B6, so copy the formula in cell B6 across the cells of row 6 as far as column M (December).

Purchases   Cash spent on the monthly Purchase of 50 tapes is given by formula:

— $B$16*$B$17

in cell C7. This formula applies to all other months and so it can be copied across row 7 as far as column M.

Replacements   The formula for February and subsequent months is of the same structure as that for January in cell B8. Therefore it can be copied from B8 to the cell range C8..M8.

Rent   Since rent is paid quarterly, there is no rent to pay in February. To complete the entries for Rent, put the pointer on B9 and copy the formula into cells E9, H9 and K9.

Total, Interest, Closing Cash   The formulae for January apply for all subsequent months and so they can be copied across the spreadsheet to column M.

The resulting values should correspond to those shown in Figure 4.5. If the numbers in the spreadsheet are not integers, the Range Format Fixed command can be employed to change the display.

Before moving on to the sensitivity analysis, it is sensible to save the Skywalker model to disc. A name such as VIDEO will avoid the original SKY file being overwritten. On the disc, there is a file SKY2 which corresponds to the model shown in Figure 4.5. It contains a pre-set graph of the monthly closing cash which appears on screen when the Graph key (f10) is pressed.

4.5   Sensitivity analysis

At first sight, the results in Figure 4.5 appear to support Skywalker's statement that £50,000 can be earned in the first year. However, at the start of the year, a large loan (of about £22,000) will have to be negotiated with the bank.

However, more importantly, sensitivity to assumptions about tape life, plays per month and rent per day should be examined. For example, suppose the rent per day is dropped to £2.00 as opposed to £2.50. Does this have much effect on cashflow? What increase in usage (plays per month) would compensate for this reduction in rental income?

The final Closing Cash figure in Figure 4.5 depends on the various 'planning values' shown in cells B16 to B22. If one or more of these planning values is changed, the immediate effect on monthly cashflow can be seen. This type of experimentation with a model is usually called sensitivity analysis.

Windows

Here, splitting the screen into two separate windows helps us to see the results of such alterations. Figure 4.6 shows two windows with the cashflow values in the upper window and the planning values in the lower window. The pointer was positioned thirteen rows down from the top of the spreadsheet and the Worksheet Window command was used to split the screen Horizontally. The Window key (f6) jumps the pointer from upper to lower window, etc. If the final Closing Cash cell (M13) is linked to cell D16, as shown in Figure 4.6, the effect on Closing Cash of changing planning values can be immediately seen on screen without the necessity to pan across to column M.

The Worksheet Window command was issued for a second time to make scrolling of the two windows Unsynchronized. The results can be seen in Figure 4.7. In the upper window, the final months' figures are displayed, whereas the focus is on column B in the lower window.

Figure 4.7 shows the Final Cash figure for a 'pessimistic' set of assumptions: although Rent per Day is down to £2.00, Plays per Month and Tape Life are also low (at 2.00 and 25 respectively) whereas new tapes cost more (£35). Instead of the vaunted £50,000 in the first year, if things go wrong with the business, it looks more like bancruptcy with debts of over £40,000.

A	B	C	D	E	F	G	H	I	J	K	L	M
1 Skywalker Video												
2	Jan	Feb	Mar	Apr	May	Jun	Jul	Aug	Sep	Oct	Nov	Dec
3 Average Stock	1000	1050	1100	1150	1200	1250	1300	1350	1400	1450	1500	1550
4 ---												
5 Opening Cash	3000	-22188	-17009	-11459	-7048	-761	5907	11445	18869	26683	33376	41966
6 Rental recpts	10825	11366	11908	12449	12990	13531	14073	14614	15155	15696	16238	16779
7 Purchases	-30000	-1500	-1500	-1500	-1500	-1500	-1500	-1500	-1500	-1500	-1500	-1500
8 Replacements	-4330	-4547	-4763	-4980	-5196	-5413	-5629	-5846	-6062	-6279	-6495	-6712
9 Rent qtrly	-1500			-1500			-1500			-1500		
10 ---												
11 Total	-22005	-16869	-11365	-6990	-754	5858	11350	18713	26462	33100	41619	50533
12 Interest	-183	-141	-95	-58	-6	49	95	156	221	276	347	421
13 Closing Cash	-22188	-17009	-11459	-7048	-761	5907	11445	18869	26683	33376	41966	50954
14												
15 Planning Values												
16 MonthlyPurchase	50	Fin Cash	50954									
17 Tape Price	30											
18 Tape Life	30											
19 Plays per Mth	4.33											
20 Rent per Day	2.50											
21 Shop Rent p a	6000											
22 Interest p a	10											

Figure 4.5   Completed model showing cashflow for Skywalker

	A	B	C	D	E	F	G
2		Jan	Feb	Mar	Apr	May	Jun
3	Average Stock	1000	1050	1100	1150	1200	1250
4	----						
5	Opening Cash	3000	-22188	-17009	-11459	-7048	-761
6	Rental recpts	10825	11366	11908	12449	12990	13531
7	Purchases	-30000	-1500	-1500	-1500	-1500	-1500
8	Replacements	-4330	-4547	-4763	-4980	-5196	-5413
9	Rent qtrly	-1500			-1500		
10	----						
11	Total	-22005	-16869	-11365	-6990	-754	5858
12	Interest	-183	-141	-95	-58	-6	49
16	MonthlyPurchase	50 Fin Cash	50954				
17	Tape Price	30					
18	Tape Life	30					
19	Plays per Mth	4.33					
20	Rent per Day	2.50					
21	Shop Rent p a	6000					
22	Interest p a	10					

Figure 4.6 Model withs two windows: 'base' case

	A	H	I	J	K	L	M
2		Jul	Aug	Sep	Oct	Nov	Dec
3	Average Stock	1300	1350	1400	1450	1500	1550
4	----						
5	Opening Cash	-37389	-39404	-39864	-40267	-42125	-42425
6	Rental recpts	5200	5400	5600	5800	6000	6200
7	Purchases	-1750	-1750	-1750	-1750	-1750	-1750
8	Replacements	-3640	-3780	-3920	-4060	-4200	-4340
9	Rent qtrly	-1500			-1500		
10	----						
11	Total	-39079	-39534	-39934	-41777	-42075	-42315
12	Interest	-326	-329	-333	-348	-351	-353
13	Closing Cash	-39404	-39864	-40267	-42125	-42425	-42668
16	MonthlyPurchase	50 Fin Cash	-42668				
17	Tape Price	35					
18	Tape Life	25					
19	Plays per Mth	2.00					
20	Rent per Day	2.00					
21	Shop Rent p a	6000					
22	Interest p a	10					

Figure 4.7 Model with two windows: 'Pessimistic' case

Data Tables

The Closing Cash position is very dependent on assumptions about Plays per Month and the Rent per Day charged for tapes. One way of examining the size of this dependence is to change the values for Rent per Day and for Plays per Month. The Data Table command in 1-2-3 enables us to carry out the procedure systematically and to retain the numerical results for different cases. The Data Table command operates as follows.

Some typical values for Rent per Day are set out in a column and some typical values for Plays per Month are arranged in a neighbouring row, as shown in Figure 4.8. The Final Cash expression is chosen as the measure of interest and it appears in the top left-hand corner cell of the Data Table. Its value will be calculated for each pair of values for Rent per Day and Plays per Month. Look carefully at the layout in Figure 4.8. The Data Table command with two Inputs (Rent per Day and Plays per Month) results in 1-2-3 producing all the Final Cash figures shown in Figure 4.9.

The Final Cash entries evaluated by the Data Table procedure and shown in Figure 4.9 are values (as opposed to formulae). A graph of these values will not change its inputs if further sensitivity analyses are undertaken because the cell entries are no longer 'linked' into the model. In contrast, graphs of cells containing formulae, such as the range B13 to M13 where Closing Cash formulae are stored in row 13 of the Skywalker model, will continually change as input values change, making visual comparison of different cases difficult. The Data Table results are therefore particularly useful where graphical comparisons are required. Figure 4.10 shows the rows of the Data Table graphed as the A range, the B range, etc. The graph Type is an XY plot with both the horizontal axis (Plays/Month) and the vertical axis (Final Cash) scaled.

	A	B	C	D	E	F	G			
2		Jan	Feb	Mar	Apr	May	Jun			
3	Average Stock	1000	1050	1100	1150	1200	1250			
4	--------									
5	Opening Cash	3000	-22188	-17009	-11459	-7048	-761			
6	Rental recpts	10825	11366	11908	12449	12990	13531			
7	Purchases	-30000	-1500	-1500	-1500	-1500	-1500			
8	Replacements	-4330	-4547	-4763	-4980	-5196	-5413			
9	Rent qtrly	-1500			-1500					
10	--------									
11	Total	-22005	-16869	-11365	-6990	-754	5858			
12	Interest	-183	-141	-95	-58	-6	49			
13	Closing Cash	-22188	-17009	-11459	-7048	-761	5907			
15	Planning Values					Plays per Month				
16	MonthlyPurchase	50	Fin Cash	50954	2.0	3.0	4.0	4.3	5.0	7.0
17	Tape Price	30		1.5						
18	Tape Life	30		2.0						
19	Plays per Mth	4.33	Rental	2.5						
20	Rent per Day	2.50		3.0						
21	Shop Rent p a	6000								

Figure 4.8 Layout for a Data Table to evaluate Final Cash for different rental–plays per month combinations

51

	C	D	E	F	G	H	I	J
15				Plays per Month				
16	Fin Cash	50954	2.0	3.0	4.0	4.3	5.0	7.0
17		1.5	-37471	-29425	-21379	-18966	-13333	2758
18		2.0	-21379	-5287	10804	15632	26896	59080
19	Rental	2.5	-5287	18850	42988	50230	67126	115402
20		3.0	10804	42988	75172	84828	107356	171724

Figure 4.9   Final Cash results after Data Table evaluation

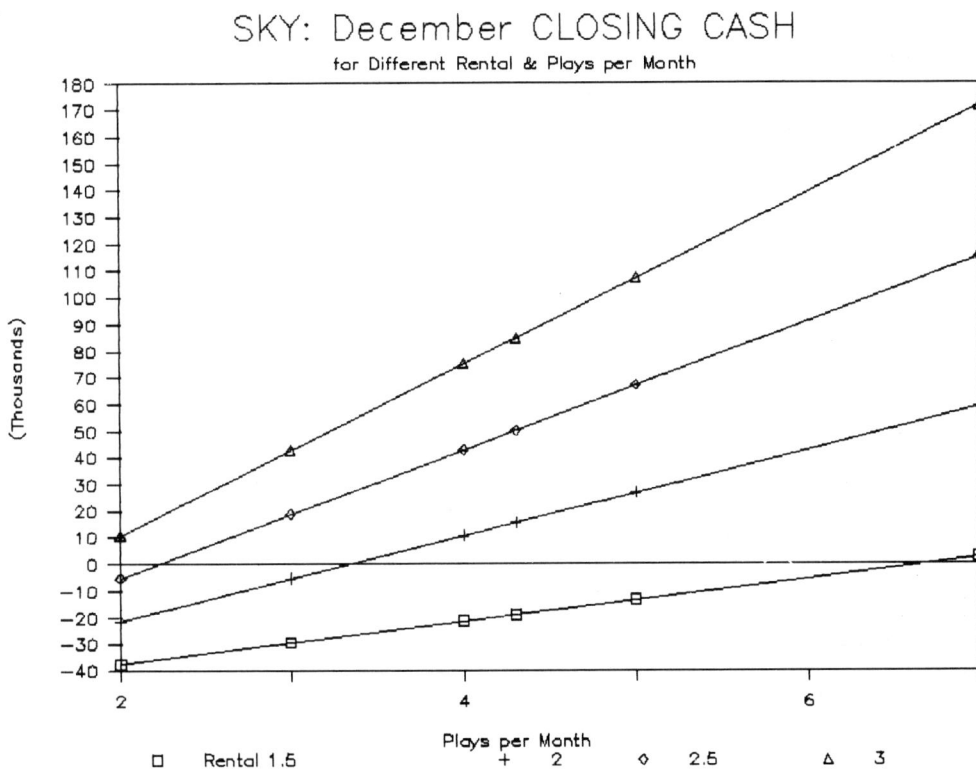

Figure 4.10   Graph based on Data Table results

Taking the £2 per day Rent, the breakeven value for usage is about 3.4 Plays per Month. For £2.50 per day Rent, the equivalent value is much lower of course (about 2.2 Plays per Month).

The 'base case' with Rent per Day at £2.50 gives rise to a Final Cash figure of approximately £51000. If the Rent figure is dropped to £2.00, average tape usage (Plays per Month) must rise to about seven to give the same Final Cash figure.

Datafile SKY3 on your disc shows the Data Table and contains the graph (G2) which corresponds to Figure 4.10.

Optimistic, pessimistic and most likely scenarios

Data Tables are useful when judging the sensitivity of cashflow to changes in one or two planning values. However, variables such as Rent per Day and Plays per Month are likely to be related and not all combinations of values will be of interest. For example, high Rent per Day combined with high Plays per Month might be judged to be unlikely to occur and be deemed of little interest therefore. Also, we may want to investigate the effect of changing more than two 'inputs'.

Another approach is to decide a set of values which constitute a 'pessimistic scenario', a worst case, and another set which makes up a best case, an 'optimistic scenario'. For example:

	Pessimistic	Most Likely	Optimistic
Tape Price	35	30	30
Tape Life	25	30	30
Plays per Month	2.00	4.33	5.00
Rent per Day	2.00	2.50	3.00

It is assumed in the following discussion that the values in the original problem formulation can be taken as the 'most likely' estimates.

To retain the numerical values for the twelve cashflow periods assuming the 'most likely' scenario, use the Range Value command to copy the numbers down to a storage area of the spreadsheet (say row 30). Change the planning values to take their 'pessimistic' values. Retain the new (lower) cashflow values using the Range Value command to copy the 'pessimistic' cashflow values down to row 31. In a similar fashion, copy the 'optimistic' cashflow values down to row 32. A comparative graph, such as that shown in Figure 4.11, can be obtained by graphing rows 30, 31 and 32. The graph illustrates the dire consequences for cashflow if the 'pessimistic' scenario were to occur.

'Guesstimating' relationships

The Skywalker model treats Plays per Month for tapes as independent of the Rent per Day charged. In practice, it would seem likely that Plays per Month would decline as rental increased. It is instructive to posit some kind of relationship between the two variables. Figure 4.12 shows a scatter of points purporting to show how Plays per Month decline as Rental increases. A straight line has been fitted to the 'data' and its slope estimated. The equation of this relationship is very approximately:

Plays per month $= 13.05 - 3.58 *$ Rent per Day

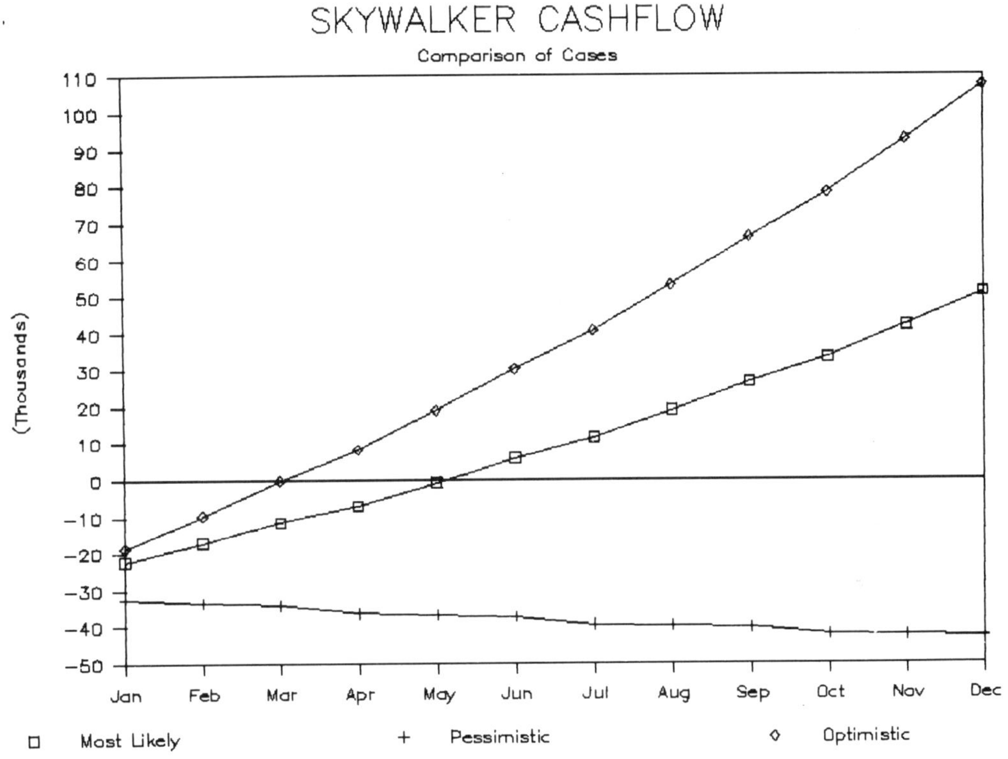

SKYWALKER CASHFLOW
Comparison of Cases

Figure 4.11   Comparison of most likely, optimistic and pessimistic scenarios

Note. It must be emphasized that the relationship is based on much guesswork and should not be taken too seriously. Returning to the original Skywalker model of Figure 4.5, the Plays per Month figure of 4.33 is now replaced by the equation above, substituting the cell address (B20) for Rent per Day.

The effect on Final Cash of holding the Rental at different levels is to be examined. One way of doing this is to evaluate Final Cash via a Data Table with one Input, Rent per Day. (Given a particular value for Rent per Day, the corresponding value of Plays per Month is determined by the equation given above.) Figure 4.13 shows the results of varying Rent per Day represented graphically. It suggests that Closing Cash is greatest if a Rental of about £2.25 is charged.

Datafile SKY4 on your ASM disc illustrates some of the analyses discussed. The named graphs, G2, G3 and G4, relate to Figures 4.11, 4.12 and 4.13. The data for the graphs is set out in the rows well below the monthly cashflow figures.

Skywalker has been used to display a variety of different sensitivity analyses. An underlying assumption has been that tape usage (or 'sales') remain constant over the period of the model. In a new business, it might be more realistic to allow plays per month to 'grow' over time as the video business establishes itself. In the next example, Glowworm Lamps, the growth in sales for a new product is modelled. The spreadsheet model allows for both planned growth and actual growth, departures from planning being explicitly modelled. The development of the model for Glowworm is outlined in the next section and then a range of sensitivity analyses is described.

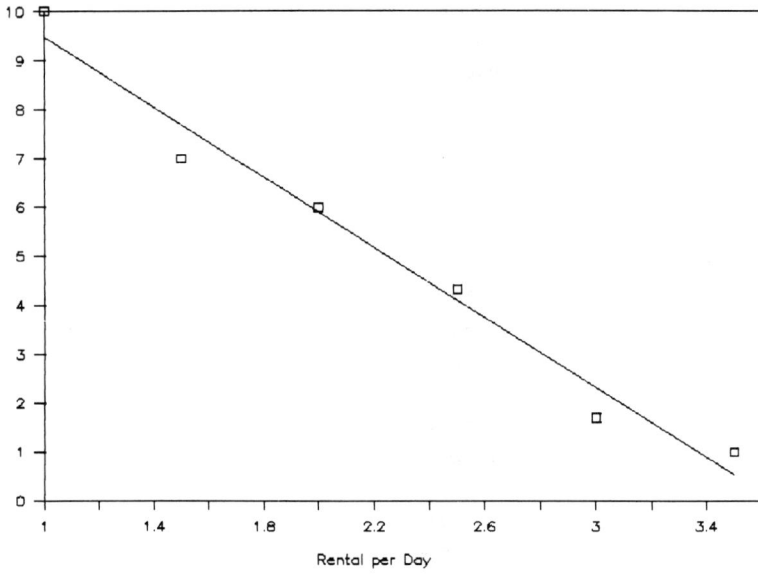

Figure 4.12   Possible relationship between Plays per Month and Rental

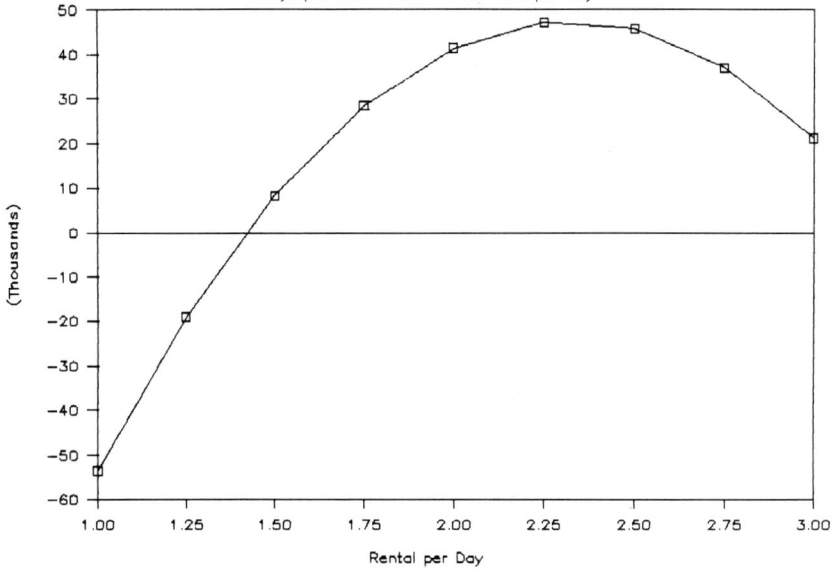

Figure 4.13   Final Cash for different rental values using the linear relationship of Figure 4.12

4.6   Example: Glowworm Lamps

Glowworm Lamps is a small manufacturer of lamps and torches. It is currently considering the production and marketing of a new type of car torch. Initial estimates suggest that the company could sell 50 000 units in the first year and expect to increase sales by as much as 15 per cent per annum thereafter. The variable costs per unit are estimated as follows:

Raw materials   £5   Packaging   £0.50
Direct labour   £2   Distribution   £0.75

The inflation rates for the next three years are forecast to be 5 per cent, 7 per cent and 8 per cent. Inflation will affect variable costs but the fixed costs for the product are likely to remain at roughly the same level over the next four years. The fixed costs consist of factory costs (£25 000) and other costs (£15 000).

In calculating profits over four years, the tax rate can be taken as 25 per cent. Glowworm are thinking in terms of a selling price of £10 for the first year increasing by £0.50 per annum.

For Glowworm, it is crucial to be able to explore the effect on Profits of changes in the planned Sales Volume and Price. The estimates made so far can be regarded as

the 'base case' (probably the most likely scenario). It makes sense to build the planning model in terms of 'percentage changes' from the base case. For this reason the model built for Glowworm includes '%Change' factors for Sales Volume and Price.

4.7   Modelling Glowworm

Figure 4.14 shows one spreadsheet layout suitable for Glowworm. It includes the starting assumptions ('planning values') which are separated out in column B and the initial entries in columns C and (where structurally different) in column D. These model all the different items of revenue and expense for the four years.

Figure 4.15 shows the formulae that underly the numerical entries in Figure 4.14. These are the formulae that have to be keyed in. All the other entries for the second to fourth planning year can be dealt with by the Copy command.

Notice in particular, that there are rows for both the Planned Sales Volume (Pl Sales Vol) and the Actual Sales Volume (Act Sales Vol). The relation between them is :

Actual Sales Vol = (Planned Sales Vol) * (1 + 'Change' Proportion)

In cell B4 is the 'change proportion' for Sales Volume: it is displayed as a percentage, but the entry is a decimal such as 0.05 for a 5 per cent change. The value of this 'change proportion' is currently zero: this is appropriate for the base case.

The entries on row 5 show the Planned Sales Volumes year by year, assuming the volume in the first year is 50000 and that sales increase by 15 per cent per annum thereafter. However, if the Actual Sales Volumes differ from plan, by say, +5 per cent, the values shown on row 6 will represent the actual values for sales.

Similarly, on row 11, the Planned Price is set out (starting at £10 and increasing by £0.50 each year). In cell B10 is the 'change proportion' for Price: once again it is

	A	B	C	D	E	F	G
1	GLOWWORM LAMPS		1988	1989	1990	1991	Total
2	Sales volume	50,000					
3	Planned growth	15%					
4	%Change vol	0%					
5	Pl Sales Vol		50,000	57,500			
6	Act Sales Vol		50,000				
7							
8	Price	10					
9	Planned growth	0.5					
10	%Change price	0.0%					
11	Planned Price		10.00	10.50			
12	Actual Price		10.00				
13							
14	Sales revenue		500,000				
15							
16	Inflation		5%	7%	8%		
17							
18	Variable unit costs						
19	Raw material	5	5	5.25			
20	Labour cost	2	2	2.10			
21	Packaging	0.5	0.5	0.53			
22	Distribution	0.75	0.75	0.79			
23	Total unit cost		8.25	8.66			
24							
25	Direct costs		412,500	0			
26							
27	Gross profit		87,500				
28							
29	Fixed costs						
30	Factory	25,000	25,000				
31	Other	15,000	15,000				
32			40,000				
33							
34	Tax rate	25%					
35	Profit before Tax		47,500				
36	Tax		11,875				
37							
38	Profit after Tax		35,625				
39							

Figure 4.14   Spreadsheet layout for Glowworm

	A	B	C	D
1	GLOWWORM LAMPS		1988	1989
2	Sales volume	50,000		
3	Planned growth	15%		
4	%Change vol	0%		
5	Pl Sales Vol		+B2	(1+$B$3)*C5
6	Act Sales Vol		+C5*(1+$B$4)	
7				
8	Price	10		
9	Planned growth	0.5		
10	%Change price	0.0%		
11	Planned Price		+B8	+C11+$B$9
12	Actual Price		+C11*(1+$B$10)	
13				
14	Sales revenue		+C6*C12	
15				
16	Inflation		0.05	0.07
17				
18	Variable unit costs			
19	Raw material	5	+B19	(1+C$16)*C19
20	Labour cost	2	+B20	(1+C$16)*C20
21	Packaging	0.5	+B21	(1+C$16)*C21
22	Distribution	0.75	+B22	(1+C$16)*C22
23	Total unit cost		@SUM(C19..C22)	@SUM(D19..D22)
24				
25	Direct costs		+C6*C23	+D6*D23
26				
27	Gross profit		+C14-C25	
28				
29	Fixed costs			
30	Factory	25,000	+B30	
31	Other	15,000	+B31	
32	Total fixed		+C30+C31	
33				
34	Tax rate	25%		
35	Profit before Tax		+C27-C32	
36	Tax		+C35*$B$34	
37				
38	Profit after Tax		+C35-C36	
39				

Figure 4.15   Formulae for first and second years

	A	B	C	D	E	F	G
1	GLOWWORM LAMPS		1988	1989	1990	1991	Total
2	Sales volume	50,000					
3	Planned growth	15%					
4	%Change vol	0%					
5	Planned Sales Vol		50,000	57,500	66,125	76,044	249,669
6	Actual Sales Vol		50,000	57,500	66,125	76,044	249,669
7							
8	Price	10					
9	Planned growth	0.5					
10	%Change Price	0.0%					
11	Planned Price		10.00	10.50	11.00	11.50	
12	Actual Price		10.00	10.50	11.00	11.50	
13							
14	Sales revenue		500,000	603,750	727,375	874,503	2,705,628
15							
16	Inflation		5%	7%	8%		
17							
18	Variable unit costs						
19	Raw material	5	5	5.25	5.62	6.07	
20	Labour cost	2	2	2.10	2.25	2.43	
21	Packaging	0.5	0.5	0.53	0.56	0.61	
22	Distribution	0.75	0.75	0.79	0.84	0.91	
23	Total unit cost		8.25	8.66	9.27	10.01	
24							
25	Direct costs		412,500	498,094	612,904	761,227	2,284,725
26							
27	Gross profit		87,500	105,656	114,471	113,276	420,903
28							
29	Fixed costs						
30	Factory	25,000	25,000	25,000	25,000	25,000	
31	Other	15,000	15,000	15,000	15,000	15,000	
32			40,000	40,000	40,000	40,000	
33							
34	Tax rate	25%					
35	Profit before Tax		47,500	65,656	74,471	73,276	260,903
36	Tax		11,875	16,414	18,618	18,319	65,226
37							
38	Profit after Tax		35,625	49,242	55,853	54,957	195,677

Figure 4.16   Glowworm profit after tax: four years' results

displayed as a percentage, but the entry is a decimal. The relationship between Actual Price and Planned Price is:

Actual Price = (Planned Price) * (1 + 'Change' Proportion)

Currently, the 'change proportion' is zero so Actual and Planned Sales are identical. However, these 'change proportions' in the model will enable Glowworm to discover the effect on profits of, say, 5 per cent or 10 per cent departures from plan.

Figure 4.16 shows the finished model for Glowworm after the formulae have been copied across to the fourth year and Totals added where appropriate. The corresponding datafile on your ASM disc is called GLOW1.

The spreadsheet model suggests, after tax, profits over the next four years of approximately £36 000, £49 000, £56 000 and £55 000 respectively (see Profit after Tax, row 38 of the model). This assumes of course that Sales Volume and Price are as planned and that all the other estimates turn out to be 'on target'.

4.8   Sensitivity analysis for Glowworm

The Glowworm model involves many assumptions and estimates. Therefore it is only proper to examine the sensitivity of projected profits to changes in these assumptions. In reporting the results of the sensitivity analyses, it sometimes helps to present results in the form of graphical comparisons. This approach sometimes circumvents the problem of an overload of numerical information. Graphs are good for bold effects and can enliven the presentation of results. The approach is illustrated in the following paragraphs.

For example, suppose inflation is 8 per cent during the first year and 10 per cent thereafter. What would the profitability of the new torch be in these circumstances? The numerical answers are easily obtained by changing the inflation figures in row 16. However, in comparing these results with the earlier 'base case' profits, it is useful to save the original profit figures and graph them together with the profits from the case with the higher inflation figures. Once again, the Range Value command allows values (such as Profit in row 38) to be transferred to a storage area in the spreadsheet. Year by year profit figures for different cases can be retained in the spreadsheet for subsequent graphing. Figure 4.17 compares Profits for the original estimates, the 'base case', with those for the higher inflation figures.

Next suppose the company were to sell 3 per cent more units per year and they were to increase the selling price by 10 per cent per year more than anticipated? What would be the effect on Profit after Tax year by year. Figure 4.18 shows how Profits would compare with the 'base case' and the high inflation case.

It is interesting to see how profits change as we vary the projected Sales Volume over a range from −10 per cent to 5 per cent of the initial assumption. This is most easily achieved by means of a Data Table. Profit after Tax for the four years and the Total Profit are set out along a row as shown in Figure 4.19. A set of values for the %Change in Sales Volume is keyed into the left-hand column. The Data Table command for a Table with one Input (%Change in Sales Volume in cell B4) is invoked and the values shown in Figure 4.19, rows 48 to 51, are obtained.

These results can also be displayed graphically (Figure 4.20). A 5 per cent change in Sales Volume gives rise to roughly an 8 per cent change in Profits.

GLOWWORM PROFITS AFTER TAX
Inflation (8,10,10%)

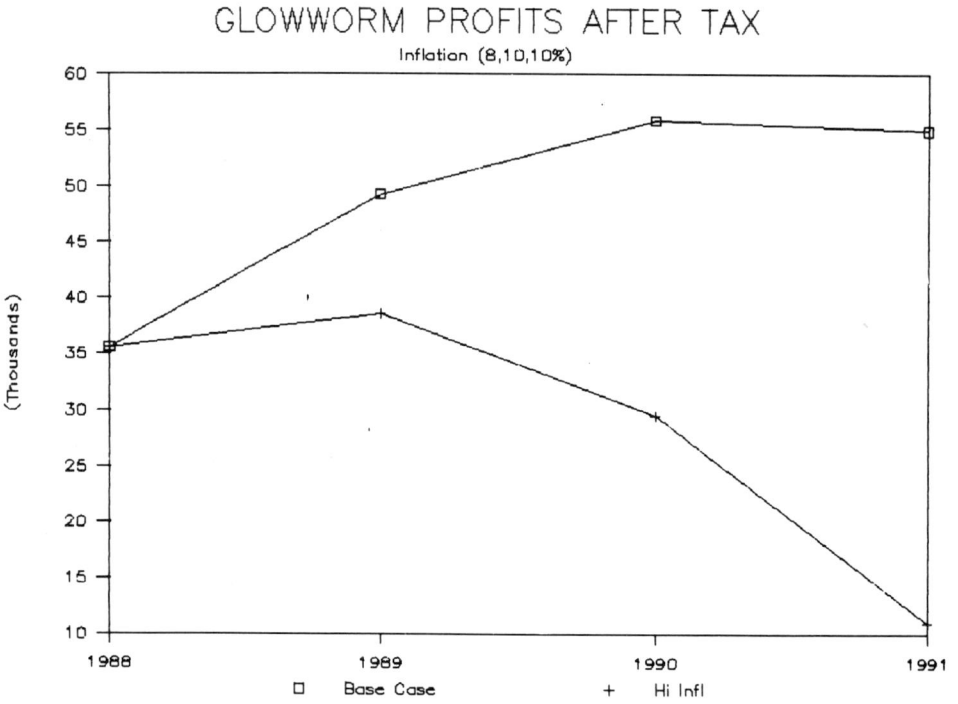

Figure 4.17 Comparison of high inflation case with base case

GLOWWORM PROFITS AFTER TAX
%Change in Vol (3%) in Price (10%)

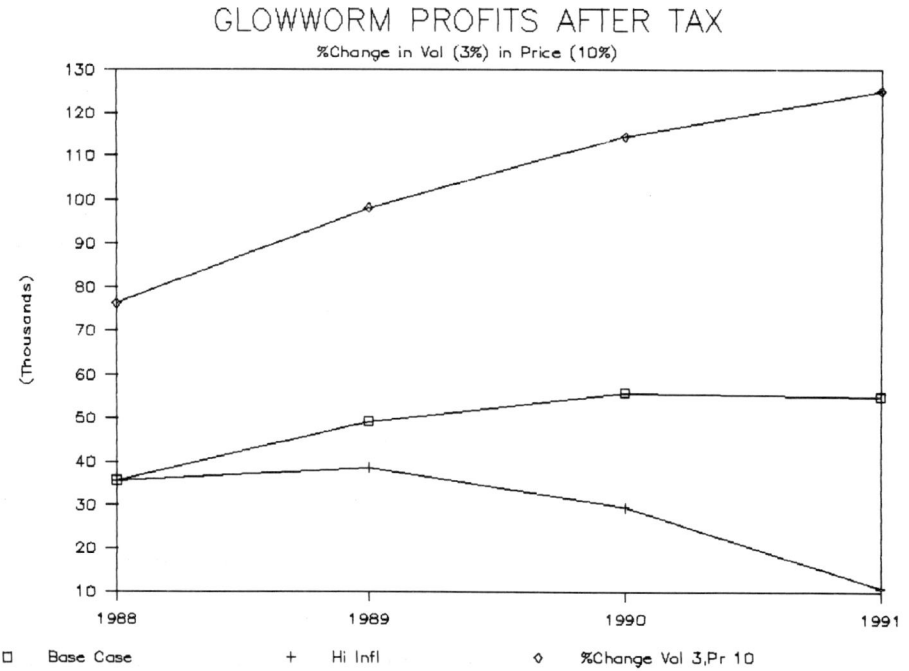

Figure 4.18 Comparison of case with increased volume and price with base case

	A	B	C	D	E	F	G
38	Profit after Tax		35,625	49,242	55,853	54,957	195,677
39							
40	RESULTS		1988	1989	1990	1991	Total
41	Base Case		35,625	49,242	55,853	54,957	195,677
42	DATA for G1						
43	Infl 8,10,10%		35,625	38,569	29,463	11,001	114,658
44	DATA for G2						
45	%Change Vol 3 Price 10%		76,219	98,259	114,618	125,061	414,157
46	DATA for G3						
47	DTab Prof after Tax		35,625	49,242	55,853	54,957	195,677
48		-10%	29,063	41,318	47,268	46,461	164,109
49	%Change S Vol	-5%	32,344	45,280	51,560	50,709	179,893
50		0%	35,625	49,242	55,853	54,957	195,677
51		5%	38,906	53,204	60,146	59,205	211,461
52	DATA for G4 &G4A						
53	Infl 12%,%Ch Vol -10%		29,063	18,904	(934)	(34,653)	12,379
54	Price Incr(B9) 1.15		29,063	44,132	57,091	65,439	195,724

Figure 4.19   Data store for %Change Sales Volume (rows 47 to 51)

As well as containing the results of the Data Table, Figure 4.19 shows the store of numerical results on which the comparative graphs are based. Row 38 contains the Profit after Tax formulae at the bottom of the spreadsheet model. Each time a 'what-if' is carried out, the Profit values are transferred to the RESULTS area (row 40 and below) using the Range Value command. Each graph that is set up is based on data ranges contained in this 'storage' part of the spreadsheet. The graphs are given 'names' (using Graph Name Create) so that they can be redisplayed with ease without having to alter planning values again.

Continuing with the sensitivity analysis, suppose inflation is exceptionally high (12 per cent per annum) and unit sales are 10 per cent below the original estimate. Figure 4.21 shows the effect on Profits. The upper line-graph represents Profits for the base case. The lowest line-graph shows the depressed Profits resulting from the above changes. The third line-graph represents the Profit cells in row 38 which are linked into the model. By experimenting with the cell for Price Planned Growth (B9), the third line-graph can be adjusted by a trial and error procedure until it overlaps the upper (base case) line graph. This leads to the price increase that would maintain roughly the same total profit over the next four years. This is 'goal-seeking'. If the value in cell B9 is increased gradually from the base case value of £0.50 up to £1.15, the Profits are 'restored', roughly speaking, to their former levels.

Once again, it would be worth while investigating any relationship between pricing and sales (as was done for Skywalker). The model for Glowworm's new product would be potentially more powerful if the two variables were linked.

The datafile GLOW2 on your disc contains the analysis discussed in this section and it contains named graphs which relate to Figures 4.17, 4.18, 4.20 and 4.21.

GLOWWORM PROFIT AFTER TAX

Different Projected Sales Figures

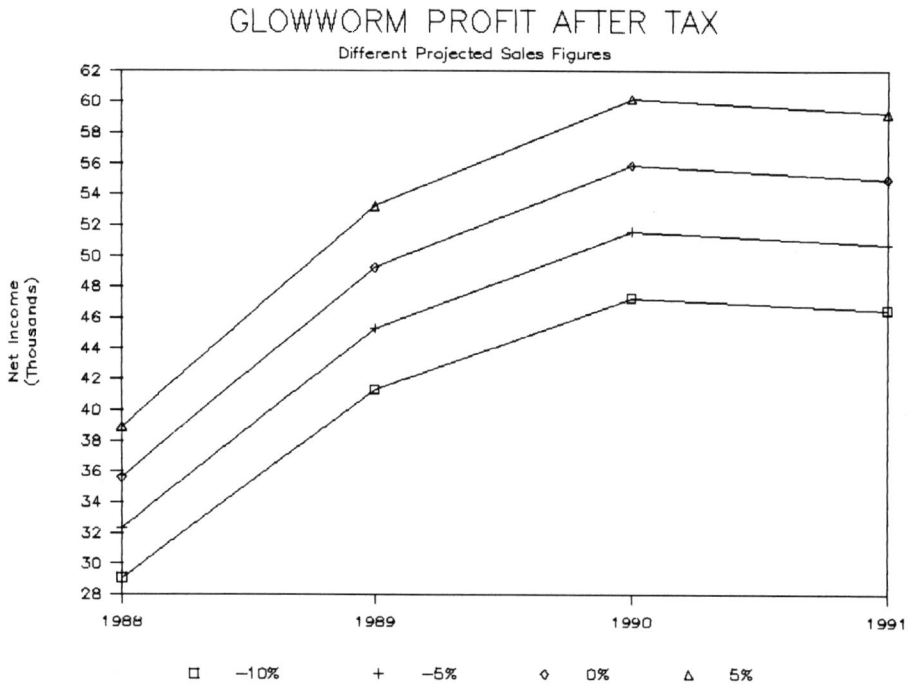

Figure 4.20   Comparison of profits for different sales volumes

GLOWWORM:Goal Seeking

Varying Price Growth (B9)

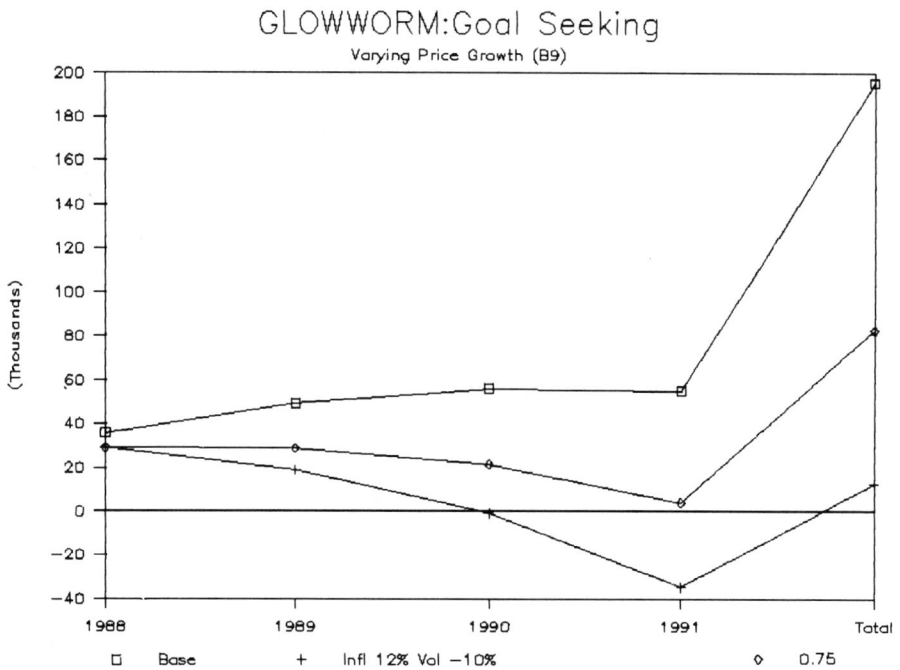

Figure 4.21   Goal seeking to find necessary price growth

CHAPTER 5

Financial Modelling — Budgeting

5.1 Introduction

Budgeting is the process whereby plans are consolidated into financial targets for the period ahead. Although the preparation of annual budgets can be something of a ritual, they do provide a framework for setting out the path to be followed and the yardsticks by which progress should be measured. One major advantage of using a budget to express future plans is that the format is pretty much standard and is therefore likely to be understood by nearly all those connected with business.

There is nothing worse than a budget with an arithmetical error in it. (People cannot resist the temptation to add up rows and columns to check for errors.) Budgets must also be comprehensive, showing the profit and loss (P & L) account, balance sheet and cashflow to give a complete representation of the firm's financial health. Again, these requirements make budgeting an ideal spreadsheet application.

The model described in this chapter meets these objectives but, in addition to this, it greatly improves the effectiveness of the whole budgeting exercise by enabling 'what-if' questions to be answered. Ideally it should be used to finalize a plan that has already been developed using the sort of profit planning model described in the previous chapter.

The accounting principles on which the budget worksheet is based will not be described here in any great depth. If you are unfamiliar with the rudiments of accountancy, you may need to read up on the subject before embarking on the description that follows.

5.2 Example: Ash Electronics

Ash is a fairly typical small business involved in electronics assembly work. Its balance sheet at 31st December looked like this:

Fixed assets: £200

Current assets:

Stock	£250	Creditors	£216
Debtors	£600	Overdraft	£0
Cash	£120	Equity	£954
Total	£1170		£1170

Sales for the coming months have been estimated as follows:

January	£650	April	£700
February	£500	May	£960
March	£900	June	£1000

Materials costs can be assumed to be roughly 36 per cent of sales and other variable expenses a further 10 per cent of sales. There are fixed expenses each month of approximately £350. All Ash's sales are for credit. Debtors take on average about 60 days to pay whereas Ash has to pay its creditors within 30 days. Depreciation works out at about 1 per cent per month of fixed assets and the interest rate on any overdraft is also 1 per cent per month. Ash want to work out their forward budgets for the next few months to see what levels of overdraft are required at the bank. They have sales estimates but would also like to know how sensitive profits are to changes in these estimates.

5.3 The Budget Worksheet

The central tool in developing budgets for Ash is the Budget Worksheet. The Worksheet is a combined P & L Account and Balance Sheet. It is an extremely useful way of modelling the interrelationships between the various conventional accounting statements and can highlight the distinction between cashflow and accounting profit. It can be drawn up month by month (or annually) over the future planning period. Figure 5.1 shows a completed worksheet for Ash's transactions during the month of January.

```
ASH ELECTRONICS:
Budget Worksheet                                                                            !
------------------------<<<---------------------  ASSETS  ----->>> <<<--------LIABILITIES----------------->>>!
January = Month 0     Fixed Assts   Stock    Debtors   Cash    Overdraft  Creditors  Equity   P & L Acct !
-----------------------------------------------------------------------------------------------------------!
Opening Balance    !    £200       £250      £600     £120       £0        £216      £954        £0 !
Sales              !                         £650                                              £650 !
Cost of Materials  !              (£234)                                                      (£234)!
Variable Expenses  !                                 (£65)                                     (£65)!
Fixed Expenses     !                                 (£350)                                   (£350)!
Depreciation       !     (£2)                                                                   (£2)!
Purchases          !               £180                                     £180                £0 !
Payment to Creditors !                               (£216)               (£216)                £0 !
Receipts from Debtor !                     (£600)     £600                                      £0 !
Interest           !                                   £0                                       £0 !
Overdraft          !                                   £0        £0                             £0 !
P & L              !                                                                  (£1)      £1 !
Closing Balance    !    £198       £196      £650      £89       £0         £180      £953       £0 !
-----------------------------------------------------------------------------------------------------------!
                                                                                                   !
```

Figure 5.1   Completed Budget Worksheet for Ash Electronics

Columns represent the different Balance Sheet items on which monthly transactions impact, for example Fixed Assets, Stock, Debtors, etc. The Balance Sheet headings are across the top with 'assets' on the left-hand side and 'liabilities' on the right. Immediately below are the Opening Balances for each Balance Sheet item; for example Fixed Assets of £200, Stock at £250, Debtors at £600 and Cash at £120 on the Asset side: Overdraft at £0, Creditors at £216, Equity at £954 on the liabilities side. The P & L Account column acts as a sump in which profit/loss for the period is collected and then transferred to the Equity column at the end of the period. Its value is therefore zero at the start of the financial period, January. An alternative interpretation says that the P & L entry ensures that the left-hand (assets) and right-hand side, (liabilities) balance. Since:

assets = (liabilities + equity)

at the start of the accounting period, the P & L Account value must be zero.

Rows represent the different types of transactions involving income and expense, for example Sales, Materials Cost, Purchases, etc. Many of these appear on the P & L Account. Each transaction gives rise to two entries in the worksheet. Usually these are equal entries one on each side of the worksheet. For example, Sales in the month of £650 appear on the asset side of the worksheet as a Debtor entry and on the right-hand side as a P & L entry. Material Costs of £234 appear in the P & L and cause the Stock balance to be reduced. Both Variable and Fixed Expenses appear in the P & L and cause Cash to be reduced. The transactions in some rows do not have entries in the P & L column, but they are required to provide additional links in the model. For example, Payment to Creditors triggers a reduction in Cash and a corresponding reduction in Creditors. Transactions such as this as well as Purchases and Receipts from Debtors do affect cashflow, which in turn determines the level of overdraft required. The resulting Interest transaction has two entries on the right-hand side of the worksheet, one under Overdraft with an equal but opposite sign entry in the P & L column to maintain the balance.

The last transaction involves clearing out the profit (loss) at the end of the month's transactions and adding it to the Equity column. Notice that the entry in the P & L column is numerically equal to the profit but the sign is reversed. It is balanced by the entry of profit in the Equity column.

The last row is the Closing Balance, that is the Opening Balance plus or minus any transaction entries in the column above. The Closing Balance for the P & L column is of course zero since the profit has been cleared to the Equity column.

If you are familiar with debits and credits you will have no trouble with the sign of the transaction entries in the worksheet. If debits and credits are one of life's great mysteries, the best thing is to fix the ones that are obvious and sort the rest out by trial and error in the confident knowledge that the Opening and Closing Balances in the P & L column have to be zero!

Figure 5.1 shows the planned profit and cash requirements for one month's operations, and the budgeting can be continued in the same way for subsequent months. The Closing Balance row forms the starting point for the next month's Budget Worksheet. Implicit in the Budget Worksheet figures are various central assumptions: in particular, assumptions about sales in the coming months and percentages used for judging costs of various kinds.

Usually the objective is to make several projections of the profits over the January to March period and on beyond on the basis of different assumptions. It is important to be explicit about the assumptions to be tested. The assumptions in Ash's case are estimates of sales over the coming months and of cost of goods sold, etc. These are the Planning Values and they are variables that can be altered by the user as the implications of the model are explored.

5.4 Building the Budget Worksheet

The steps in setting up the Budget Worksheet are described in this section. The starting datafile is called BUDGET1. After retrieving this file, explore the layout using the pointer keys and the Tab and Shift Tab keys for horizontal 'page' jumps.

Figure 5.2 shows the layout in 1-2-3 for the Budget Worksheet for Ash at the start of January. This corresponds with the datafile BUDGET1 on your disc. (Alternatively, you may prefer to key the layout in. To do this, copy the headings and boundary lines from Figure 5.2 and set the Global Format to Currency. Enter the Planning Values (where necessary changing the Range Format) and the Opening Balances.)

The worksheet is ready for modelling January's transactions. Row 6 contains the Opening Balance for each Balance Sheet item, for example Fixed Assets of £200, Stock at £250, etc. Of course, the balances on the left-hand 'assets' side are balanced out by the 'liability' balances on the right. This concept of balance underlies the zero entry in cell J6, the P & L Account entry.

The assumptions (Planning Values) are shown in Figure 5.2 positioned to the right of the main calculation area in columns L and M. The actual values are in cells M4 to M18. Firstly, there are the sales estimates in cells M4 to M11. The notation used is: 0 denotes the current month, -1 the previous month and 1 next month. Therefore, in the January worksheet, Sales(0) denotes January sales, Sales(1) February sales and Sales(-1) December sales. (In the February worksheet, Sales(0) will represent February sales, etc.) Below the sales estimates are the other Planning Values. Cell M12 contains the cost of materials percentage (36 per cent), M13 the variable expenses percentage (10 per cent) and M14 the fixed expenses (£350). In M17 and M18 are the percentages for calculating interest on overdraft and depreciation on fixed assets. Figures for 'debtor days' and 'creditor days' also are displayed. Strictly speaking, these cells are not proper planning values; that is if the values in these cells are changed, the model will not adjust automatically to reflect the new values. The assumptions about debtor days, etc., are built into the way the modelling of debtors is carried out. Changed assumptions will require a fundamental reworking of the model. Nevertheless, the debtor and creditor days assumptions are set out here for completeness.

Formulae for Closing Balances

The Closing Balances are in row 18. Each Closing Balance is calculated by summing the appropriate column, so it is the Opening Balance net of the transactions in the month. For example, in the Fixed Assets column, the Closing Balance equals the Opening Balance plus any entries in column B. Therefore cell C18 contains the formula:

@SUM(C6..C17)

This is a general formula which applies for all columns in the Budget Worksheet. Therefore it has been copied across row 18 as far as column J to provide Closing Balances for all the worksheet columns.

The Closing Balances equal the Opening Balances at present since no transactions have been modelled yet. Notice, however, that formulae-like sums can be entered in advance of the entries that make up the sum.

	A	B	C	D	E	F
1	ASH ELECTRONICS:					
2	Budget Worksheet					
3	----------------------<<<----------------------				ASSETS	------->>>
4	January = Month 0		Fixed Assts	Stock	Debtors	Cash
5	---					
6	Opening Balance	!	200	250	600	120
7	Sales	!			+M9	
8	Cost of Materials	!		-M12*M9		
9	Variable Expenses	!				-M13*M9
10	Fixed Expenses	!				-M14
11	Depreciation	! -M18*C6				
12	Purchases	!		+M12*M8		
13	Payment to Creditors	!				-M10*M12
14	Receipts from Debtor	!			-M11	-E14
15	Interest	!				-G6*M17
16	Overdraft	!				-M19*M20
17	P & L	!				
18	Closing Balance	!	£198	£196	£650	£89
19	---					

	G	H	I	J	K	L	M
						PLANNNING VALUES	
3	<<<--------LIABILITIES--------------------->>>					------------------------	
4	Overdraft	Creditors	Equity		P & L Acct !	Sales(5)	£1,000
5	--!					Sales(4)	£960
6	0	216	954		£0 !	Sales(3)	£700
7					£650 !	Sales(2)	£900
8					(£234)!	Sales(1)	£500
9					(£65)!	Sales(0)	£650
10					(£350)!	Sales(-1)	£600
11					(£2)!	Sales(-2)	£600
12		+D12			£0 !	Mat/Sales	36%
13		+F13			£0 !	Var/Sales	10%
14					£0 !	Fixed Exp	£350
15					£0 !	Dtr Days	60
16	+F16				£0 !	Ctr Days	30
17			@SUM(J6..J16)		£0 !	Int Rate /Mo	1.00%
18	£0	£180	£954		(£1)!	Depn /Mo	1.00%
19	--					Cash Calc	£89
20						O/D (0=No 0/D)	0

Figure 5.2   Layout of January Budget Worksheet in 1-2-3

68

Formulae for the P & L column

Changes in assets are either reflected in changes in liabilities or they result in flows reported in the P & L account. Thus entries in the P & L column (column J) act to 'balance' asset side entries against liability side entries. In any row, the P & L entry is the sum of the entries on the 'assets' side of the spreadsheet (that is columns C to F) minus the entries on the 'liabilities' side (that is columns G to I). With spreadsheet modelling, we can perform this balancing operation by means of a general formula. Therefore the formula in cell J7 is:

@SUM(C7..F7)—@SUM(G7..I7)

and similar formulae will be found in the P & L column down to row 16. Cell J17 is blank at present, but will be dealt with in the following section.

This completes the layout and general formulae for the Budget Formulae. The next step is to model the income and expenditure transactions for January.

5.5 Modelling January's transactions

Having set up the general framework, we now turn to the detailed transactions. It is important to express these entries in terms of formulae based on the Planning Values where possible. With formulae, you will be able to answer 'what-if' questions about the effect of changing your assumptions at a later stage.

Worksheet Titles and Windows

At this point, it may help to 'freeze' the headings and row labels so that they remain on screen in entering the formulae for the transactions. To effect this, put the pointer in cell B6 and choose:

/ Worksheet Titles Both

(The frozen titles can be released when required by choosing:

/ Worksheet Titles Clear)

In keying in formulae, it is advisable where possible to 'point' to cells to include them in formulae, rather than type in the cell addresses. Splitting the screen into two parts and using the Window key (f6) to jump from window to window can help. Position the pointer one column in from the edge of the right-hand side of the screen in the L column. Then use the sequence:

/ Worksheet Window Vertical

to leave the Planning Values in the right-hand window and a portion of the Budget Worksheet in the left-hand window. To return to one window, the sequence of commands is:

/ Worksheet Window Clear

Working down row by row, January's transactions are entered in the appropriate columns. Because of the way the Budget Worksheet is extended to other periods (to be described in Section 5.6), it is better *not* to make the references to Planning Value cells absolute, i.e. not to use $ signs in the cell addresses.

Sales (row 7)

Sales in January (month 0) are forecast to be £650 (in cell M9). All sales are for credit and hence are entered in the Debtors column. The entry under Debtors in cell E7 is the formula:

+ M9

The balancing entry is in the P & L column and is taken care of by the formula already in the P & L column.

Cost of materials (row 8)

Defined as a percentage of Sales, the percentage is given in cell M12. The formula for the reduction in Stock in cell D8 is:

− M12*M9

which is currently −£234. The offsetting entry is in the P & L column and is taken care of by the formula already in cell J8.

Variable expenses (row 9)

This is again a percentage of Sales—the percentage is in cell M13. The formula under Cash in cell F9 is:

− M13*M9
which evaluates to −£65. The balancing entry is in the P & L column in cell J9.

Fixed expenses (row 10)

The amount is in cell M14 and the entry to Cash in cell F10 is simply:

− M14

Again the offsetting entry is in the P & L column.

Depreciation (row 11)

The rate per month is in cell M18 and the Fixed Assets in cell C6. Depreciation is deducted from the Fixed Assets column. The formula in cell C11 is:

— M18*C6

The corresponding entry is in the P & L column.

Purchases (row 12)

Purchases arise because stock that is consumed has to be replaced. It is for the modeller to decide what determines purchasing patterns. Here, it is assumed that the amount purchased in the current month (denoted month 0) is the Material cost of sales (in M12) for the month ahead (in cell M8). The effect of purchasing is to increase stock, so cell D12 contains the formula:

+ M12*M8

which has the value £180. The balancing entry in cell H12 under Creditors is:

+ D12

Payment to creditors (row 13)

Again, the modelling assumptions for handling creditors have to be decided. Here, it is assumed that purchases are paid for a month in arrears. Payment in the current month is therefore for purchases made last month (month - 1). The formula in cell F13 under Cash is:

— M12*M10

which evaluates to —£216. A similar entry is made in cell H13 under Creditors by entering:

+ F13   in cell H13

Receipts from debtors (row 14)

Here it is assumed that receipts this month are from sales two months ago (in cell M11). Therefore the entry under Debtors in cell E14 is:

—M11

which displays as —£600. The balancing entry is an addition to the Cash column, so cell F14 contains the entry:

—E14

Interest (row 15)

This is calculated on the opening Overdraft (in cell G6) using the interest rate shown in cell M17. Thus the Cash outflow is given by the formula in cell F15:

$- M17*G6$

and the corresponding entry is in the P & L column.

Overdraft (row 16)

This is a little more complicated. The Opening Cash Balance is in cell F6. The month's cash transactions are in column F from F7 to F15 so the Closing Cash Balance is the sum of entries in the range F6..F15. If the consequence of these transactions is that the end-of-period Cash Balance is negative, then the Overdraft has to be increased. Cell M19 calculates the end-of-period Cash Balance:

@SUM(F6..F15)

In cell M20, the @IF special function tests for a negative Cash Balance. The formula:

@IF(M19>0,0,1)

will display as 0 if the Cash Balance is positive and 1 otherwise. In other words, it will display 1 if additional Overdraft is required and 0 if no Overdraft is required. The product of these two cells, M19 and M20, gives the Overdraft required to get the Cash Balance back to zero whatever the circumstances with respect to Cash.
Hence the entry for the overdraft in cell F16 under Cash is:

$-M19*M20$

and in cell G16 the balancing entry is +F16.

P & L account (row 17)

In the P & L row, the month's Profit (or Loss) is transferred to the Equity column. The entry in cell I17 under Equity is the sum of entries in the P & L column, that is:

@SUM(J7..J16)

which evaluates to $-£1$. The balancing entry (in cell J17) of:

$- I17$

clears the P & L account balance to zero. The sign of the entry in cell I17 is positive for Profit and negative for Loss (that is shareholders' equity increases if you make a profit).

```
         A              B      C       D         E          F
 1 ASH ELECTRONICS:
 2 Budget Worksheet
 3 ------------------------<<<---------------------    ASSETS    ------->>>
 4 January = Month 0      Fixed Assts    Stock     Debtors     Cash
 5 ----------------------------------------------------------------------
 6 Opening Balance     !    £200       £250       £600        £120
 7 Sales               !                          £650
 8 Cost of Materials   !               (£234)
 9 Variable Expenses   !                                      (£65)
10 Fixed Expenses      !                                      (£350)
11 Depreciation        !    (£2)
12 Purchases           !               £180
13 Payment to Creditors!                                      (£216)
14 Receipts from Debtor!                          (£600)      £600
15 Interest            !                                      £0
16 Overdraft           !                                      £0
17 P & L               !
18 Closing Balance     !    £198       £196       £650        £89
19 ----------------------------------------------------------------------
```

```
         G          H         I        J        K              L            M
                                                         PLANNNING VALUES
 3 <<<--------LIABILITIES--------------------->>>    ----------------------
 4 Overdraft  Creditors   Equity    P & L Acct !   Sales(5)        £1,000
 5 -------------------------------------------- !   Sales(4)          £960
 6    £0        £216       £954          £0    !   Sales(3)          £700
 7                                     £650    !   Sales(2)          £900
 8                                   (£234)    !   Sales(1)          £500
 9                                    (£65)    !   Sales(0)          £650
10                                   (£350)    !   Sales(-1)         £600
11                                     (£2)    !   Sales(-2)         £600
12               £180                    £0    !   Mat/Sales          36%
13             (£216)                    £0    !   Var/Sales          10%
14                                       £0    !   Fixed Exp         £350
15                                       £0    !   Dtr Days           60
16    £0                                 £0    !   Ctr Days           30
17                          (£1)         £1    !   Int Rate /Mo     1.00%
18    £0        £180        £953         £0    !   Depn /Mo         1.00%
19 --------------------------------------------    Cash Calc          £89
20                                                O/D (0=No O/D)       0
```

Figure 5.3   Completed worksheet for January's transactions

```
        A              B       C         D          E          F
 1 ASH ELECTRONICS:
 2 Budget Worksheet
 3 ----------------------<<<---------------------  ASSETS   ------->>>
 4 January = Month 0      Fixed Assts   Stock    Debtors     Cash
 5 ------------------------------------------------------------------------
 6 Opening Balance    !      £200       £250       £600       £120
 7 Sales              !
 8 Cost of Materials  !
 9 Variable Expenses  !
10 Fixed Expenses     !
11 Depreciation       !
12 Purchases          !
13 Payment to Creditors !
14 Receipts from Debtor !
15 Interest           !
16 Overdraft          !
17 P & L              !
18 Closing Balance    !      £200       £250       £600       £120
19 ------------------------------------------------------------------------
```

```
           G        H        I        J        K         L          M
                                                     PLANNNING VALUES
     <<<--------LIABILITIES-------------------->>>   -------------------------
  4  Overdraft  Creditors  Equity   P & L Acct !  Sales(5)   £1,000   4
  5 -------------------------------------------!  Sales(4)    £960    5
  6     £0       £216      £954        £0 !       Sales(3)    £700    6
  7                                     £0 !       Sales(2)    £900    7
  8                                     £0 !       Sales(1)    £500    8
  9                                     £0 !       Sales(0)    £650    9
 10                                     £0 !       Sales(-1)   £600   10
 11                                     £0 !       Sales(-2)   £600   11
 12                                     £0 !       Mat/Sales    36%   12
 13                                     £0 !       Var/Sales    10%   13
 14                                     £0 !       Fixed Exp   £350   14
 15                                     £0 !       Dtr Days     60    15
 16                                     £0 !       Ctr Days     30    16
 17                                        !       Int Rate /Mo 1.00% 17
 18     £0       £216      £954        £0 !       Depn /Mo    1.00%  18
 19 ----------------------------------------------  Cash Calc   £120   19
                                                   O/D (0=No 0/D)  0  20
```

Figure 5.4   Formulae in January Budget Worksheet

This concludes the modelling of January's transactions. The Balance Sheet for the end of January can be read off from row 18, the Profit and Loss account for January can be seen in column J and the Cash position (with the Overdraft requirement) is shown in column F. Figure 5.3 shows the display at this stage in the modelling and the formulae are summarised in Figure 5.4.

The model with all the formulae for January is also on the disc, and is called BUDGET2.

Before proceeding to extend the model for February and future months, clear the 'frozen' titles (/ Worksheet Titles Clear) and return to a single window (/ Worksheet Window Clear).

5.6 Extending the model for February

A moment's reflection will confirm that the basic structure of the transactions in January will hold good for February, March and other subsequent periods. The current level of sales will change month by month but the relationships between the various elements in the Budget Worksheet will not. Therefore, it is relatively easy to extend the model to cover future months simply by copying the worksheet for January and by making a few simple adjustments.

A schematic diagram of the arrangement of the multiple period model is shown in Figure 5.5. The Budget Worksheets for four consecutive months lie under one another. The four worksheets are connected together by making the Closing Balances of one

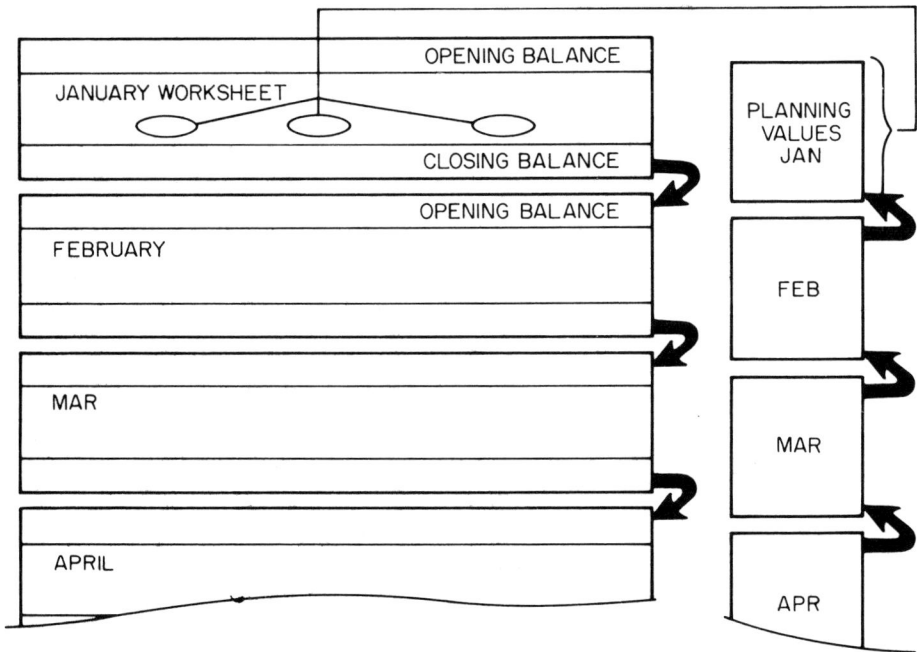

Figure 5.5   Layout for multiple period Budget Worksheet

	A	B	C	D	E	F
22	Budget Worksheet					
23	-----------------------<<<---------------------				ASSETS	------->>>
24	February = Month 0		Fixed Assts	Stock	Debtors	Cash
25	---					
26	Opening Balance	!	£198	£196	£650	£89
27	Sales	!			£500	
28	Cost of Materials	!		(£180)		
29	Variable Expenses	!				(£50)
30	Fixed Expenses	!				(£350)
31	Depreciation	!	(£2)			
32	Purchases	!		£324		
33	Payment to Creditors	!				(£234)
34	Receipts from Debtor	!			(£600)	£600
35	Interest	!				£0
36	Overdraft	!				£0
37	P & L	!				
38	Closing Balance	!	£196	£340	£550	£55
39	---					

	G	H	I	J	K	L PLANNNING VALUES	M
23	<<<--------LIABILITIES--------------------->>>					------------------------	
24	Overdraft	Creditors	Equity	P & L Acct !		Sales(5)	NA
25	---!					Sales(4)	£1,000
26	£0	£180	£953	£0 !		Sales(3)	£960
27				£500 !		Sales(2)	£700
28				(£180)!		Sales(1)	£900
29				(£50)!		Sales(0)	£500
30				(£350)!		Sales(-1)	£650
31				(£2)!		Sales(-2)	£600
32		£324		£0 !		Mat/Sales	36%
33		(£234)		£0 !		Var/Sales	10%
34				£0 !		Fixed Exp	£350
35				£0 !		Dtr Days	60
36	£0			£0 !		Ctr Days	30
37			(£82)	£82 !		Int Rate /Mo	1%
38	£0	£270	£871	£0 !		Depn /Mo	1%
	--					Cash Calc	£55
						O/D (0=No 0/D)	0

Figure 5.6 Completed worksheet for February's transactions

month become the Opening Balances of the next month so that changes in one month are reflected through into subsequent months.

The procedure for extending the model to be described below minimizes the amount of keyboard entry required of the user. The basic idea is to copy down the whole model and then adjust the Planning Values to reflect the fact that the model has moved on another month. Some of the entries have to be adjusted the first time you copy the worksheet down; after that it all becomes automatic. The procedure for extending the model to the second month will be described first.

Suppose the Budget Worksheet for February is to start in cell A22:

1. Copy the whole of the model down to the new location. Use / Copy from the cell range A2..M20 to cell A22 one 'page' down in the spreadsheet.
2. Edit the heading in cell A24 to read February = Month 0.
3. Now connect the February set of Sales Planning Values to the January set by putting the formula +M4 into cell M25 and then copying all the way down to cell M31.

   This has two effects. Firstly, any changes to the January Planning Values are carried through to the February worksheet, so you can change the whole model via the January column of Planning Values. Secondly, the sales for February are aligned with the model, so Month 0 is now February with sales of £500. If the estimated sales five months ahead (Sales(5)) is not available, enter the special function @NA into cell M24. This entry indicates that the cell entry is not yet available. Any cell that uses cell M24 as part of a formula will display NA (as opposed to giving an incorrect answer).
4. Now connect the rest of the Planning Values for February to those of January. Do this by putting +M12 in cell M32 and copying the formula down to row 38. You will find that some of the values appear in the wrong format, so correct them using the Range Format command. The Cashcalc and O/D entries do not need amending.
5. Lastly, link the Closing Balances for January to the Opening Balances for February by putting +C18 in cell C26 and copying this formula across to column J.

The resulting values are shown in Figure 5.6. To check that the worksheets are properly linked, try changing some of the Planning Values adjacent to the January worksheet and watch the effect on the February Closing Balance.

5.7 Extending the model to March, April etc.

All the cells of the February model now refer directly or indirectly to the January model. If February is now copied to become March (that is if the range A22..M40 is copied down a 'page' to A42), all the references will be transferred intact. The only change you have to make is to alter the title to read March = Month 0. Observe that the first two Planning Values now display NA for Not Available. If further estimates exist, they should be entered.

5.8 Adding summary accounts

The model in its Budget Worksheet form is not very easy to interpret. When presenting conclusions, it is much better if the output is summarized in the form of conventional accounts.

	O	P	Q	R	S	T
1 !	P & L Account					!
2 !	============					!
3 !						!
4 !	MONTH --->	January	February	March	April	!
5 !						!
6 !	Sales	£650	£500	£900	£700	!
7 !	Material	(£234)	(£180)	(£324)	(£252)	!
8 !						!
9 !	Contribution	£416	£320	£576	£448	!
10 !						!
11 !	Var. Exp.	(£65)	(£50)	(£90)	(£70)	!
12 !	Fixed Exp.	(£350)	(£350)	(£350)	(£350)	!
13 !	Depn.	(£2)	(£2)	(£2)	(£2)	!
14 !	Interest	£0	£0	£0	£0	!
15 !						!
16 !	Total Exp.	(£417)	(£402)	(£442)	(£422)	!
17 !						!
18 !	PROFIT	(£1)	(£82)	£134	£26	!
19 !						!
20 !						!

	U	V	W	X	Y	Z
1	Balance Sheet					!
2	============					!
3						!
4	AT MONTH END	January	February	March	April	!
5						!
6	Fixed Assets	£198	£196	£194	£192	!
7						!
8	Cash	£89	£55	£85	£0	!
9	Debtors	£650	£550	£800	£1,000	!
10	Stock	£196	£340	£268	£362	!
11	NET C. ASSET	£935	£945	£1,153	£1,362	!
12						!
13	Creditors	(£180)	(£270)	(£342)	(£364)	!
14	Overdraft	£0	£0	£0	(£159)	!
15	NET C. LIAB.	(£180)	(£270)	(£342)	(£523)	!
16						!
17	NET ASSETS	£953	£871	£1,005	£1,031	!
18						!
19	EQUITY	£953	£871	£1,005	£1,031	!
20						!

	Z	AA	AB	AC	AD
1 !	Net Cash Flow				
2 !	============				
3 !					
4 !	IN MONTH -->	January	February	March	
5 !		(£31)	(£34)	£30	
6 !					
7 !					

Figure 5.7   Summary of P&L account, Balance Sheet and Net Cash Flow

Figure 5.7 shows the budget projections in the form of a P & L account, a Balance Sheet and the Net Cash Flow Statement. The P & L account has been constructed from the P & L columns in each of the Budget Worksheets. The Balance Sheet has come from the Closing Balance rows of the worksheets. The cashflow is calculated from the difference between the opening and closing Cash position after allowing for any change in Overdraft.

Most of the entries for transferring data over from the Budget Worksheets to the Summary statements are cell addresses and have to be entered individually. There are no labour-saving tricks for doing this. Datafile BUDGETS on your disc contains the Budget Worksheets and summary accounts described above. File Retrieve BUDGET3 and explore the model before proceeding to the next section.

5.9   Using the model

The general idea is to use the Planning Values alongside the first Budget Worksheet (January) to input different assumptions as to future trends. For example, Ash are intersted to know the effect on profits and the level of overdraft if sales estimates are raised by 15 per cent. They also want to know the effects of sales which are 10 per cent lower than the estimates. How serious will the position be if the Cost of Materials percentage is 45 per cent rather than the assumed 36 per cent.

The effects of changes such as these can be traced through each worksheet or, alternatively, they can be observed on the summary accounts. In this latter case, it is very helpful to split the screen so the Planning Values and the summary accounts are visible at the same time. To do this, position the pointer in the third column in from the left of the window and use the Worksheet Window command to split the screen vertically. It may also help to be able to scroll the two windows separately. To do this, use the Worksheet Window command again for Unsynchronized scrolling. As mentioned before, you can jump the pointer from the left to right window with the Window key (f6).

If you do not want certain Planning Values to remain the same for all periods covered by the model, 'disconnect' the reference from one month to the next and simply enter the appropriate values directly into each cell. Similarly, you can alter the formulae that define the relationship between the different elements within a budget worksheet. If, for example, part of the plan is to improve cashflow, it might be necessary to alter the formulae that control the debtor/creditor transactions.

CHAPTER 6

Business Forecasting

6.1 Introduction

One fruitful avenue for applying spreadsheeting skills is in business forecasting, both in elementary causal modelling and in time series analysis. Many of the popular forecasting techniques can be implemented via spreadsheets. In this chapter, spreadsheet models for trend curve fitting, time series decomposition and causal modelling are described.

A forecasting model must take into account the underlying characteristics of a time series. One of the easiest ways to discover these characteristics is to plot the series. This is a simple operation if the data is entered into a spreadsheet. The graphics capability in Lotus 1-2-3 encourages the forecaster to look at his data. Graphs also help in judging the appropriateness of the models used in forecasting (is the trend really linear or will the upward growth tail off?, does the fitted model track all the significant patterns in the data?, etc.).

The simple methods of forecasting are easy to implement with spreadsheets because many repetitive calculations are involved. At a very basic level, spreadsheet modelling allows easy adjustment of sales figures for factors such as inflation or varying numbers of working days from period to period.

Often the objective is to establish the long-term trend (growth or decline) in sales of a product or product group. The chapter starts with some illustrations of trend-fitting. The first McInver Whisky example demonstrates how a linear trend is handled and sets out the steps required in using 1-2-3's regression facility. The Microwave Ovens sales data is more complex and a transformation is required before the regression technique can be used for trend-fitting.

Another approach to forcasting is time series decomposition in which some sales data is 'decomposed' into trend, seasonal and random variation. Often the objective is to estimate 'seasonal indices' for a sales series so that these together with the estimated trend can be combined to produce forecasts. The McInver monthly sales data is used to explain the decomposition method of analysis.

Finally, a forecasting model which tries to 'explain' sales in terms of causal variables will be described. Lytham Glass sells its product to car manufacturers and the construction industry. It wants to use an explanatory forecasting model to predict glass sales when good forecasts of the levels of the car production and construction activity are available.

6.2 Example: McInver Whisky

McInver Whisky have large amounts of sales data which they would like to use to forecast the future levels of sales for their product, quality malt whisky.

Figure 6.1 shows some annual sales data for McInver malt whisky. The graph of sales over a thirteen year period shows a steady growth with some irregular variation about the trend. If the past can be used as a guide to the future, forecasts can be produced by extrapolating the straight line trend. The trend equation can be roughly estimated from the plot (as outlined in Chapter 3 on graphs in modelling) or produced by regression. The regression approach is particularly useful when the irregular variation is sizeable.

The objective of regression put at its simplest is to find the 'best fitting' line that enables Sales to be predicted from Time. Since regression analysis is available in Release 2 of 1-2-3, it is extremely easy to carry out. The explanation that follows attempts to be as non-technical as possible. However, the reader may wish to consult any one of the many standard statistics textbooks on the detail of regression. (The author's previous book on 1-2-3 applications, *Creative Modelling*, showed how regression could be carried out using the LINREG 'template' with the earlier version of Lotus 1-2-3.)

The steps involved in fitting the trend line for McInver are described one by one in the following paragraphs

1. The data shown in Figure 6.1 is stored in datafile MCINVER , so first:

     / File Retrieve MCINVER

    Notice that as well as the Years in the column denoted (1), the Time periods have also been labelled 1, 2, 3, etc., where Time=1 means 1974, Time=2 means 1975, etc. This representation is more usual, when fitting a trend curve.

2. Press the Graph key (f10) to see the current graph which should be similar to that in Figure 6.1.

    This graph was set up previously via the Graph command, taking Years (in column A in the spreadsheet) and Sales (in column C) as the X range and the A range respectively.

    Looking at the graph, it seems sensible to fit a straight line trend to the data. To do regression within 1-2-3, it is necessary to specify the Y-Range, the X-Range and the Output Range. The Y-Range is the location of the cells holding the values of the variable to be predicted (here Sales in column C). The X-Range is the location of the values of the 'predictor' variable (here Time in column B). The Output range is the area of the spreadsheet in which the regression results will be displayed, for example one page down starting in cell A21.

3. To carry out regression of Sales on Time, use the sequence:

     / Data Regression

    Select the Y-Range and specify it as the range C4..C16.
    Select the X-Range and specify it as the range B4..B16.
    Select the Output range and specify it as A21.
    Select Go to carry out the regression.

	A	B	C
1	ANNUAL WHISKY SALES		thousands of cases
2	(1)	(2)	(3)
3	Year	Time	Sales
4	1974	1	70
5	1975	2	81
6	1976	3	94
7	1977	4	110
8	1978	5	121
9	1979	6	132
10	1980	7	131
11	1981	8	145
12	1982	9	155
13	1983	10	147
14	1984	11	178
15	1985	12	186
16	1986	13	170
17	1987	14	
18	1988	15	

McINVER ANNUAL WHISKY SALES

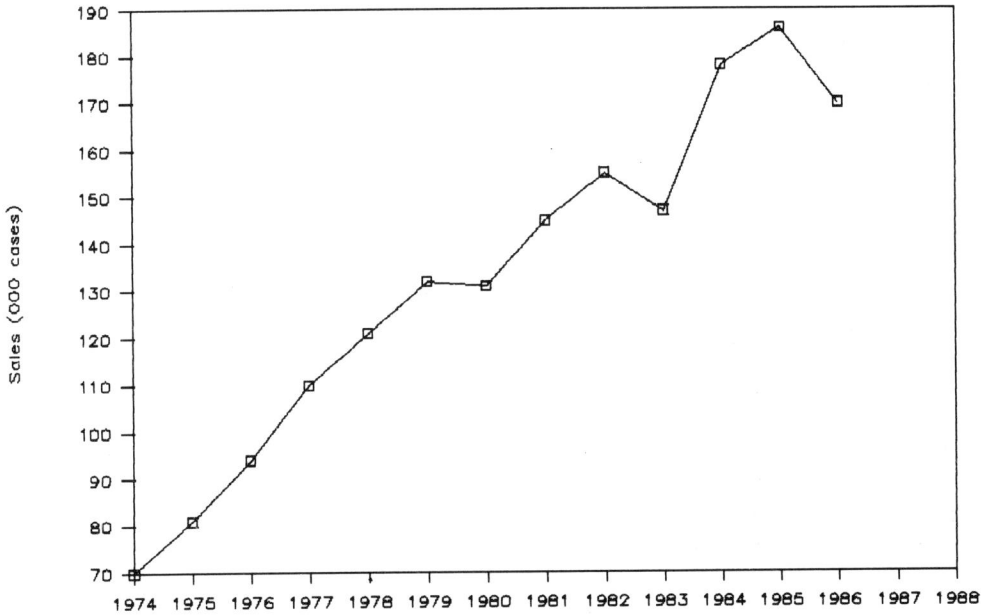

Figure 6.1   McInver annual whisky sales in the worksheet

The results are displayed starting in cell A21. It helps to use Range Format on parts of the output to reduce the number of decimal places, say to two.

The regression results suitably rounded are shown at the bottom of Figure 6.2. The regression output gives the coefficients for the regression line together with various measures that summarize how well the line fits the data. The equation of the regression line can be constructed from the 'Constant' or intercept (68.73 in cell D22) and the 'X Coefficient' or slope (9.08 in cell C28). Thus the trend equation for annual whisky sales is:

Predicted Sales = 68.73 + 9.08 * Time   where Time = 1 means 1974, etc.

One 'global' measure of the goodness of fit of the trend equation to the data is provided by 'R Squared' in cell D24. This quantity takes a value between 0 and 1. Provided there

```
            A        B        C        D        E
 1 ANNUAL WHISKY SALES   thousands of cases
 2        (1)      (2)      (3)      (4)      (5)
 3       Year     Time    Sales   Fitted  Residual
 4       1974      1        70   → 77.81    -7.81 ←
 5       1975      2        81     86.90    -5.90
 6       1976      3        94     95.98    -1.98
 7       1977      4       110    105.06     4.94
 8       1978      5       121    114.14     6.86
 9       1979      6       132    123.23     8.77
10       1980      7       131    132.31    -1.31
11       1981      8       145    141.39     3.61
12       1982      9       155    150.47     4.53
13       1983     10       147    159.55   -12.55
14       1984     11       178    168.64     9.36
15       1985     12       186    177.72     8.28
16       1986     13       170    186.80   -16.80
17       1987     14              195.88
18       1988     15              204.97
19
20                          +$D$22+$C$28*B4
21              Regression Output:
22 Constant                        68.73
23 Std Err of Y Est                 8.94  +C4-D4
24 R Squared                        0.94
25 No. of Observations               13
26 Degrees of Freedom                11
27
28 X Coefficient(s)       9.08
29 Std Err of Coef.       0.66
```

Figure 6.2   Estimating the trend line with 'data regression'

is plenty of data, high values close to 1 occur when the time series is more or less a straight line: values near zero suggest no straight line trend at all. The value of 0.97 in cell D24 suggests that this trend line fits the data quite closely.

As well as the regression results, Figure 6.2 shows two additional columns of figures headed 'Fitted' values and 'Residual' values. A 'Fitted' value for Sales is obtained from the trend equation by substituting the appropriate Time value. A 'Residual' value is the difference between the actual Sales and the Fitted value for Sales. (In fact the regression line is the one for which the sum of squared residuals is least: hence the criterion for choosing the regression line is called 'least squares').

Continuing with the 1-2-3 modelling therefore:

4. Calculate Fitted and Residual values for the regression.
   In cell D4, enter the formula for the first of the Fitted values:

   $+\$D\$22+\$C\$28*B4$

   to give the value given by the trend equation when Time=1 (as in cell B4).

   In cell E4, enter the formula for the first Residual value:

   $+C4-D4$

   Use / Range Format Fixed on D4..E4 to reduce the number of decimal places to 2, say.
   Copy the formulae in range D4..E4 down columns D and E to row 16.

The top part of the worksheet should now correspond with Figure 6.2 rows 1 to 16.

5. Extrapolate the trend by Copying the formula in D16 into D17, D18, etc.

Thus, predicted sales for 1987 and 1988 are approximately 196 and 205 thousand cases respectively—from substituting Time=14 and then Time=15 into the above trend equation.

This 'best fitting' trend equation is shown fitted to the whisky sales data in Figure 6.3. Working from the current graph (shown in Figure 6.1), which can be accessed by pressing the Graph key, the steps to get the graph in Figure 6.3 are as follows:

6. Add a B range defined as the cell range D4..D18 (the Fitted values) and View. To display the Fitted values as a line and the actual Sales as symbols only, choose the Options on the Graph menu then Format the A range to be Symbols only. You also need to add a second Title again from the Options menu.

A datafile called MCINVER1 containing the regression analysis and graphs (named as G1 and G2) is on your ASM disc. You may wish to examine it if you have had any difficulty in following any of the steps outlined above.

This linear regression routine can be extended to cover a variety of trend equations, not necessarily only linear ones. The objective is to fit a mathematical equation to the trend displayed by the sales values over time. Provided that the relationship with time

84

McINVER ANNUAL WHISKY SALES
Fitted Trend

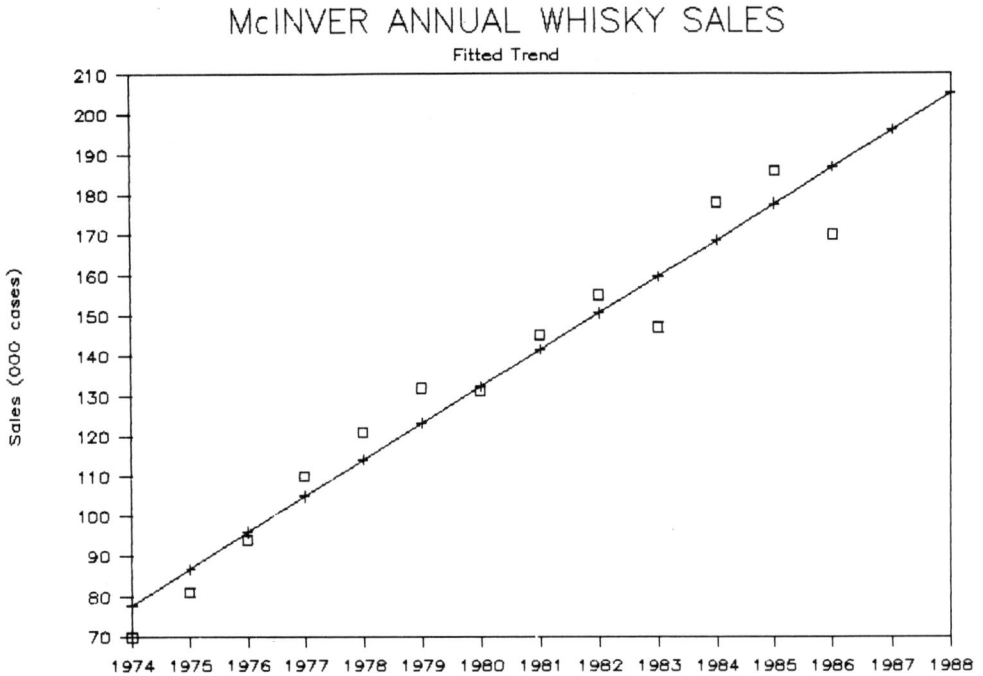

Figure 6.3   Trend line fitted by regression

can be transformed to a straight line one on some transformed scale(s), the regression command in 1-2-3 can be employed for estimating the best fitting relationship. Transformations of one or both of the variables (Sales and Time) are easily carried out with the mathematical functions in Lotus 1-2-3 (logs, exponents, square roots, etc.). The approach is demonstrated in the following example.

6.3   Example: microwave ovens

Data has been collected for sales of one company's brand of microwave oven over several periods. Figure 6.4 shows that the trend in sales of ovens is not linear as in the previous case. The data displays a curved trend. In fact, sales in any period are roughly 8 per cent higher than sales in the previous period, resulting in a so-called exponential trend curve. To use regression to fit the trend equation, rescaling is required so that the relationship between sales and time is roughly linear on the transformed scale. As we shall see, this linearity is achieved for exponential data by transforming sales to the log scale.

The argument runs as follows. The general relationship between Sales in period t and the previous period (t-1) can be written:

Sales in period $t = r$ * Sales in period (t-1)

For example, if sales increase proportionately by 5 per cent each period, the multiplier r takes the value 1.05; for sales increasing by 10 per cent, r would be 1.10, etc.

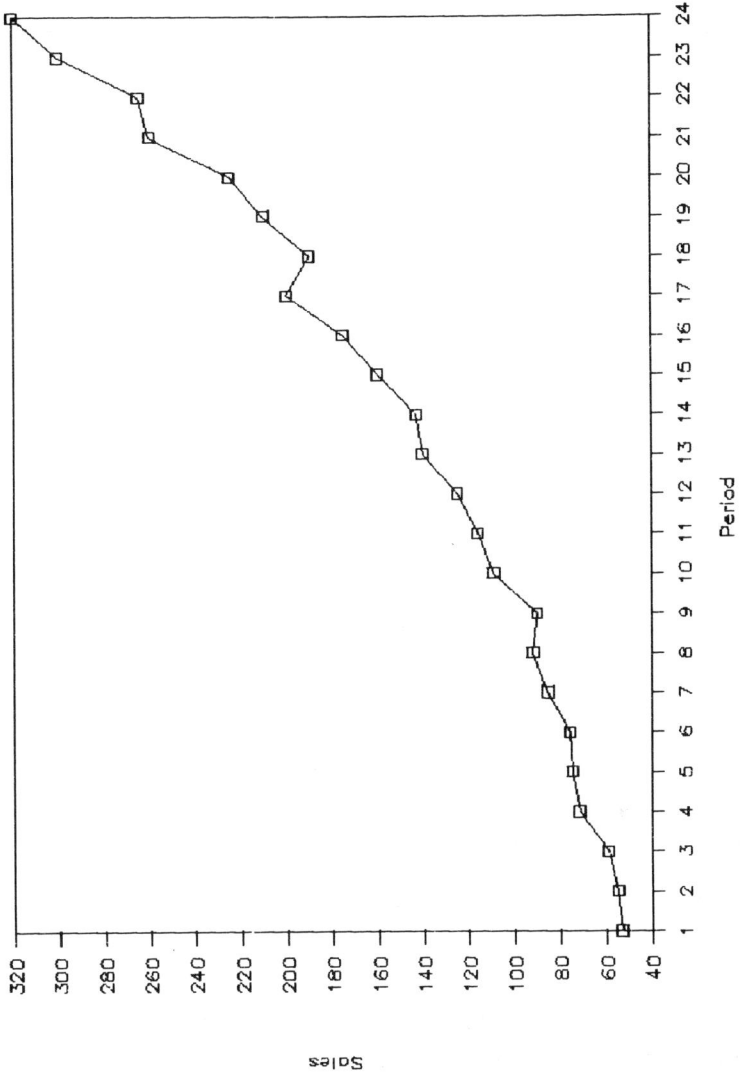

Figure 6.4   Microwave sales showing a curved (non-linear) trend

	A	B
1	MICROWAVE OVENS	SALES
2	Period	Sales
3	1	53
4	2	55
5	3	59
6	4	72
7	5	75
8	6	76
9	7	86
10	8	92
11	9	90
12	10	109
13	11	116
14	12	125
15	13	140
16	14	143
17	15	160
18	16	175
19	17	200
20	18	190
21	19	210
22	20	225
23	21	260
24	22	265
25	23	300
26	24	320

Using notation $S(t)$ to denote Sales in period t, we have

$S(t)=r*S(t-1)$

This implies that $S(1) =r*S(0)$ and $S(2) =r*S(1)= r^2 *S(0)$ and hence that:

$S(t) = r^t *S(0)$.

This is the type of equation that underlies exponential growth (or decline if r is between 0 and 1). Taking logs of both sides,

$\log [S(t)] = \log[r^t *S(0)]$

that is

$\log [S(t)] = t*\log r + \log[S(0)]$

since 'logs of products' turn into 'sums of logs'. Thus $\log S(t)$ is linearly related to t, all the other expressions in the above equation being constants rather than variables.

In non-mathematical terms, if the percentage increase in sales stays roughly the same from period to period, then the plot of log(Sales) against time should be roughly a straight line.

1-2-3 has three special functions which calculate logs and exponents (or powers): @LOG() which converts numbers into their ordinary logs (to the base 10), @LN() for natural logs (to the base e) and @EXP() which calculates powers of the number e (where e is a special mathematical constant with value 2.718...). @EXP() and @LN() are mathematical opposites: @EXP() evaluates powers of e whereas the @LN() expresses numbers as powers of e. The opposite operation to @LOG() is working out 10 raised to different powers. This can be done using the 'caret' key ^ in Lotus 1-2-3: for example,

$10^2=100$, $7^2=49$, $6^3=216$, $81^{0.5}=9$, etc.

The microwave oven sales data is in datafile MWO1 on your ASM disc, so the steps are:

1. / File Retrieve MWO1 to load the data.
2. Press the Graph key to see the graph of Sales over time.
3. Point to cell C3 which contains the natural log of the Sales in period 1. The formula in cell C3 is:

    @LN(B3)

4. Copy this formula down to the cell range C4..C26.
5. View the named graph G2 (with Log(Sales) plotted) by choosing:

    / Graph Name Use G2

Figure 6.5 shows the transformation of the Sales data (column B) into Log(Sales) data (column C). For example, the formula @LN(B3) in cell C3 converts the Sales of 53 units in B3 into its 'natural' log of 3.97 units. (Reversing this operation to explain the link between 3.97 and 53, you can demonstrate that @EXP(3.97) is approximately equal to 53. When the number e (2.718...) is raised to the power 3.97 the result is about 53. As a further check, note that 2.75 raised to the power 4 has a value of about 57.) The transformation to the log scale can be done equally well with the function @LOG which gives ordinary logs to the base 10. (The intermediate numbers will be different of course.)

The plot of log(Sales) in Figure 6.5 shows the linear relationship between log(Sales) and Time for the microwave data. To get the equation, use Regression (on the Data menu) taking Log(Sales) as the Y-Range and Time as the X-Range; that is use:

/ Data Regression

Select the X-Range and specify it as the range A3..A26.
Select the Y-Range and specify it as the range C3..C26.
Select the Output range and specify it as A41.
Select Go to carry out the regression.

The Regression output is shown (after some rounding) starting in cell A41 at the bottom of Figure 6.6. (At this stage, ignore the text starting in cell E42 which has been added subsequently.) Taking the 'Constant' from cell C42 and 'X Coefficient' from C48, linear regression gives the prediction equation:

Log Sales(t) = 3.89 + 0.08*t where t is the period

Figure 6.6 also shows the formula for the Fitted value for Log(Sales) in period 1 in cell D3, namely:

+$D$42+$C$48*A3

which is the regression equation with the period filled in as A3, which contains the value '1'. Figure 6.6 also contains the expression for the first Residual value in cell E3. As with the McInver data, these formulae are copied down for all the data lines. Thus, all the Fitted values (for Log Sales) in column D have been calculated from the regression equation given above. The Residual values in column E show the difference between actual Log(Sales) values and Fitted Log(Sales) values.

Reversing the log transformation by making each side an exponent to return to the original scale of measurement, the trend equation has the form:

Predicted Sales(t) = exp (3.89) * exp(0.08*t)

Using the @EXP() to evaluate the numbers exp(3.89) and exp(0.08), this gives:

Predicted Sales(t) = 49 * $(1.08)^t$

Therefore sales increase by 8 per cent per period since r equals (1 + 0.08).

88

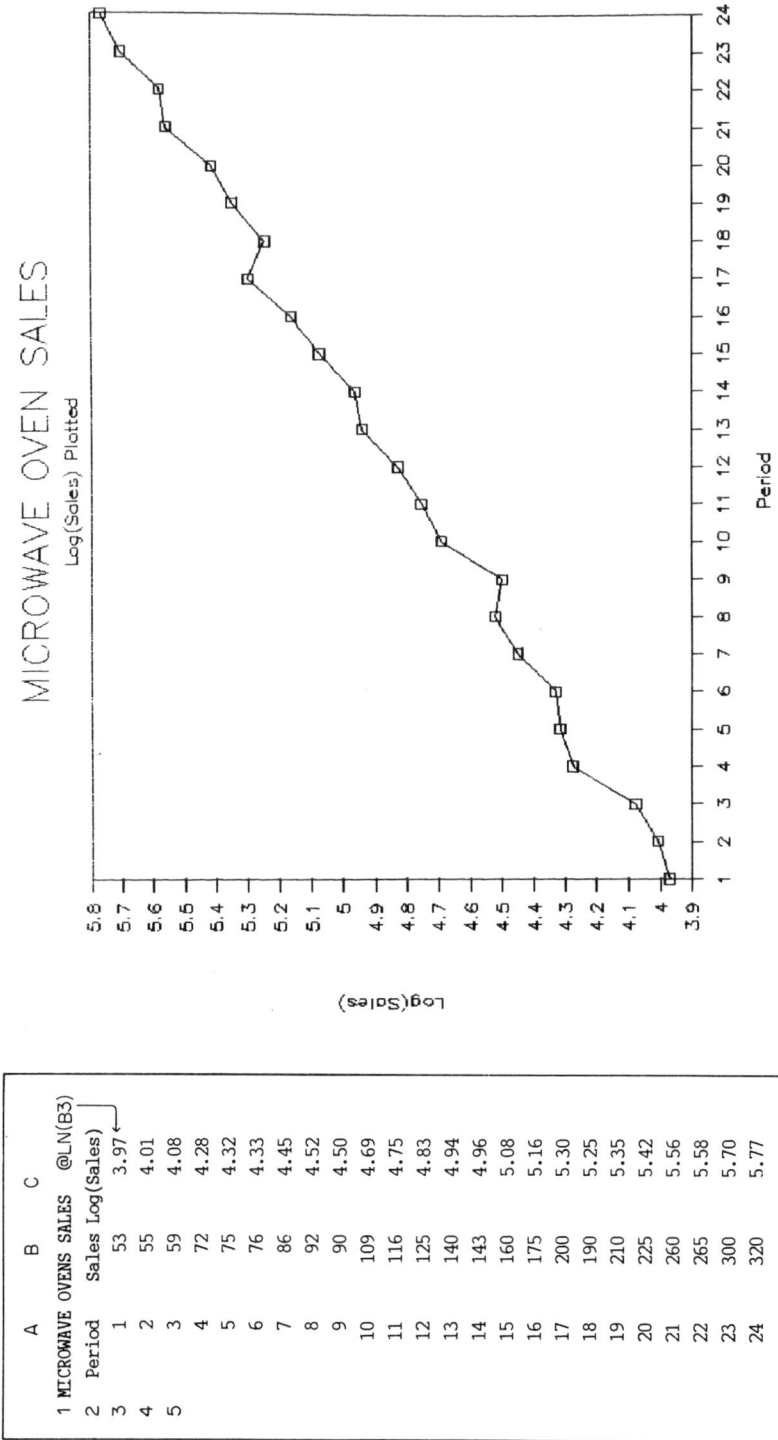

	A	B	C
1	MICROWAVE OVENS SALES		@LN(B3)
2	Period	Sales	Log(Sales)
3	1	53	3.97
4	2	55	4.01
5	3	59	4.08
	4	72	4.28
	5	75	4.32
	6	76	4.33
	7	86	4.45
	8	92	4.52
	9	90	4.50
	10	109	4.69
	11	116	4.75
	12	125	4.83
	13	140	4.94
	14	143	4.96
	15	160	5.08
	16	175	5.16
	17	200	5.30
	18	190	5.25
	19	210	5.35
	20	225	5.42
	21	260	5.56
	22	265	5.58
	23	300	5.70
	24	320	5.77

Figure 6.5 The transformed relationship (Log(Sales) versus Time)

	A	B	C	D	E	F
1	MICROWAVE OVENS SALES					Sales
2	Period	Sales	Log(Sales)	Fitted	Residual	Fitted
3	1	53	3.97	→ 3.97	0.005 ←	53 ←
	2	55	4.01	4.04	-0.037 +B3-D3	57 @EXP(D3)
	3	59	4.08	4.12	-0.045	62
	4	72	4.28	4.20	0.076	67
	5	75	4.32	4.28	0.038	72
	6	76	4.33	4.36	-0.027	78
	7	86	4.45	4.44	0.015	84
	8	92	4.52	4.51	0.008	91
	9	90	4.50	4.59	-0.092	99
	10	109	4.69	4.67	0.021	107
	11	116	4.75	4.75	0.005	115
	12	125	4.83	4.83	0.001	125
	13	140	4.94	4.91	0.036	135
	14	143	4.96	4.98	-0.021	146
	15	160	5.08	5.06	0.013	158
	16	175	5.16	5.14	0.024	171
	17	200	5.30	5.22	0.080	185
	18	190	5.25	5.30	-0.050	200
	19	210	5.35	5.38	-0.028	216
	20	225	5.42	5.45	-0.037	234
	21	260	5.56	5.53	0.029	253
	22	265	5.58	5.61	-0.030	273
	23	300	5.70	5.69	0.015	295
26	24	320	5.77	5.77	0.001	320
	25			5.85		346
	26			5.92		374
	27			6.00		404
	28			6.08		437
	29			6.16		473
32	30			6.24		511

+$D$42+$C$48*A3

41	Regression Output:			
42	Constant		3.89	LogSales=3.89+0.0783*Period
43	Std Err of Y Est		0.04	Anti 48.79 1.08
44	R Squared		0.99	
45	No. of Observations		24	Sales=49*(1.08)^t
46	Degrees of Freedom		22	
48	X Coefficient(s)	0.078		
49	Std Err of Coef.	0.001		

Figure 6.6   Regression calculations to estimate the best fitting curve

The Fitted Log(Sales) values can also be transformed back to the original scale of measurement. The values in column F shown in Figure 6.6 are obtained from the column D values using @EXP. If actual Sales values and Fitted values (computed as described above and shown in Figure 6.6 column F) are graphed against time as in Figure 6.7, the closeness of the model can be judged.

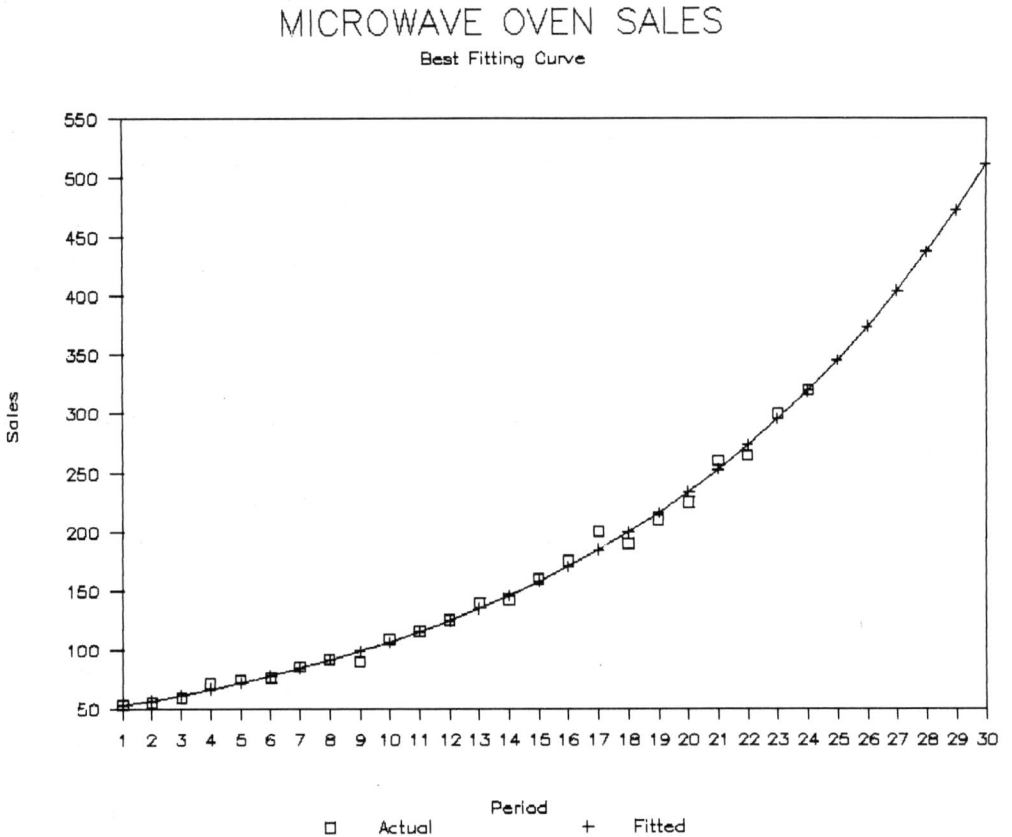

Figure 6.7   Microwave ovens trend curve and forecast sales

For practice, you may wish to evaluate the Fitted and Residual values for your Log(Sales) regression equation. The steps are exactly the same as those outlined for the McInver data. To get the appropriate Fitted Sales values in the worksheet, it is merely necessary to transform the Fitted Log(Sales) values using @EXP. Therefore the first Fitted Sales value in cell F3 is given by:

@EXP(D3)

This formula can be copied down to transform all the other Fitted Log(Sales) values.

Next add these Fitted Sales values to the first graph (that is the graph shown in Figure 6.4). The result should tie up with the plot in Figure 6.7.

To extrapolate the trend curve, add additional periods (in cell A27 and below). Copy the formulae in cells D26 and F26 down for these additional time periods, as illustrated in rows 27 to 32 in Figure 6.6.

Your ASM disc contains a datafile called MWO2 which illustrates the analysis just described. In addition, the named graphs (G3 and G4) embedded in this datafile show the trend curves for Fitted Log(Sales) (straight line) and Fitted Sales (exponential in form).

6.4 Adjusting for seasonal effects

Frequently the graph of a business series will reveal a trend in the overall level of sales and, in addition, a seasonal pattern. To estimate and extrapolate the trend properly, past sales figures must be adjusted for season or be 'deseasonalized'. This requires us to 'decompose' sales into a trend component and a seasonal component, and then to estimate 'seasonal indices'. The approach is illustrated on monthly data for McInver whisky sales.

Retrieve the datafile MCIN1 from your ASM disc. It contains a worksheet with the monthly sales data in the second column in units of thousands of cases. The other columns contain some of the calculations for decomposition to be described below. Press the Graph key (f10) to see a plot of the monthly whisky sales, which should correspond to Figure 6.8.

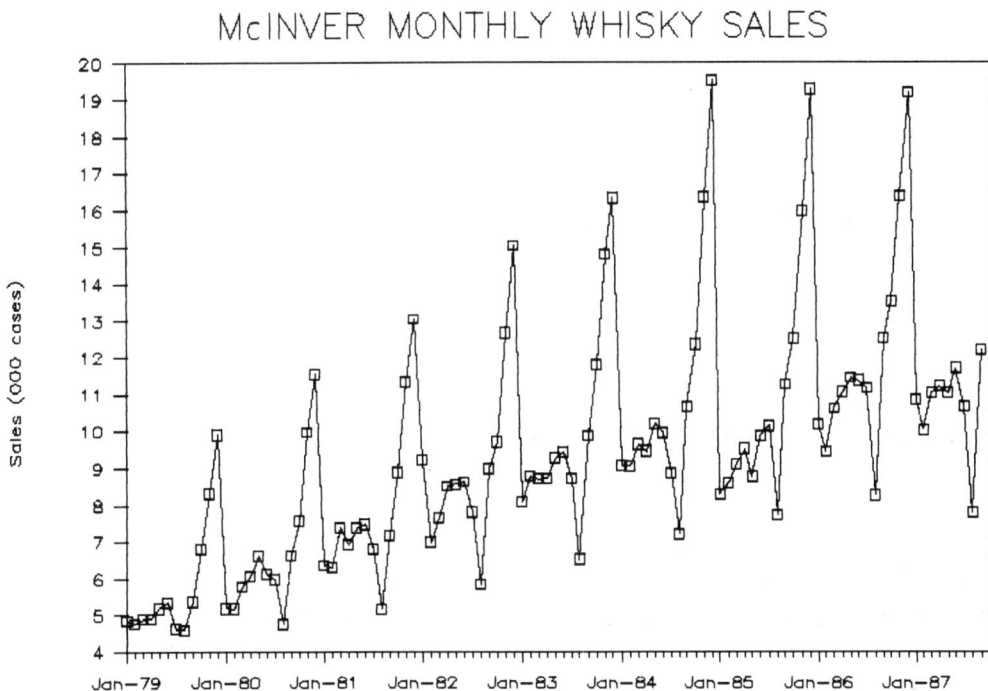

Figure 6.8 McInver monthly whisky sales

The plot displays a marked seasonal pattern superimposed on the strong upward trend in the overall level of whisky sales. The size of the seasonal fluctuation appears to vary with the average level of sales: it becomes larger as the average level of sales increases. This suggests that a 'multiplicative' model for sales (that is one where the fitted trend curve is multiplied by the seasonal factors to get the sales figures) would be appropriate:

Sales = Trend * Seasonality

Earlier in the chapter, trend estimation by regression was described. Another way of isolating the trend is to calculate moving averages of the data. The steps to work out a centred moving average are illustrated in Figure 6.9 and can be followed by exploring columns C and D in the MCIN1 worksheet.

In column C, the twelve month moving averages are calculated. The average for the first twelve months is evaluated by the special function:

@AVG(B4..B15)

entered in cell C10. As an average, it applies to the time-point halfway between row 9 and row 10. However, this slight problem is resolved by 'centering', that is averaging the twelve-month moving averages in rows 10 and 11. The resultant centred moving average can be placed in cell D10. These formulae have been copied down to all the rows that have data. An extract of the MCIN1 worksheet at this stage is shown in Figure 6.9. (The ratios in column E will be explained below.)

```
            A        B        C        D        E
     1 MONTHLY WHISKY SALES
     2    (1)      (2)      (3)      (4)       (5)
     3   Period    Sales 12 Mth MA 12 Mth MA   Ratio
     4   Jan-79    4.865            Centred   (2)/(4)
     5   Feb-79    4.772
     6   Mar-79    4.905  @AVG(B4.B15)
     7   Apr-79    4.921            @AVG(C10.C11)
     8   May-79    5.196                      +B10/D10
     9   Jun-79    5.336                         ↓
    10   Jul-79    4.632   5.803    5.817      0.796
    11   Aug-79    4.612   5.830    5.847      0.789
    12   Sep-79    5.372   5.864    5.900      0.910
    13   Oct-79    6.801   5.937    5.985      1.136
    14   Nov-79    8.314   6.032    6.092      1.365
    15   Dec-79    9.912   6.152    6.185      1.603
    16   Jan-80    5.191   6.218    6.274      0.827
    17   Feb-80    5.175   6.330    6.336      0.817
    18   Mar-80    5.781   6.342    6.395      0.904
    19   Apr-80    6.066   6.448    6.480      0.936
    20   May-80    6.626   6.513    6.582      1.007
    21   Jun-80    6.13    6.652    6.721      0.912
```

Figure 6.9 Worksheet showing calculations for moving averages and seasonal ratios

To avoid problems with the averaging at the bottom of the data column, it is advisable to work temporarily with an entry of @NA below the last sales reading. If this entry is involved in the calculation of any cell entry, the formula will cause NA for 'Not Available' to be displayed.

The choice of twelve-month averages ensures that the seasonal pattern is averaged out and the trend isolated. Figure 6.10 shows the moving averages superimposed on the original whisky sales. The plot suggests a linear trend in the level of sales.

Figure 6.10   Moving averages superimposed on sales

(You can see this graph by choosing the sequence:

/ Graph Name Use G2

The named graph G2 corresponds to Figure 6.10).

Dividing the sales values by the corresponding moving averages de-trends the series and gives the ratios (Figure 6.9, column E). These ratios form the basis for calculating monthly seasonal indices since for the multiplicative model:

Sales/Trend = Seasonality.

Estimating Seasonal Indices

The seasonal indices can be estimated within the spreadsheet by averaging all the ratios for January, all the ratios for February, etc. The steps are as follows:

94

1. In cell F10, enter the average of all the July ratios, that is:

@AVG(E10,E22,E34,E46,E58,E70,E82,E94)

and display the seasonal factor to at most three decimal places.
2. Copy this formula for the July seasonal factor down to the cell range F11..F21 to get the other months' seasonal factors.
3. Edit the formulae in cells F19, F20 and F21 to remove any cell references below cell E102 (which is where the ratios stop).
4. Plot the seasonal indices in a graph to display their pattern over the twelve months.

It is desirable to present the seasonal indices graphically (as in Figure 6.11) so that special features such as the low August index and the high December index stand out. Datafile MCIN2 contains the calculations for the seasonal indices. The formulae are in cells F10..F21. The resultant values are repeated in cells J4 to J15 in the order January to December. The named graph G3 within file MCIN2 shows the pattern graphically. So the steps are:

/ File Retrieve MCIN2

/ Graph Name Use G3

Figure 6.11   Seasonal indices displayed graphically

Deseasonalising whisky sales

If sales (in Column B) are divided by the appropriate seasonal index (in Column F), deseasonalised sales figures (Column G) are obtained. To see how this is done, point at cell G10 to see the formula entered:

+B10/$F$10

for the July-79 deseasonalised sales reading. Then choose:

/ Graph Name Use G4

to see the graph of deseasonalised whisky sales.

Forecasting one year ahead

If forecasts are required from the decomposition, the equation of the linear trend can be estimated and extrapolated. Here the Data Regression procedure can be used to fit a trend line (as on the annual data). It can be extrapolated one year ahead (to cover 1988 in this case). The seasonal indices are then applied as multipliers to inflate or deflate sales from the trend line according to the month of the year. Thus superimposing the seasonal indices leads to forecasts of sales for the coming year.

The results of Data Regression (Sales (Column B) on Period (Column A)) are displayed starting in cell L3. Forecasts using the trend equation inflated by the appropriate seasonal index are displayed in cells N17 and below. To see the results:

1. Point at cell N17 to explore the forecast Sales for October 1987:

   ($0$4+$N$10*L17)*F13

   i.e. (trend value for October 87)*Oct seasonal index.

2. To see forecasts superimposed on whisky sales graph, choose:

   / Graph Name Use G5

6.5 Causal modelling

The decomposition approach described for the McInver monthly sales establishes the main trends and seasonal patterns in the past. These past patterns can be projected into the future to obtain forecasts. However, note that with this approach there is no attempt to understand the mechanism driving McInver sales. In contrast, a causal model tries to establish which factors cause sales and to estimate relationships which can be used to produce forecasts. The crucial method for estimating relationships is, as we have seen, regression analysis.

The development of a forecasting model consists of visual inspection of the data to detect meaningful relationships. This is followed by carefully chosen regression analysis. Thus, the graphics facility together with the Data Regression command allow us to carry out all the necessary steps in Lotus 1-2-3 for simple cases. The Lytham Glass example is used to illustrate the causal modelling approach.

6.6   Example: Lytham Glass

Lytham Glass, a company in the glass-making industry, sells mainly to car manufacturers and major building contractors. Therefore in building a forecasting model to help predict future sales, the objective is to attempt to relate annual sales in the past to the levels of activity in the automotive and construction industries. Industry statistics exist for the automotive activity (number of Cars produced each year) and for building activity (number of construction Contracts each year). Goverment forecasts are also available for these measures for the next two years. If a forecasting equation can be estimated, predictions of sales can be derived using government forecasts.

The relevant data is shown tabulated in Figure 6.12. Sales are millions of pounds, car production units are ten thousands and contracts hundred thousands of contracts. The three time series are presented together on a graph in Figure 6.13. The Lytham sales figures have already been adjusted for price inflation. Note that the units chosen for the three variables have been scaled (into millions, ten thousands, etc.) in such a way that they can be displayed together on a graph without one variable swamping the effect of the others.

LYTHAM GLASS SALES

(1)	(2)	(3)	(4)
Year	Sales	Car Prod	Contracts
1971	385.0	390.9	94.3
1972	386.5	511.9	103.6
1973	442.4	666.6	145.0
1974	509.2	533.8	157.5
1975	507.1	432.1	167.8
1976	557.0	611.7	174.4
1977	536.7	555.9	197.7
1978	687.3	792.0	237.6
1979	701.6	581.6	316.1
1980	725.8	611.3	321.7
1981	618.6	425.8	350.9
1982	711.9	559.1	364.2
1983	734.0	667.5	365.8
1984	707.7	554.3	371.4
1985	761.7	693.3	413.0
1986	883.5	763.8	456.2
1987	982.6	775.2	473.8

Figure 6.12   Data for Lytham Glass

Before describing how to develop the forecasting model in detail, a summary of the main steps involved may help. Firstly, graphs are employed to reveal the main features of the data. As will be seen, the graphs suggest exploring the relationship between Lytham Sales (Y) and building Contracts (X(2)) to start. The Data Regression command is then used to calculate the regression of Y on X(2), that is the equation of the line that best fits the relationship between Sales and Contracts. Next, an improved equation (or model) is sought which contains both building Contracts (X(2)) and Car production (X(1)) as explanatory variables. Again, the Data Regression command is used to regress Y on X(1) and X(2).

6.7   Looking at the Lytham sales data with 1-2-3

To carry out the analysis outlined above, the steps are:

1. Start by loading the LYTH1 datafile (which contains data on all three variables), that is type:

/ File Retrieve LYTH1

The layout of the data is exactly the same as shown in Figure 6.12 with Sales (the dependent variable) in column B and Cars and Contracts (the so-called independent variables) in columns C and D.

It helps to give 'names' to the various cell ranges that contain the data. Since it is conventional to call the dependent variable (here Sales) the Y variable and all the explanatory variables (such as Cars and Contracts) the X variables, we choose these types of names. Therefore Sales takes the name Y and Cars the name X(1) and Contracts the name X(2). (The brackets are important in Lotus 1-2-3 or else the variable names will be interpreted as cell addresses). Hence:

2. / Range Name Create Y B4..B20 to Name the Sales readings Y.

Similarly, name Cars (as X(1)) and Contracts (as X(2)).

Before embarking on regression, first look at the data. Line graphs of all three variables plotted over time as shown in Figure 6.13 can easily be set up from the Graph menu. Scatter plots (XY graphs) can also be constructed by plotting Sales against Cars (see Figure 6.14) and Sales against Contracts (Figure 6.15). It is important to emphasize that in looking for relationships between variables visually, we work with graphs for which both axes are numerically scaled, that is the XY type of graphs within Lotus 1-2-3, known in statistical parlance as scatter plots.

In fact, the file LYTH1 contains the settings for these graphs. They have been set up via the Graph menu using the steps outlined in Chapter 3. To view them, they can be recalled from the Graph menu by Naming and Using graphs G1 to G4.

3. To view the pre-set graphs, type:

/ Graph Name Use to Use the Named Graphs called G1 (a line graph), and G2 to G4 (scatter plots (or XY graphs) of Y versus X(1), etc.).

LYTHAM GLASS
Plots of Sales, Cars & Contracts

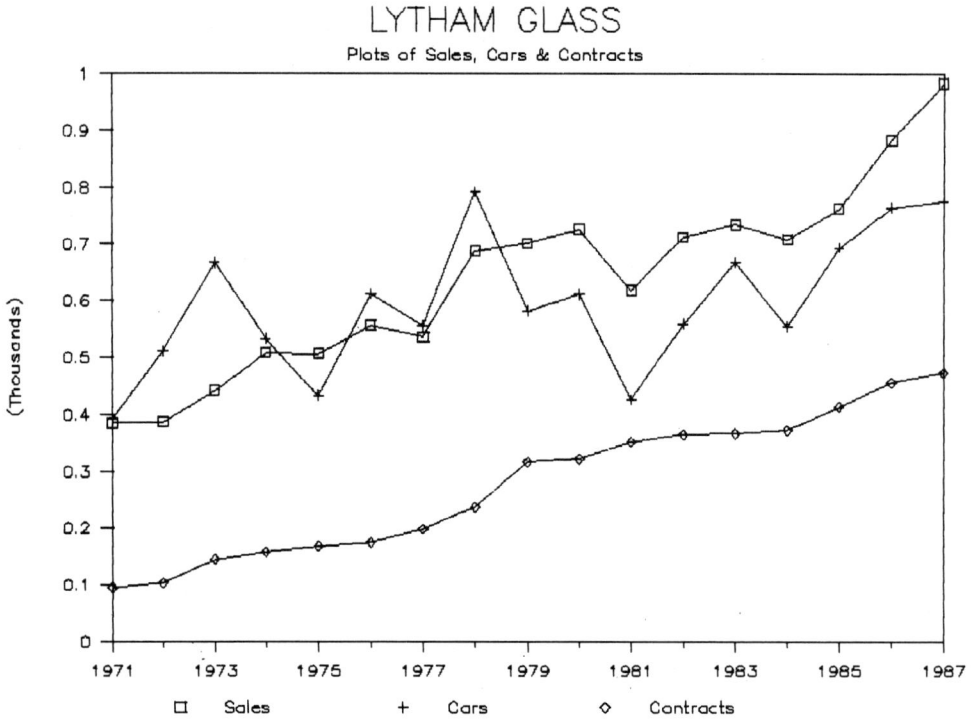

Figure 6.13   Line graph showing all variables plotted over time

LYTHAM: SALES v CARS

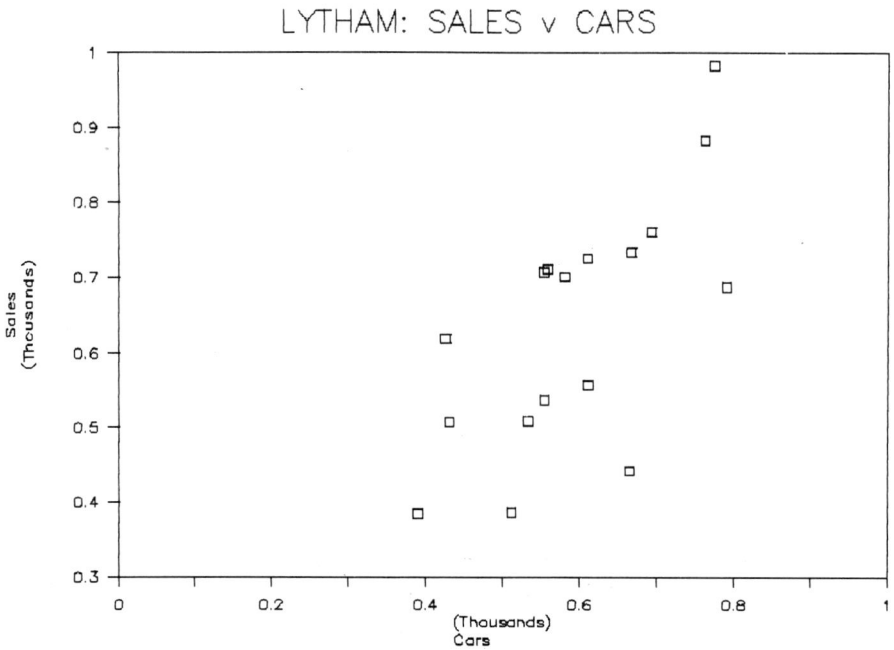

Figure 6.14   Lytham sales plotted against car production

LYTHAM: SALES v CONTRACTS

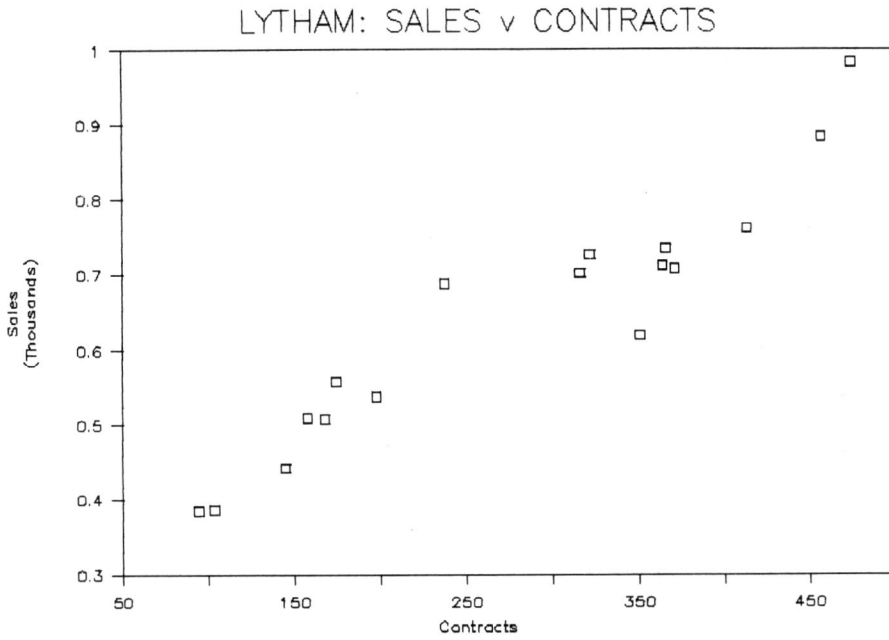

Figure 6.15 Lytham sales plotted against building contracts

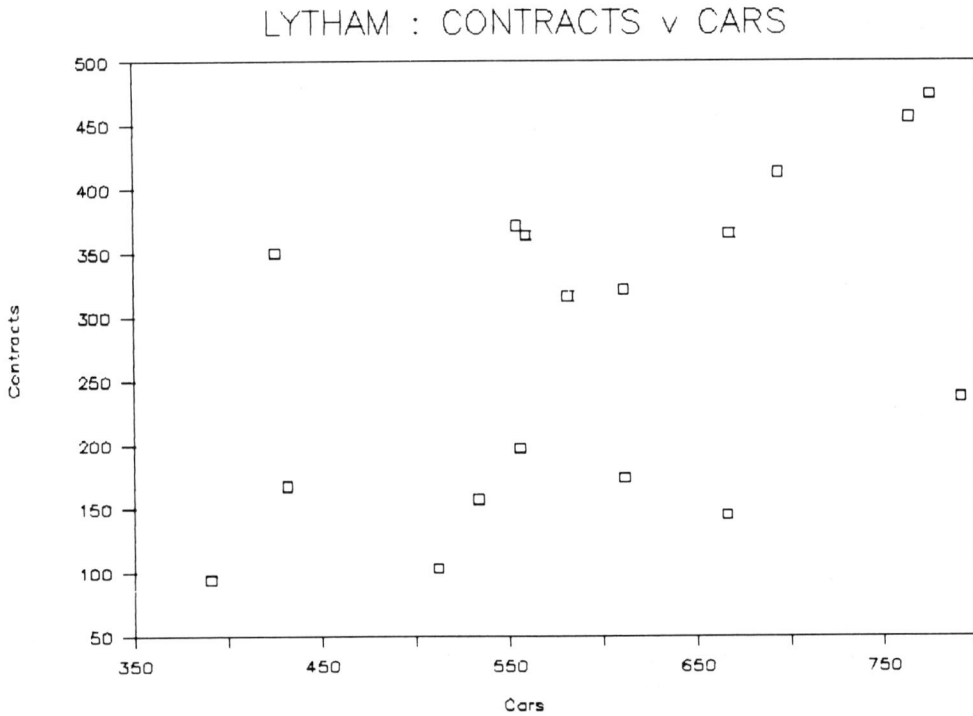

LYTHAM : CONTRACTS v CARS

Figure 6.16 Car production plotted against building contracts

The graphs show that the Contracts variable appears to be more closely related to Lytham Sales than Cars. Hence, this leads us to estimate the relationship between Y and X(2) first, that is to regress Y on X(2) (Contracts). The regression calculations give us the equation of the 'best fitting' line relating Sales and Contracts together with some measures that express the 'goodness of fit' of the relationship to the data. Then, possibly, the equation may be extended to include the Cars variable if the fit of the equation can be improved. For this extension to be possible, the Cars variable must not be too closely related to the Contracts variable. Figure 6.16 which is an XY graph of Contracts against Cars suggests that the two variables are not strongly related.

6.8 Carrying out the regressions

We start by estimating the relationship between Sales and Contracts. The resulting equation will be referred to as model 1. The main steps are:

1. To get the regression menu:

    / Data Regression

2. Specify the Y-Range as Y (that is Sales values in B4..B20).
   Specify the X-Range as X(2) (that is Contracts in D4..D20).
   Specify the Output-Range as J4 (that is say where you want 1-2-3 to put the regression results by specifying the top left-hand corner).

    Choose Go to carry out the regression calculations.

The regression results are output on the second page of the spreadsheet, starting in cell J4. They are displayed in Figure 6.17, after rounding the coefficients with Range Format Fixed and expressing numbers to two decimal places. The best fitting line turns out to have an intercept of 285.93 (cell M5) and a slope of 1.27 (cell L11). Simplifying, the relationship (model 1) takes the form:

Predicted Sales = 286 + 1.27*Contracts

Therefore, interpreting the equation, if building Contracts increase by 2 million (20 hundred thousand), the equation predicts that Lytham Sales will increase by 1.27*20 or 25.4 million pounds.

Figure 6.17 also shows the calculations required in the spreadsheet to get the fitted and residual values for the regression. The steps are:

3. Enter the Fitted value for 1971 Sales in cell E4, namely:

    +$M$5+$L$11*D4

    which is the value of Sales given by the prediction equation for the 1971 value of building Contracts.
4. Calculate the Residual for 1971, that is the difference between actual Sales and Fitted Sales in 1971.
5. Round the Fitted value and Residual for 1971 using Range Format Fixed to 0 decimal places.

LYTHAM GLASS SALES   LYTHAM: SALES on CONTRACTS

	A (1) Year	B (2) Sales	C (3) Car Prod	D (4) Contracts	E (5) Fitted	F (6) Residual
4	1971	385.0	390.9	94.3	406	-21
5	1972	386.5	511.9	103.6	417	-31
6	1973	442.4	666.6	145.0	470	-28
7	1974	509.2	533.8	157.5	486	23
8	1975	507.1	432.1	167.8	499	8
9	1976	557.0	611.7	174.4	507	50
10	1977	536.7	555.9	197.7	537	0
11	1978	687.3	792.0	237.6	587	100
12	1979	701.6	581.6	316.1	687	15
13	1980	725.8	611.3	321.7	694	32
14	1981	618.6	425.8	350.9	731	-113
15	1982	711.9	559.1	364.2	748	-36
16	1933	734.0	667.5	365.8	750	-16
17	1984	707.7	554.3	371.4	757	-49
18	1985	761.7	693.3	413.0	810	-48
19	1986	883.5	763.8	456.2	865	19
20	1987	982.6	775.2	473.8	887	95

Fitted: +$M$5+$L$11*D4
Residual: +B4-E4

Regression Output:

J K L	M	
Constant	285.93	5
Std Err of Y Est	54.72	6
R Squared	0.90	7
No. of Observations	17	8
Degrees of Freedom	15	9
X Coefficient(s)	1.27	11
Std Err of Coef.	0.11	12

Sales = 286 + 1.27*Contracts

Figure 6.17 Regression results for model 1 (sales on contracts)

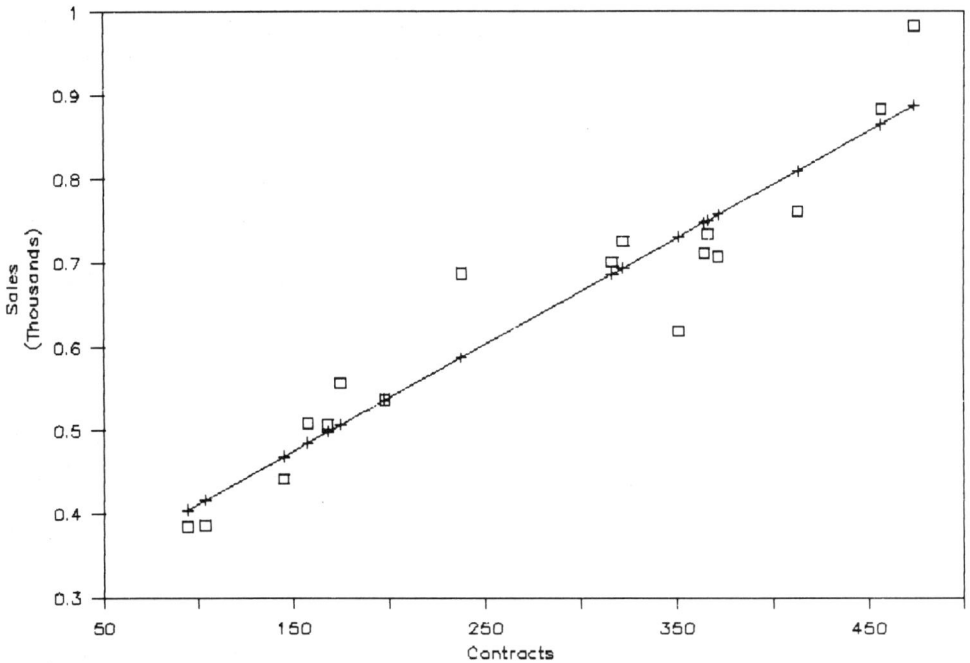

Figure 6.18 Best fitting sales–contracts relationship

6. Copy these formulae down as far as row 20. Check that the residuals look random and that there are no obvious patterns in sequence.
7. Add the Fitted Sales as the B range to the XY graph of Sales against Contracts (originally shown in Figure 6.15).

The fit of the regression line is quite good, as can be seen from the last graph, given here as Figure 6.18. The statistical measure of fit, namely R Squared, is reasonable (0.90 in M7) and confirms what we can see in the graph, namely satisfactory fit. There is a tendency for high Sales years to be associated with high levels of the Contracts variable. However, there is also some residual scatter about the line 'unexplained' by the level of building activity.

This residual variation can be measured by calculating its standard deviation. (In fact, the regression line is the line for which this residual standard deviation is least.) Before doing this calculation though, the residuals should be checked to ensure that they appear to be irregular, both in size and sign. It is not sensible to summarize the residual variation into a measure such as the standard deviation if the residuals display a systematic pattern. Looking at Figure 6.18, the residuals appear to be satisfactorily random in size and sign for the Lytham sales data.

It would be easy to apply the special function @STD() to the residuals in column F to calculate their standard deviation. In practice, a slightly more efficient estimation procedure is used. The result of this is given in the Regression Output shown in Figure 6.17. Cell M6 labelled as 'Std Err of Y Est' contains the value 54.72 for the estimated residual standard deviation. The size of the residual scatter about the line tells us how well the line fits the data, particularly when we judge its size relative to, say, the mean value or standard deviation of the Sales figures (Y). (You may wish to evaluate the standard deviation of the Sales figures using @STD(Y), where Y is the name given to the range of Lytham Sales figures (B4..B20). The units are sales units, namely, millions of pounds.)

For this regression, the residual standard devation is still moderately high, 55, as compared with 162 (million pounds), the standard deviation of the Sales figures. In other words, even when we make an allowance for Sales to be higher in years in which Contracts are high, there is still some 'unexplained' variablilty in the Sales figures.

Datafile LYTH2 on disc contains the regression analysis at this stage and after saving your own file, you may wish to load LYTH2 and check the formulae and layout.

In passing, it is worth mentioning that 1-2-3's regression algorithm does allow the estimation of the best fitting line through the origin, that is the line with 'Zero intercept'. Intuitively, it may seem more sensible to fit a line through the origin so that 'zero Contracts' will result in 'zero Sales' (rather than 286). In practice, statisticians prefer the best fitting relationship overall without constraining the line to pass through the origin. Their preference is based on much practical experience, which shows that many relationships, which are satisfactory over normally observed data values, often change in structure as variables approach zero.

Returning to the equation explaining variation in glass Sales in terms of variation in building activity, data is also available on the level of activity in the automotive industry, namely Cars produced per annum. Therefore, it is worth seeing if this second variable accounts for any of the residual variation in Sales. We obtain the best fitting linear relationship relating Sales to Contracts and Cars by an extension of simple linear regression, namely multiple regression. Working in three dimensions with the observations on three variables, the problem is to find the best fitting plane. The 'least squares' principle is used to determine the plane about which residual scatter (measured by standard deviation) is least.

You may wish to reload your Lytham file again: this was saved just after completing the regression of Sales on Contracts. Alternatively, you may continue with the LYTH2 datafile.

Returning to the menu for Data Regression, it is merely necessary to respecify the X-Range and also say where the Output Range is to be located. In particular, the X-Range must now be defined as the column of Contracts values and the adjacent column of Cars values, that is the cell range C4..D20. Suppose that the Output Range for this regression of Sales on Cars and Contracts (model 2) is to be located two pages across the spreadsheet, namely starting in cell R4.

The main steps in carrying out the multiple regression analysis are therefore:

1. Choose / Data Regression.
2. Check that the Y-Range is specified as B4.B20.
3. Specify the X-Range as C4..D20.
4. Specify the Output Range as R4.
5. Choose Go to regress Sales on Contracts and Cars and get the results for model 2 output in cell R4 and beyond.

6. Round the regression results, for example use / Range Format Fixed with two decimal places on the cell ranges U5..U7 and T11..U12.

The general form of the prediction equation for the regression of Y on X(1) and X(2) is:

Predicted Y = Constant + [Slope for X(1)]*X(1) + [Slope for X(2)] * X(2)

The results for the Lytham Sales data should tally with the Regression Output shown in Figure 6.19. Interpreting the output values, the best fitting linear equation is:

Predicted Sales = 124 + 0.36*Cars + 1.09*Contracts

where the constant (124) comes from cell U5 and the slopes or 'X Coefficients' come from cells T11 and U11 in the worksheet. Thus for years with much the same level of building activity, an additional unit increase (that is ten thousand cars) puts glass Sales up by 0.36 (million pounds). The coefficient for Contracts (1.09) can be interpreted in the same fashion.

The next step is to evaluate the Fitted values and Residuals for Sales using the model 2 prediction equation.

7. Applying the equation, the formula for the Fitted value for 1971 to enter in cell G4 is:

+$U$5+$T$11*C4+$U$11*D4

and the formula for the corresponding Residual value in cell H4 is:

+B4−G4

8. To improve the legibility of these values, use / Range Format Fixed to round them to zero decimal places.
9. Lastly, Copy the formulae in cells G4 and H4 down to the data rows below.

The Fitted and Residual values should tie up with those in Figure 6.19.

It is important to check down column H to ensure that the residuals look reasonably irregular and random. A more rigorous approach would be to plot Residual values against Fitted values using the Graph menu.

10. Plot actual Sales (column B) and Fitted sales (column G) year by year; That is:

/ Graph Type Line   to choose a Line Type of Graph.

Specify the X range as the Years, that is A4..A20.
Specify the A range as actual Sales, that is B4..B20.
Specify the B range as Fitted sales, that is G4..G20.

Then View the graph.

	A	B	C	D	E	F	G	H
1	LYTHAM GLASS SALES				-----Model 1----------Model 2------			
2	(1)	(2)	(3)	(4)	(5)	(6)	(7)	(8)
3	Year	Sales	Car Prod	Contracts	Fitted	Residual	Fitted	Residual
4	1971	385.0	390.9	94.3	406	-21	366	19
5	1972	386.5	511.9	103.6	417	-31	419	-33
6	1973	442.4	666.6	145.0	470	-28	519	-77
7	1974	509.2	533.8	157.5	486	23	486	24
8	1975	507.1	432.1	167.8	499	8	460	47
9	1976	557.0	611.7	174.4	507	50	532	25
10	1977	536.7	555.9	197.7	537	0	537	0
11	1978	687.3	792.0	237.6	587	100	665	23
12	1979	701.6	581.6	316.1	687	15	675	27
13	1980	725.8	611.3	321.7	694	32	692	34
14	1981	618.6	425.8	350.9	731	-113	657	-38
15	1982	711.9	559.1	364.2	748	-36	719	-7
16	1983	734.0	667.5	365.8	750	-16	759	-25
17	1984	707.7	554.3	371.4	757	-49	725	-17
18	1985	761.7	693.3	413.0	810	-48	820	-58
19	1986	883.5	763.8	456.2	865	19	892	-9
20	1987	982.6	775.2	473.8	887	95	915	67

+B4-G4

+$U$5+$T$11*C4+$U$11*D4

	J	K	L	M
1	LYTHAM: MODEL 1			
2	Sales on Contracts			
3	------------------			
4		Regression Output:		
5	Constant			285.93
6	Std Err of Y Est			54.72
7	R Squared			0.90
8	No. of Observations			17
9	Degrees of Freedom			15
10				
11	X Coefficient(s)		1.27	
12	Std Err of Coef.		0.11	
13				
14	Regression Equation			
15	------------------			
16	Sales = 286 + 1.27*Contracts			

	R	S	T	U
1	LYTHAM: MODEL 2			
2	Sales on Cars & Contracts			
3	------------------			
4		Regression Output:		
5	Constant			124.12
6	Std Err of Y Est			41.08
7	R Squared			0.95
8	No. of Observations			17
9	Degrees of Freedom			14
10				
11	X Coefficient(s)		0.36	1.09
12	Std Err of Coef.		0.10	0.10
13				
14	Regression Equation			
15	------------------			
16	Sales = 124 + 0.36*Cars + 1.09*Contracts			

Figure 6.19   Regression results for model 2 (sales on cars and contracts)

LYTHAM: ACTUAL v FITTED SALES

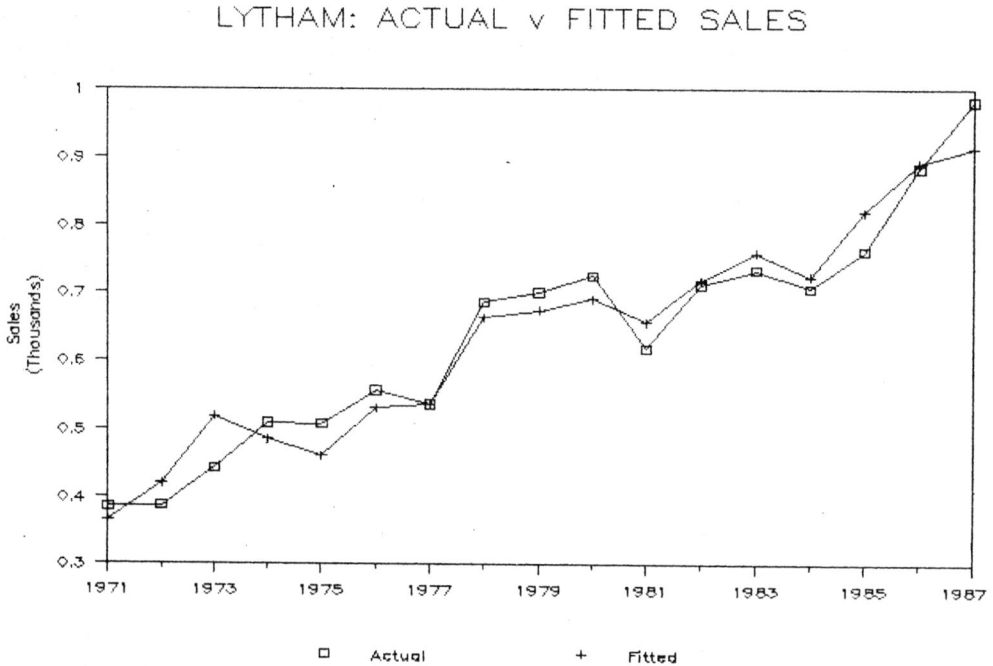

Figure 6.20   Best fitting sales forecasting model versus actual sales

Figure 6.20 shows the resulting graph. The fitted values are exceedingly close to the actual values. Note that without three-dimensional graphics it is not possible to superimpose the fitted equation on the data.

The numerical results of the regression are shown in Figure 6.19. The fitted values have been calculated from the linear equation:

Fitted Sales $= 124 + 0.36*$Cars $+ 1.09*$Contracts

where the coefficients come from cells U5, T11 and U11 in the worksheet.

The visual impression of the graph in Figure 6.20 is confirmed by the statistical measures conventionally used to judge the goodness of fit. R Squared is high (0.95 in cell U7) and the residual standard deviation is about 41 million pounds (in U6).

The regression coefficients (or X Coefficients as Lotus calls them) are set out in cells T11 and U11. Underneath in row 12 are their standard errors (which are similar to standard deviations). Taking the ratio of each regression coefficient to its standard error, namely:

(X Coefficient)/(Standard Err of Coef.)

we get the so-called *t*-values. You need to refer to a statistics book to understand the 'significance' of these values. Basically, the t values help in deciding whether the individual variables are 'contributing' to the model. A very rough and ready test is to say that a variable is worth including in the model if its t value is 2 or more: otherwise, the variable is best excluded and the analysis re-run without it. Here, both variables have t values which exceed 2. (The values are 0.36/0.10 and 1.09/0.10.) We conclude that the addition of Cars as another explanatory variable is an improvement: that is, model 2 outperforms model 1.

To summarize, the model with Cars as well as Contracts as explanatory variables (denoted model 2) has a higher R-squared value compared with the earlier model including only Contracts (0.95 versus 0.90). The 'unexplained' variation, measured in terms of the residual standard deviation has, been reduced from 55 to 41 million pounds by including Cars in the equation.

Lastly, suppose government forecasts are available for the Cars and Contracts variables for 1988 and 1989 as shown below:

Year (£mill)	Cars (0 000s)	Contracts (00 000s)
1988	640.0	485.1
1989	790.0	512.3

Then the model 2 equation would be used with these values to give predictions for 1988 and 1989. The formula in cell G20 can be copied down into cells G21 and G22, and the government estimates entered in the corresponding cells C21,C22 and D21, D22 to get predicted sales from model 2.

You may wish to make forecasts for Sales in 1988 and 1989 as suggested above. Alternatively, retrieve datafile LYTH3 from your disc and look at the forecasts given in cells G21 and G22. The graphs shown in Figures 6.15, 6.17 and 6.19 have been 'named' and saved with the worksheet. In particular, graph G3 contains the two forecasts for Sales given by model 2 for the years 1988 and 1989.

6.9   Concluding remarks

Spreadsheets are a convenient way of demonstrating how the simple methods of forecasting can be carried out. However, in practice, there are many occasions when specialist forecasting software is preferable. Where forecasts are required for a large number of series, processing the data in spreadsheets is inefficient. For the more complicated methods, the spreadsheet approach can sometimes be clumsy and inelegant and is not a substitute for proper forecasting software.

CHAPTER 7

Decision Models

7.1 Decision tree modelling

Often a decision problem involves a sequence of related decisions spread out over months and even years rather than a single one-off decision. For example, although the initial decision facing a business may involve investment in new processing plant, later decisions might be concerned with whether capacity should be expanded or the mode of operation changed, say, from two- to three-shift working. This type of decision situation is particularly suitable for structuring in terms of a decision tree diagram. The approach is illustrated by the following simplified example.

7.2 Example: Montson Industrial Chemicals

The board of Montson has to decide whether to build manufacturing facilities for a new chemical product. When first set up in the seventies, the Montson Industrial Chemicals enjoyed buoyant sales from new products, but in the early eighties was less successful in bringing new products to the market. Given the current dearth of new offerings, Montson is anxious to exploit its first major product development to the full. Once the board has decided to go ahead with the project, Montson has to decide whether to build a small plant (£2.6 million investment) or a large one (£6 million) to manufacture the new product. The economics of this decision depend partly on the size of the market the company can obtain for the product.

Best forecasts suggest that the market life of the product will be about ten years. Initial demand is expected to be high. Most customers are likely to try out the product within the first two years. However, if they do not find it a major improvement, demand could fall to a low level thereafter. On the other hand, high initial demand could indicate the existence of a high-volume market over the entire ten years of the product's life. If the high demand is sustained and Montson is unable to satisfy it because of insufficient capacity within the first two years, competitive products will almost certainly be introduced by other manufacturers.

In an attempt to be more specific, Montson's marketing people have come up with the probability assessments shown in Table 7.1 for demand initially and in the long term.

Table 7.1 Probability assessments for Montson's new product

Demand scenario	Notation	Probability (%)
Initially high, sustained high demand	'High–high'	60
Initially high, long-term low demand	'High–low'	10
Initially low, continuing low demand	'Low–low'	30
Initially low, subsequently high demand	'Low–high'	0

That is, there is a 60 per cent chance of high demand over the product life and a 40 per cent (10+30 per cent) chance of low demand in the long run.

If Montson decides to build a big plant, it has no room for manouevre if the high-volume market does not materialize. The capital investment would have been committed and the plant forced to run with idle capacity and consequently low profits for the whole ten years.

On the other hand, if Montson decides on a small plant, it could possibly be expanded in two years' time if demand were high during the introductory period. This would require further investment of £4.4 million and be less efficient to operate than a large plant. The company would need to move promptly to fill the demand that would develop, because competing firms would be tempted to move in with equivalent products. If demand was found to be lower than anticipated during the introductory period, the company would continue operations in the small plant and make a reasonable profit on the low-volume throughput.

Montson's corporate planners have produced some estimates of the annual cashflows (in millions of pounds) for each of the plant sizes and each of the demand scenarios (see Table 7.2). Cashflows are shown for the first two years (Initial Cashflow) and the remaining eight (Later Cashflow) on a per annum basis. The figures in the Profit column are derived from the simple formulae:

Profit over 10 years = 2* Initial Cashflow + 8* Later Cashflow − Capital Costs

Table 7.2 Capital Costs and Cashflows (in £Millions) for Montson

Decisions	Outcomes (demand)	Capital costs	Initial cashflow	Later cashflow	Profit (millions)
Big plant	High–high	6	2	2	14
Big plant	High–low	6	2	0.2	-0.4
Big plant	Low–low	6	0.2	0.2	-4
Small, expand	High–high	7	0.9	1.4	6
Small, expand	High–low	7	0.9	0.1	-4.4
Small, no expand	High–high	2.6	0.9	0.5	3.2
Small, no expand	High–low	2.6	0.9	0.8	5.6
Small plant	Low–low	2.6	0.8	0.8	5.4

The cashflows have not been discounted but if desired this could easily be done.

7.3 Decision tree approach

Figure 7.1 shows Montson's decision problem set out in the form of a decision tree. The tree is a diagrammatic representation of Montson's decisions together with all the possible outcomes with regard to demand level. It shows the sequences of decisions and 'chance' events in chronological order over ten years, laid out from left to right.

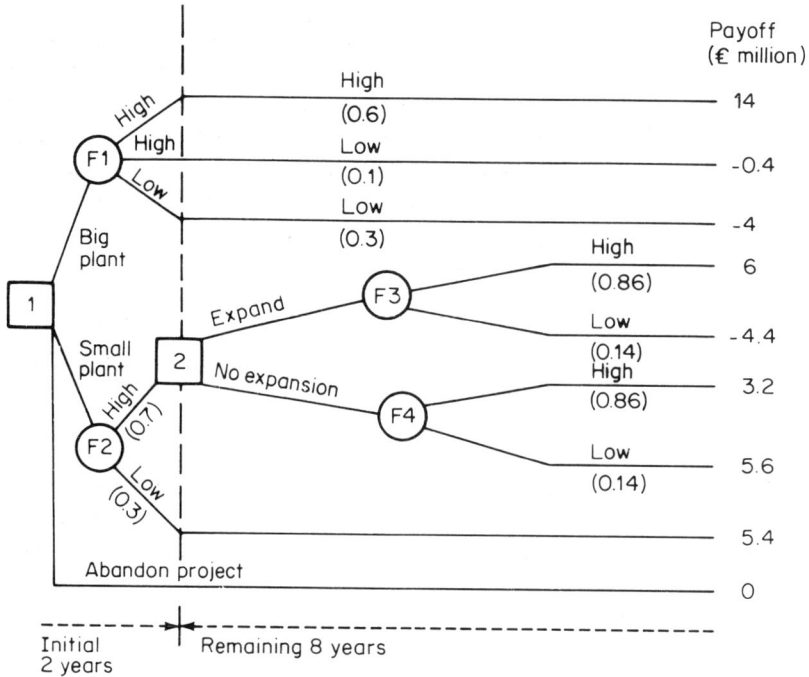

Figure 7.1   Decision tree for Montson Industrial Chemicals

The tree structure consists of branches and nodes. The nodes may be either decision nodes or event nodes shown diagrammatically by squares and circles respectively. At a decision node, a decision must be made; at an event node, chance takes over and essentially the decision maker has no control over the outcome of the event. To avoid confusion, event nodes will be referred to as 'chance forks' in the following exposition.

Looking at Figure 7.1, initially there is a decision node denoted diagrammatically by a square box and labelled 1. The node gives rise to three branches representing the alternative decisions open to Montson at the start: namely 'big plant', 'small plant' or 'abandon the project'. Note that at this type of node Montson can decide itself which alternative to choose.

The 'big plant' branch leads on to a second node from which three further branches emanate, labelled 'high–high demand', high–low demand' and 'low–low demand'. The branches represent the possible demand levels for the product both initially for the first two years and thereafter for the remaining eight years. Montson has no direct control over which branch is followed from this node. This is a chance fork represented here by a circle labelled F1. The outcome (or choice of branch) at this node is determined by factors outside the control of Montson, that is as if by chance. The probability values for each outcome as assessed by Montson are attached to the branches. The probability that demand is high for the product over all ten years is 60 per cent shown here as 0.6 (given in brackets). Notice that the probabilities on the three branches emanating from chance fork F1 sum to unity: demand must be either high–high (0.6) or high–low (0.1) or low–low (0.3); there are no other possibilities.

Following the 'small plant' branch, a chance fork (F2) representing initial demand is reached. The probability of demand being low initially is 30 per cent, shown on the tree as 0.3 in brackets. The other outcome, high initial demand, is shown with probability 0.7. If the demand is low initially, it will remain low throughout the life of the product. Montson will not consider expanding: in other words, no further decisions are made along this branch of the tree. However, following the 'high' initial demand branch, decision node 2 is reached at which Montson can decide whether to 'expand' the small plant or on 'no expansion'. Along both of these branches there is a further chance fork (labelled F3 and F4) representing the level of demand ('high' or 'low') for the remaining eight years of the project.

A note of explanation is needed about the probabilities in this part of the tree. In general, the probability attached to the branch of a chance fork represents the probability of occurrence of that event, conditional on having arrived at the associated chance fork in the tree. Thus, the probability that after expanding the small plant the demand remains high for the remaining eight years is shown as 0.86. Here, demand has been high for the first two years (probability $0.6+0.1=0.7$) and there is a 6 to 1 chance that it will remain high for the remaining years. Hence the conditional probability on this branch of the tree is $0.6/(0.6+0.1)$ or 0.86. Similarly, the probability that demand will be low, given that it has been high for the first two years, is $0.1/(0.6+0.1)$ or 0.14. Notice again that the probabilities on the branches of a chance fork sum to unity.

It is sometimes convenient to refer to a sequence of decisions and outcomes stretching from the starting node to the conclusion of the tree as a 'decision path'. Thus the sequence 'big plant' followed by 'high–high demand' is a path, as is the sequence:

'small plant' − 'high initial demand' − 'expand' − 'low demand'

Thus there are nine distinct paths through the tree shown in Figure 7.1, if 'abandon the project' is included. If the decisions 'small plant' followed by 'no expansion' are taken, three paths through the tree are possible outcomes. A sequence of decisions such as 'small plant' followed by 'no expansion' if initial demand is 'high' is conveniently referred to as a decision strategy. Inspection of Figure 7.1 will show that there are four distinct decision strategies in Montson's tree.

To analyse a tree, a method of choosing between the different decisions is needed. To this end, the 'payoffs' along each decision path are added at the right-hand side. In the case of Montson, the payoffs are cashflows over ten years less capital investment, and these have already been evaluated (see the column headed Profit in Table 7.2). Thus the figure 14 (representing £14 million) is attached to the right-hand side of the path 'big plant'–'high–high' demand, and similarly for the remaining payoffs in Table 7.2.

A typical decision tree therefore consists of a sequence of branches emanating from decision nodes and chance forks. Usually the two types of node alternate, starting with a decision node and ending with a chance fork. All the branches of the tree stemming from a decision node are labelled with an action; those from a chance fork are labelled with chance outcomes. Probabilities are attached to all the chance outcomes. Finally the payoffs resulting from passing down each of the paths in the tree are displayed at the ends of the paths.

Many decision problems can be simplified and represented in the form of decision trees. The diagrammatic approach is particularly useful when the problem can be broken down into a sequence of interrelated subproblems as in the case of Montson.

7.4 Analysing Montson's tree

The decision tree shown in Figure 7.1 consists of nine different paths, each having a payoff attached. The problem is to determine which sequence of decisions (strategy) is best in some sense. One possible criterion is to choose the strategy that contributes most 'payoff' (here most profit) or more generally most 'monetary value'. In the face of uncertainty about the level of demand, maximization of 'expected' profit or 'expected monetary value' is more appropriate.

To illustrate the idea of expected value, consider the expected monetary value (EMV) of the decision 'big plant' shown in detail in Figure 7.2. The payoff for this decision is £14 or -0.4 or -4 million according to whether demand is high throughout, high initially then low or low throughout. Montson have assessed the probablility of high demand throughout as 60 per cent or 0.6. Similarly, the probabilities of the other two demand outcomes have been assessed as 0.1 and 0.3 respectively. A composite measure called 'expected payoff' or 'expected monetary value' can be constructed by weighting each payoff by the probability of its occurrence. Thus, the expected monetary value (EMV) of building a big plant is given by:

$$
\begin{aligned}
\text{EMV (big plant)} &= \quad 0.6*14 \quad + \quad 0.1*(-0.4) \quad + \quad 0.3*(-4) \\
&\qquad \text{(high--high)} \quad \text{(high--low)} \quad \text{(low--low)} \\
&= 8.4 - 0.04 - 1.2 \\
&= 7.16 \ (\text{£million})
\end{aligned}
$$

This EMV figure, 7.16, is displayed adjacent to chance fork F1 in the tree, as shown in Figure 7.2. It is the expected value of the decision to build a big plant. It can be interpreted as a special kind of average payoff.

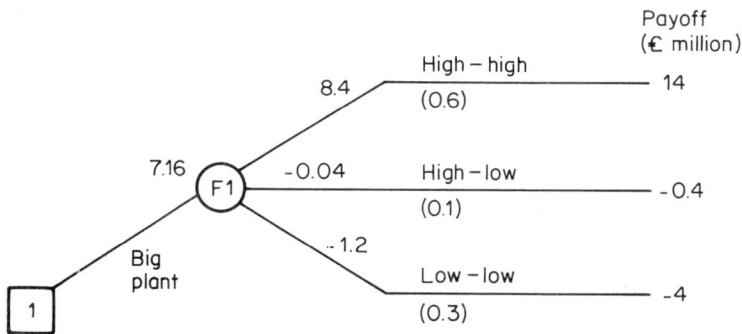

Figure 7.2 Analysis of 'big plant' decision

To evaluate the 'small plant' alternative, we first need to know the best decision at node 2: Montson needs to know if expansion is good or bad, given that the initial demand is high. (Notice that this forces us to evaluate nodes from the right to the left across the tree.)

The tree from decision node 2 onwards is shown separately in Figure 7.3. Working out the expected monetary value (EMV) of expansion at chance node F3, we have:

EMV (expand) = 0.86*6 + 0.14*(-4.4)
          (high)   (low)
       = 5.14 - 0.63
       = 4.51 (£million)

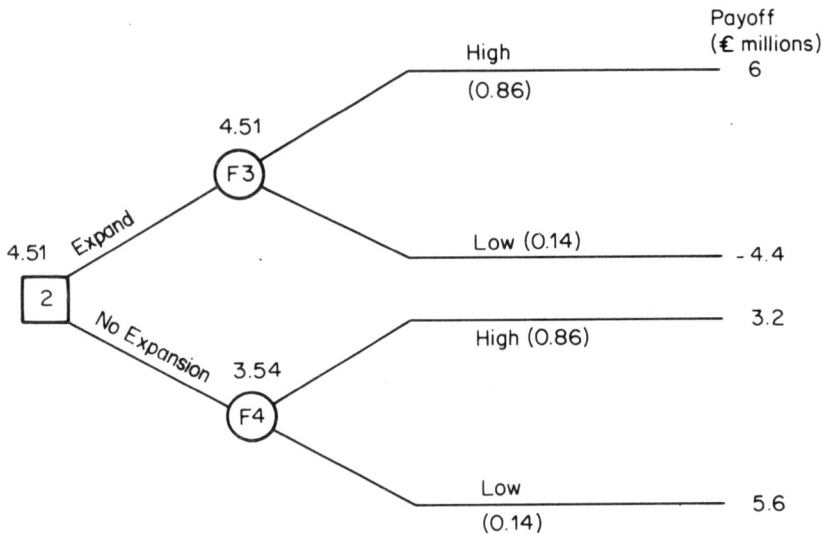

Figure 7.3   Decision node expansion or no expansion

In passing, we may note that it is sometimes convenient to refer to a payoff multiplied by its probability as a 'conditional expected value' (or CEV). Thus the CEVs for the two branches of fork F3 are 5.41 and -0.63 (£millions) respectively. The expected value at a chance fork is thus calculated by summing all the CEVs at the fork. These terms, EV and CEV, will be used later in the chapter to label cells in the spreadsheet model.

Applying the same method at chance fork F4, the expected value for no expansion is:

EMV (no expansion) = 0.86*3.2 + 0.14*5.6
              (high)   (low)
       = 3.44 + 0.90
       = 3.54 (£million)

Since the EMV is higher for expansion than no expansion (£4.51 million versus £3.54 million), the decision if this node were reached would be to expand the plant. This is signified in Figure 7.3 by displaying the highest EMV (4.51) close to decision node 2 and lopping off all other branches with lower EMVs. If node 2 were to be reached, the best decision thereafter (expansion) would have an expected value of £4.51 million. In any further analysis, the tree to the right of the decision node 2 is effectively replaced by the EMV figure of 4.51. This is demonstrated in Figure 7.4, which also displays the results of the remaining calculations.

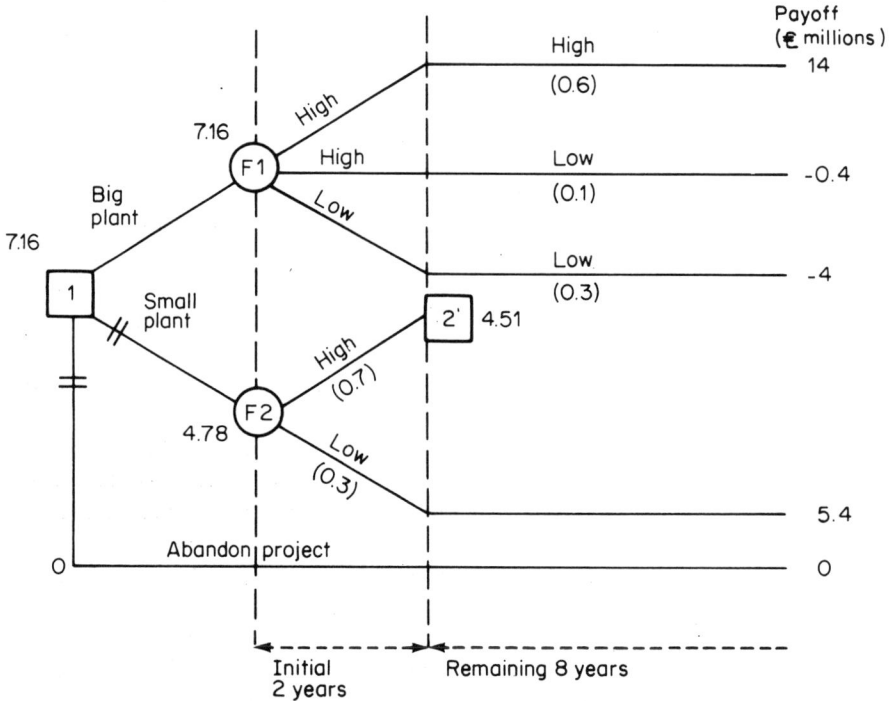

Figure 7.4   Completed tree for Montson

Evaluating the expected value of building a small plant (fork F2), the high demand branch has yielded the expected value 4.51, and so:

$$\text{EMV (small plant)} = \underset{\text{(high)}}{0.7*4.51} + \underset{\text{(low)}}{0.3*5.4}$$
$$= 3.16 + 1.62$$
$$= 4.78 \text{ (£million)}$$

Finally, the decision with the highest EMV at node 1 is identified. The expected value of building a big plant has already been calculated as 7.16 (£million). Since this EMV figure exceeds that for the small plant option (£4.78 million) and also abandoning the project (£0), the best decision (in EMV terms) would be to build a big plant. To complete the tree, this maximum EMV figure 7.16 (£millions) is displayed at node 1 and the other branches 'lopped' off the tree.

Thus, analysing a decision tree consists of starting at the end of the decision paths and working back to the start of the tree (from right to left). At each chance fork, the expected payoff (or monetary value) is calculated. It is often called the expected value (or EMV) at that fork. At each decision node, the branch with the highest EMV is identified. All other branches from that node are 'lopped off' (in effect, removed from the analysis) and the highest EMV attached to the node. The best decision path from the node onwards is thus identified. The process is repeated gradually moving from right to left through the tree. Finally, the starting decision node is reached and the decision with the highest EMV identified. This also identifies the best decision strategy to be followed through the entire tree.

7.5   Modelling Montson's decision tree in 1-2-3

The sequence of analysis in the previous section depends on the tree diagram. In structuring the EMV calculations and the search for the best decisions to solve Montson's problem, the tree representation is central. Its layout determines the sequence of calculations and ensures that they are correctly ordered. The choice of a best decision strategy can be justified by displaying the intervening calculations clearly on the tree diagram. Therefore it is worth pausing to ask if anything further is to gained by putting the calculations into a spreadsheet. If it is, what is the best way of adapting the tree analysis to the spreadsheet format?

At the elementary level, a spreadsheet implementation should ensure that the EMV calculations in the decision tree are carried out correctly. However, it is the treatment of the assumptions and the ability to undertake sensitivity analysis that makes a spreadsheet version worth having. Often analysts are worried about some of the 'softer' assessments of probability that are required to evaluate the expected values. One line of approach is to rework the tree analysis using changed probabilities. If the probability estimates are pulled out as planning values in the spreadsheet model, it is extremely easy to do the necessary sensitivity analysis. Thus the spreadsheet model of a decision tree provides a way of checking on the robustness of the chosen decision strategy.

Another argument in favour of decision trees set up in spreadsheets is the fact that decision trees are rarely needed in isolation from other modelling. For example, the cashflows used in the Montson tree may well be derived from some other planning model, itself set up in a spreadsheet. It is therefore desirable to handle the entire model in the spreadsheet rather than have a 'pencil and paper' stage centred on the tree.

There are a number of ways of drawing up a decision tree in the spreadsheet format. One way is to attempt to draw a rudimentary structure resembling the tree with vertical and horizontal 'lines'. Although this approach is feasible, it has few advantages in terms of spreadsheet functionality when it comes to the calculations.

A preferred approach is described in the next few paragraphs. This requires the tree diagram to be drawn up first, manually, to identify the nodes, to sequence and to number them. Thereafter, the tree diagram helps to structure the layout in rows and columns, but it is not reproduced as such in the spreadsheet. Since it is more natural to work from left to right in the columns of a spreadsheet, the tree diagram is in effect turned round with the payoffs on the many branches to the left in the spreadsheet and the evaluation of the final decision node to the right.

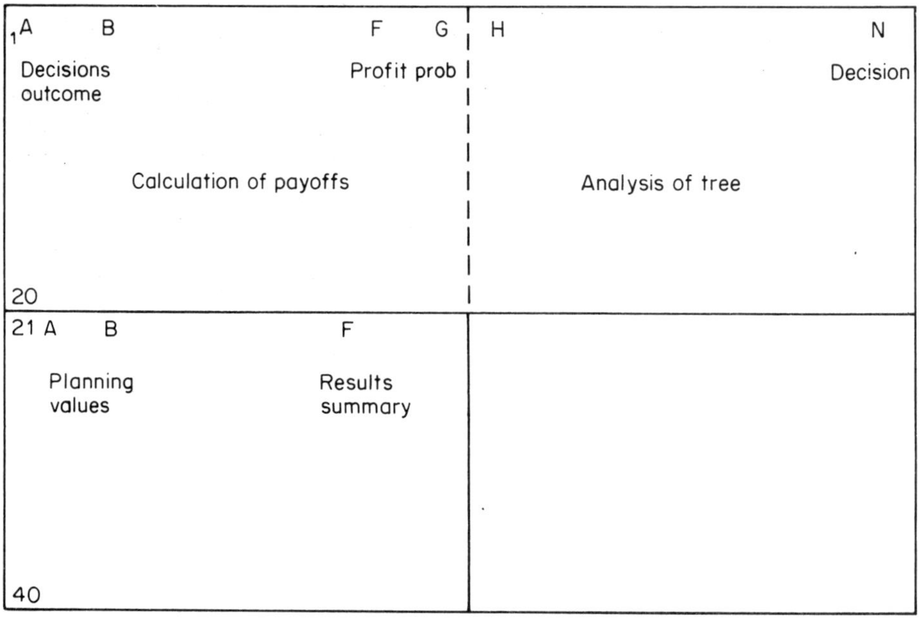

Figure 7.5 Layout of decision tree analysis in worksheet

```
MONTSON CHEMICAL
Planning Values
-----------------------------------------
Probabilities
Prob (hi-hi)        0.60
Prob (hi-lo)        0.10
Prob (lo-lo)        0.30
**Sum of Probs**    1.00

Annual Cashflows         Years to expansion
-----------------------------------------
                    mill Before          2
Big & hi               2 Life           10
Big & lo            0.2
Small, hi            0.9  Capital millions
    then hi          0.5 -----------------
Small,exp hi-hi      1.4 Big plant       6
Small,exp hi-lo      0.1 Small         2.6
Small & lo           0.8 Expansion     4.4
-----------------------------------------
```

Figure 7.6 Planning values in decision analysis spreadsheet

The overall layout of the spreadsheet model for Montson is shown in Figure 7.5. At the top, there are two main calculation areas: one for calculating the payoffs at the end of each of the decision tree paths and the other for the expected value calculations. Rows of the spreadsheet model correspond to the different decision paths. The assumptions in the analysis (the planning values) are grouped together under the computed values on a 'page' that also contains a summary of the main results. This layout makes it possible to use the model and read off the results from the planning value page without having to cursor over the tree calculations. Figure 7.6 shows the planning values in detail. The probabilities as assessed by Montson's marketing people are set out here. One important point is to ensure that the probabilities given here sum to one. This is crucial when the values are varied in any sensitivity analysis. Notice that it is also possible to change the various assumptions for annual cashflow and capital investment.

7.6   Building the decision analysis model

The steps in building the Montson model are described in this section. The starting datafile is MONT1. On retrieving this file, the first display shows the planning values and a summary (empty at this stage) of the conclusions from the analysis. Explore the layout using the pointer keys and the Tab, PgDn, PgUp and Home keys.

The detailed structure of the model is shown in Figure 7.7. Looking first at the top 20 rows of the spreadsheet, columns A and B carry labels that specify the particular decision path (DECISIONS in A, OUTCOMES in B) and the ensuing nine rows are the nine different decision paths through the tree. Columns E to F are devoted to the calculation of payoffs. The various cost and profit elements required to give the payoff along the path (PROFIT in column F) are linked to the cells in the Planning Values area one page down in the worksheet. Columns G through to O contain the decision analysis proper, that is the EMV calculations and the selection of the maximum EMV decisions. The calculations are laid out from left to right in the spreadsheet in the order that they are actually carried out in the manual decision analysis. The numbering of the nodes in the spreadsheet model corresponds to that in the manually produced tree. Columns J and O contain cells for the display of the decisions at nodes 2 and 1 respectively. The Planning Values area starts one page down below the payoff calculations, starting in row 22 of column A. The cells below F22 will be used to summarize the results of the decision analysis.

The worksheet is ready for the decision analysis in columns F and beyond to be undertaken. Probabilities linked to the planning values have already been entered. 'Freezing' the row labels helps in executing this part of the modelling. A suitable screen configuration is suggested in Figure 7.8. To effect this, first press the Home key, then point to cell C6 and choose:

/ Worksheet Titles Both

Use the pointer keys to line up the columns as shown in Figure 7.8 and point to cell H10 to start calculating the expected value for fork F3.

MONTSON CHEMICAL

	A DECISIONS	B OUTCOMES	C Capital	D Initial Revenue	E Later Revenue	F PROFIT mill	G Probs F3&4	H CEVs F3&4	I EVs F3&4	J EMVs DN2	K Probs F1	L CEVs F1	M EVs F1	N EVs 4	O DECISION DN1 5
1	MONTSON CHEMICAL									Decision Analysis					DECISION
2		Calculation of Payoffs													
6	Big Plant	Hi-hi	6	2	2	14				14	0.6	F1	F1		
7	Big Plant	Hi-lo	6	2	0.2	-0.4				-0.4	0.1				
8	Big Plant	Lo-lo	6	0.2	0.2	-4				-4	0.3				
10	Small, expand	Hi-hi	7	0.9	1.4	6	0.86	F3	F3	DN2	0.7	F2			
11	Small, expand	Hi-lo	7	0.9	0.1	-4.4	0.14						F2		
13	Small,no expand	Hi-hi	2.6	0.9	0.5	3.2	0.86	F4	F4						
14	Small,no expand	Hi-lo	2.6	0.9	0.8	5.6	0.14								
16	Small plant	Lo-lo	2.6	0.8	0.8	5.4				5.4	0.3				
18	Abandon		0	0	0	0				0	1				

RESULTS

EMV (mill)   _____

DETAILS of EVs

BIG PLANT   _____

SMALL PLANT _____

ABANDON   _____

MONTSON CHEMICAL

22 Planning Values

24 Probabilities
25 Prob (hi-hi)   0.60
26 Prob (hi-lo)   0.10
27 Prob (lo-lo)   0.30
28 **Sum of Probs**   1.00

30 Annual Cashflows   Years to expansion

	mill	Before	2
		Life	10
33 Big & hi	2		
34 Big & lo	0.2		
35 Small, hi	0.9	Capital millions	
then hi	0.5		
37 Small,exp hi-hi	1.4	Big plant	6
38 Small,exp hi-lo	0.1	Small	2.6
39 Small & lo	0.8	Expansion	4.4

Figure 7.7 Detailed layout of spreadsheet model MONT1

A	B	F	G	H	I	J
MONTSON CHEMICAL						
				Decision	Analysis	DECISION
---	---	---	---	---	---	---
4 DECISIONS	OUTCOMES	PROFIT	Probs	CEVs	EVs	EMVs
		mill	F3&4	F3&4	F3&4	DN2
6 Big Plant	Hi-hi	14				14
7 Big Plant	Hi-lo	-0.4				-0.4
8 Big Plant	Lo-lo	-4				-4
			F3	F3	F3	DN2
10 Small, expand	Hi-hi	6	0.86	5.14	4.51	4.51
11 Small, expand	Hi-lo	-4.4	0.14	-0.63		EXPAND
			F4	F4	F4	
13 Small,no expand	Hi-hi	3.2	0.86	2.74	3.54	
14 Small,no expand	Hi-lo	5.6	0.14	0.80		
16 Small plant	Lo-lo	5.4				5.4
18 Abandon		0				0

Figure 7.8 Evaluating decision node 2

Expected values for forks F3 and F4

The 'conditional expected values' (CEVs) are entered in column H, that is payoffs weighted by their probabilities. Therefore, in cell H10, enter the formula:

+F10*G10

and copy it down to H11, H13 and H14.

The expected values (EVs) are calculated in the next column. Therefore, in cell I10, enter the formula:

+H10+H11

to sum the CEVs for fork F3 and copy the formula to cell I13.

Thus the expected values for forks F3 and F4 are stored in cells I10 and I13 respectively, the displayed values being 4.51 and 3.54. It may help in the following exposition to use 'names' (for example EVF3 and EVF4) instead of cell addresses. To this end, point to cell I10 and choose:

/ Range Name Create EVF3   to attach the name EVF3 to cell I10

Similarly, attach the name EVF4 to cell I13.

Decision node 2

To calculate the best decision at node DN2, that is the alternative with the highest expected value, point to cell J10 and enter the formula:

@MAX(EVF3,EVF4)

The displayed value is 4.51, the expected value of the 'expand' alternative. As well as displaying the highest value, the associated decision should be indicated. Therefore, to describe the chosen decision, in cell J11 enter the formula:

@IF(EVF3>EVF4, "EXPAND" , "NO EXPANSION")

If the condition EVF3>EVF4 is true, the first label, EXPAND, will be displayed : otherwise NO EXPANSION will be displayed. In this case, the best decision at this node is to expand the small plant.

Figure 7.8 shows an extract of the spreadsheet after Decision node 2 has been evaluated.

Expected values for forks 1 and 2

The payoffs and probabilities for fork F1 are set out in cells J6 to K8 (in MONT1). The payoffs link to the earlier profit entries in column F and the probabilities to the planning values. Calculation of the expected value at fork F1 is carried out in the area from L6 to M8 as follows.

To evaluate the conditional expected values for fork F1 (CEVs) enter the formula in cell L6:

+J6*K6

and copy the formula to cells L7 and L8. The same formula applies for the CEVs for fork F2, so copy the formula in L6 to cells:

L10, L16 and L18.

To calculate the expected values in column M, in cell M6, enter the sum:

@SUM(L6..L8)

and +L10+L16 in cell M16.

On the 'Abandon' row, in cell M18 enter the formula:

+L18

to repeat the value displayed in cell M18.

Thus cells M6 and M16 contain the expected values at forks F1 (7.16) and F2 (4.78). Cell M18 contains the zero payoff if the project is abandoned. These three cells represent the expected values for the three alternatives at decision node 1. Again it helps to attach

	A	B	C	D	E	F	G	H	I
1	MONTSON CHEMICAL								
2			Calculation of Payoffs					Decision Analysis	

4	DECISIONS	OUTCOMES	Capital	Initial Revenue	Later Revenue	PROFIT mill	Probs F3&4	CEVs F3&4	EVs F3&4
6	Big Plant	Hi-hi	6	2	2	14			
7	Big Plant	Hi-lo	6	2	0.2	-0.4			
8	Big Plant	Lo-lo	6	0.2	0.2	-4			
							F3	F3	F3
10	Small, expand	Hi-hi	7	0.9	1.4	6	0.86	5.14	4.51
11	Small, expand	Hi-lo	7	0.9	0.1	-4.4	0.14	-0.63	
							F4	F4	F4
13	Small,no expand	Hi-hi	2.6	0.9	0.5	3.2	0.86	2.74	3.54
14	Small,no expand	Hi-lo	2.6	0.9	0.8	5.6	0.14	0.80	
16	Small plant	Lo-lo	2.6	0.8	0.8	5.4			
18	Abandon		0	0	0	0			

```
         MONTSON CHEMICAL
22       Planning Values                            RESULTS
         -----------------------------------        ---------------
24       Probabilities                            | EMV (mill)
25       Prob (hi-hi)    0.60                      |    7.16
26       Prob (hi-lo)    0.10                      | BIG PLANT
27       Prob (lo-lo)    0.30                      |
28       **Sum of Probs**  1.00                    |
                                                   | DETAILS of EVs
30       Annual Cashflows      Years to expansion  | ---------
         -----------------------------------       | BIG PLANT
                              mill Before      2   |    7.16
33       Big & hi            2 Life          10    |
34       Big & lo          0.2                     | SMALL PLANT
35       Small, hi         0.9  Capital millions   |    4.78
           then hi         0.5 ------------------  |
37       Small,exp hi-hi   1.4 Big plant      6    |
38       Small,exp hi-lo   0.1 Small        2.6    | ABANDON
39       Small & lo        0.8 Expansion    4.4    |    0.00
         -----------------------------------       | ------------------
```

Figure 7.9 Completed analysis in spreadsheet model MONT1

122

names to the cells (say EVF1, EVF2 and EVNULL) with the command sequence Range Name Create. The names suggest the contents of the cells and are easier to use in constructing formulae.

The values can be checked against those in Figure 7.9 which also gives the completed analysis.

Decision node 1

In the MONT1 spreadsheet, column N is left blank to give a narrow border between the computations and the result of the decision analysis. In cell O6, enter the formula:

@MAX(EVF1,EVF2,EVNULL)

to find the decision with the highest EMV (7.16 in this case). Give this cell the name EVMAX (with Range Name Create) as it represents the 'maximum expected value'.

In cell O7, the formula:

@IF(EVF1=EVMAX," BIG PLANT" ,(@IF(EVF2=EVMAX," SMALL PLANT", " ABANDON")))

describes the best decision at node 1. The @IF expressions are nested. The internal @IF displays SMALL PLANT or ABANDON according to whether EVF2 is the maximum EMV or not. However, this @IF will only come into play if EVF1 is *not* the largest expected value alternative.

In cell O8, it helps to record whether expansion is required if the small plant alternative is selected. A suitable formula for cell O8 is:

@IF(EVF2=EVMAX,J10," ")

The effect of this formula is to display the decision at node 2 (EXPAND or NO EXPANSION), if the small plant alternative is selected; otherwise the cell will be blank.

For easy use, it is worth displaying the main details of the results below the calculation area, for example adjacent to the planning values, to assist the sensitivity analyses.

For reference, the completed analysis is given in datafile MONT2 on the datadisc.

7.7 Sensitivity analysis

Usually the first sensitivity analysis will concentrate on the probabilities that have been assessed. It is of interest to know how low the probability of a sustained high demand over the ten years can drop before the best decision changes.

In varying the probabilities, we must guard against them failing to sum to unity. In the Montson models MONT1 and MONT2, cell A29 contains an error message that will be displayed if the Sum of Probs in cell B28 is not unity. The formula in cell A29 is:

@IF(B28<>1, "***Probs MUST sum to 1***"," ")

Thus with the help of the error message, it is possible to explore the effect of changing the probabilities on the decision in an *ad hoc* way, always ensuring that the probabilities do sum to one.

Another approach is to change only the probability in cell B24 and to adjust the probability in cell B26 accordingly. Enter the formula:

1-B24-B25   into cell B26

This ensures that the probabilities do sum to one. When this is done, we find that Prob(high–high) can fall to 0.47 before the best decision switches from 'big plant' to 'small plant'.

As well as reducing the probability of high demand for ten years, we may be interested in the effect of increased capital cost. Figure 7.10 shows what happens if the probability (denoted by Prob(hi-hi)) is slightly lower at 0.5 and the capital cost of the big plant is £7 million (instead of £6 million). It is better to start by building the small plant and then to expand it if these assumptions hold.

```
MONTSON CHEMICAL
Planning Values                                    RESULTS
-------------------------------------------        ---------------

Probabilities                            |  EMV (mill)
Prob (hi-hi)      0.50                    |     4.72
Prob (hi-lo)      0.10                    |  SMALL PLANT
Prob (lo-lo)      0.40                    |  EXPAND
**Sum of Probs**  1.00                    |
                                         |  DETAILS of EVs
Annual Cashflows        Years to expansion|  ---------
-------------------------------------------|  BIG PLANT
                     mill Before        2 |     4.36
Big & hi                2 Life         10 |
Big & lo              0.2                 |  SMALL PLANT
Small, hi             0.9 Capital millions|     4.72
    then hi           0.5 -----------------|
Small,exp hi-hi       1.4 Big plant     7 |
Small,exp hi-lo       0.1 Small       2.6 |  ABANDON
Small & lo            0.8 Expansion   4.4 |     0.00
-------------------------------------------   ------------------
```

Figure 7.10   Results for changed capital cost and probabilities

A more systematic approach would use a Data Table for this kind of analysis. Figure 7.11 shows how the best decision changes from 'small plant' to 'big plant' as the probability of high demand increases for different levels of capital cost. The formula for evaluation links to the best decision cell, namely cell O7. However, an amended form with shortened labels is preferable, namely:

124

```
MONTSON CHEMICAL
Data Table: Capital for Big Plant v Prob(hi-hi)


                                    Prob(hi-hi)
               BIG     0.3     0.4     0.5     0.6     0.7
Capital        4.50   SMALL    BIG     BIG     BIG     BIG
Big Plant      5.00   SMALL   SMALL    BIG     BIG     BIG
               6.00   SMALL   SMALL    BIG     BIG     BIG
               7.50   SMALL   SMALL   SMALL    BIG     BIG
               9.00   SMALL   SMALL   SMALL   SMALL    BIG
```

Figure 7.11   Data Table varying capital cost and probability

@IF(EVF1=EVMAX," BIG" ,@IF(EVF2=EVMAX," SMALL"," ABANDON")

The input cells for the Data Table are the probability (Prob(hi-hi)) in cell B24 and the capital cost in cell D37. The results in Figure 7.11 show the boundary (breakeven probabilities) where the best decision changes from SMALL to BIG plant.

7.8   Discussion

The analysis has been carried out using expected monetary value as the decision crite-rion. Although building the big plant has the highest expected payoff (EMV), it does entail the possibility of a loss of £4.0 million occurring with a 30 per cent chance if the demand turns out to be low. Montson may prefer the 'small plant' alternative and 'no expansion', which would give a profit of at least £3.2 million. Any other decisions could result in losses if demand is low. However, this conservative strategy ignores the possibility of profits as high as £14.0 million which could occur if a big plant were to be built. If Montson is a large firm, the EMV approach is relevant. However, if Montson is small, a possible loss of £4.0 million would be untenable and the more cautious approach is probably relevant.

The cashflows in Section 7.4 were not discounted. However, if discounting were to be applied, the principles of the analysis would be the same. The timings of the cash inflows and outflows would make the small plant with the possibility of further expansion relatively more attractive. This is because some of the capital expenditure is delayed for two years. The size of the effect would depend upon the rate of interest used in the analysis.

As we have seen, decision trees tackle problems that can have a long time-span and may involve decisions at different stages. It is important to check that conditions have not changed when a future decision node is reached. For example, even though the decision analysis of Montson might have suggested expanding the small plant after two years with high demand, it is important to check that conditions are unchanged before going for the expansion. In effect, expenditure in the past can be regarded as a sunk cost; now the name of the game is to optimise the future.

CHAPTER 8

Introductory Macro Models

8.1 Introduction

Macros are single key commands that activate a sequence of 1-2-3 commands. Any operation you can carry out with 1-2-3 can be automated with the macro facility. Macros are particularly useful for accomplishing tasks that have to be repeated many times: for example retrieving files, creating graphs, displaying named graphs, sorting and querying databases, etc. In addition, specially tailored menus can be created within macros. For example, it is easy to write a macro with a menu to control the entry of data into a model. (This is not possible with the normal manual keystroking method.)

Macros are described fully in the 1-2-3 Users' Manual. Although their effective use is slightly more difficult to master than spreadsheet modelling, they provide a wealth of further possible applications for 1-2-3. In effect, they permit the use of 1-2-3 commands in 'deferred mode' (as well as the familiar 'immediate mode'). This allows 1-2-3 models to be 'programmed' for operation by non-expert users.

A macro is created by entering the sequence of keystrokes necessary to perform some operation into a cell as a label (or column of labels). A special letter key is assigned to each macro and used to 'invoke' or activate it. Each time the activating key is typed in combination with the Alt key, the operation is performed automatically. The worksheet together with its macro(s) can be saved for future use.

8.2 Overview of stages in writing a simple macro

The main steps in building a macro to automate an operation are:

1. Perform the operation manually.
2. Enter the sequence of commands making up the macro.
3. Attach a letter key to the macro.
4. Activate the macro.

To illustrate the steps, a simple macro to erase entries in a small part of the worksheet is developed. To be specific, suppose the area given by the range A1..C7 is to be used as a workpad for calculations and the objective is to create an 'Erase' Macro to clear out entries in the workpad from time to time.

125

126

Step 1: To clear out the range A1..C7, the 1-2-3 sequence might be:

/ Range Erase A1..C7   followed by pressing Enter

Step 2: Start with an empty spreadsheet, point to cell F1 and enter (as a label) the sequence for the Erase Macro:

'/REA1..C7~   in cell F1
                                            to Range Erase the cell range A1..C7

Note, firstly, that the entry starts with an apostrophe (') so that it is a label. Secondly, the tilde symbol (~) is used to denote the Enter key.

Step 3: With the pointer on F1, name the macro cell with the sequence:

/ Range Name Create E   which attaches Name E to cell F1

As normally in 1-2-3, you press Enter after any input such as the name E.

Step 4: To try out the macro, first enter some data into some of the cells in the range A1..C7. Then activate the Erase Macro by pressing the Alt key and the E key simultaneously. The result should be that the data is erased from the screen.

To generalize, then, about developing a macro or sequence of macros to automate a procedure:

Step 1: Work through the procedure manually, noting down *every* key used.
Step 2: Choose an area of the worksheet that will not be affected by the ensuing calculations. Type each line of commands into a cell as if it were a label. It makes no difference if the entry overflows into an adjacent cell. Starting at a particular cell, for example J1, enter the first sequence of commands and continue down the same column (J say) using consecutive cells.
Step 3: The topmost cell of the sequence of 'label commands' (in J1) is given a name using the Range Name command. To distinquish a Macro from an ordinary cell range, the name must start with the backslash (e.g. M). Note that it is only necessary to name the topmost cell of the macro, not the entire cell range.
Step 4: To invoke the macro, on the IBM PC you press the Alt key together with the chosen letter key, say the M key. As soon as you simultaneously press Alt and the macro key M, 1-2-3 jumps into action and carries out the instructions (in column J) automatically.

8.3 Building a simple macro

To illustrate, we will build a second simple macro that does the following:

1) Enters the numbers 27 and 16 into cells A1 and A2.
2) Waits for a third number to be entered into A3 underneath.
3) Adds the three numbers in column A and puts the resulting sum immediately below.
4) Copies the contents of the cell range A1..A4 to C4..C7.

Firstly, decide the keystrokes to carry out part 1 above. The best method is to perform the operation noting down every one of the keys touched. (For example, pressing the Home key followed by 27 and then pressing Enter (or Return) would enter 27 in cell A1. The Down arrow key followed by 16 and then Enter would complete part 1 of the operation.)

Start with an empty worksheet. This time the macro will be situated away from the calculation area, say in column J. Point to cell J1 and type the label:

{HOME}   into cell J1

Note that the brackets must be {}. {HOME} is the macro equivalent of pressing the Home key. As we shall see, there are macro equivalents for all the other special keys used in 1-2-3 operations.

Next enter the sequence

'27~{DOWN}16~   into cell J2 as shown in Figure 8.1.

```
         I      J       K       L       M
  1             {HOME}
  2             '27~{DOWN}16~
  3
  4
  5
  6
  7
  8
  9
 10             {HOME}/REA1.C7~
 11
 12
```

Figure 8.1   First part of Number macro (also Erase macro in J10)

The label prefix ' is important—without it, 1-2-3 will not permit you to enter subsequent symbols. The apostrophe ' is shown in the illustrations in this Chapter, although the symbol will not be visible in the normal screen display. It is included in these illustrations to emphasise the process of entering macro instructions as labels.

The tilde symbol ~ is used to denote Enter. {DOWN} is the macro equivalent of the 'Down arrow' key. The first line of the macro, {HOME}, is equivalent to pressing the Home key, that is it will jump the pointer to cell A1. The second line will enter the number 27 into cell A1 and then move the pointer down one cell before entering the number 16.

To attach key N (for Number) to the macro, use the Range Name Create command. That is, point to J1 and type:

/ Range Name Create   N   to attach Name   N to the macro starting in cell J1

128

Remember that the name must start with a backslash, which tells 1-2-3 that this named cell is at the top of a macro. There is no space between the backslash and the single letter key.

Having named the macro, invoke it. On the IBM PC, you press down the Alt and N keys simultaneously. This should jump the pointer to A1 and enter the numbers 27 and 16 in cells A1 and A2. (If your macro does not function properly, press Escape to cancel any error message and then check carefully that it ties up exactly with Figure 8.1 and that its starting cell is named   N. If the screen displays the message CMD, indicating that is following a macro command, you may also need to use BREAK (that is press the Control key together with the Break key) to get back to READY mode. This is described more fully in Section 8.4 under the sub heading 'single-step execution').

For convenience, the Erase Macro developed earlier can be included in column J to help erase entries while in the building stage of macro writing. A second macro can be positioned in the worksheet below the first one provided that at least one cell is blank between the end of the first macro and the starting cell of the second one.

Point to cell J10 and enter the sequence for Macro E:

{HOME}/REA1..C7~   in J10
                                          to Range Erase the range of cells A1..C7

With the pointer on J10, name the macro that starts in J10 with the sequence:

/ Range Name Create   E   to attach the Name   E to cell J10

Then invoke the Erase macro by pressing Alt and E simultaneously.

If both macros are working satisfactorily, remember to Save your File (after using the Erase Macro). If the macros are not working properly, check out the entries against those in Figure 8.1 before saving to disc.

Returning to the original set of operations specified for the macro N, part 2 above gets input from the user. To do this, the special form {?} is used. Point to J3 and type:

{GOTO}A3~{?}~   which allows the macro user to input a
                                                              number to cell A3

When an instruction {?} occurs, the macro stops operating and control is with the user for keying in an entry until he presses Enter. Note that this Enter is not entered into the system. It is necessary to follow the {?} by a tilde (~) to force the macro to continue operating after user input. {GOTO} is the macro equivalent of the Goto key (f5). It is used to introduce another of the macro equivalents for special keys.

Again, check the macro by pressing the Alt and N keys together. When the macro pauses, type a number followed by Enter. Afterwards erase the results using macro E. (Notice that it is not necessary to name the macro again. Although the macro has been extended down column J, the location of the starting cell has not changed.)

Next, in part 3, the three entries in column A are summed and the result placed in cell A4. Having positioned the pointer on A4, the special function @SUM(A1..A3) can be used for the column sum. Part 4 involves copying from column A to column C. This could be achieved by typing in the cell addresses. Alternatively, referring to the ranges by 'pointing' would require repeated use of the Up and Right arrow keys. Continue working through these operations manually, noting down every key used. One possible sequence of keystrokes for carrying out the entire operation is shown in Figure 8.2. Notice that pressing the Up arrow key three times can be denoted {UP}{UP}{UP} or more concisely {UP 3}.

Figure 8.2 shows that every line of the macro is entered as if it were a label. In particular, the label prefix ' must be keyed in for any entry that 1-2-3 would interpret as a value or a command, for example the entry in cell J2 (which starts with a number) and in J5 (which starts with the Command key /).

```
        I       J       K       L       M       N
  1             {HOME}
  2             '27~{DOWN}16~
  3             {GOTO}A3~{?}~
  4             {DOWN}@SUM(A1.A3)~
  5             '/C.{UP 3}~{RIGHT 2}~
  6
  7
  8
  9
 10             {HOME}/REA1.C7~
 11
 12
```

Figure 8.2   Macro N (number) and E (erase)

Check that your macro carries out parts 1 to 4 above. If it fails to work check each cell carefully, making sure that all cells contain labels and that the starting cell has been named   N. If there are still problems, the single-step mode of execution described in the next section should be used.

As mentioned before, as with all spreadsheet work remember to use File Save from time to time to ensure that work is saved to disc. The best procedure would be to check that Macro N is working and then use Macro E to clear out the entries; then File Save to disc.

8.4   Documenting and debugging a macro

As with all forms of programming, it is worth observing a few rules of layout and structure right from the start when you try your hand with macros. A few conventions will ease the tasks of debugging, updating or adapting macros at a later stage. In particular, the discussion in this section concerns the layout, documentation and naming of macros and the so-called 'single-step' execution mode.

Three-column layout

Figure 8.3 shows a 'three-column' layout with macro names in column I and brief descriptions of the main steps in macro sequences in column N. The documentation is important as this form of programming rapidly becomes impossible to follow as the application develops.

```
        I       J       K       L       M       N       O
 1 Macro    Macro                           Description
 2 Names
 3 '\N      {HOME}
 4          '27~{DOWN}16~                    Enter 27 & 16
 5          {GOTO}A3~{?}~                    Wait for userinput
 6          {DOWN}@SUM(A1.A3)~               Sum
 7          '/C.{UP 3}~{RIGHT 2}~            Copy entries & sum
 8
 9
10
11
12 '\E      {HOME}/REA1.C7~                  Range Erase work
13                                           area
```

Figure 8.3   Documented versions of macros N and E

It is useful to have the names of macros stored and visible in the spreadsheet. To this end, Figure 8.3 shows the two macros N and E under a common heading 'macros' with their names stored as labels adjacent to the starting cell position for each macro. For example, the label ' N tells us that a macro associated with the N keystroke starts in the adjacent cell J3. Its entries continue in the cells below until the first blank cell is reached. Having laid out the macro names in this way, they can be named in one operation with the command Range Name Labels Right. This will attach the macro names N and E to the labels starting in J3 and J12; that is with the pointer on I3, type:

/ Range Name Labels Right I3..I12   to Name the Ranges to the Right
                                                    with the Labels in column I

Single-step execution

In testing macros, 1-2-3 has a 'single-step mode' in which it pauses after each keystroke of the macro. To try this, use the Erase macro to return to the original blank work area.

Press the Alt and Edit keys (f2) together to give the STEP indicator at the bottom of the screen. Now invoke Macro N (press Alt together with the N key) and get the flashing SST indicator as the macro progresses. To step through the macro, press any key. To leave the single-step mode when the macro is complete, use STEP again; that is press the Alt and the Edit keys together again.

If the macro requires input from the user, as Macro N does with its {?}, after keying in a number, you must press Enter to continue in single-step mode.

When you detect an error in single-step mode, press BREAK (that is the Control key together with the Break key on the IBM PC) to stop the macro. It may also be necessary to press Escape if an Error message flashes on screen. You can edit the macro and then continue stepping through it.

Note the convention in Figure 8.3 of typing the macro commands in upper case letters to distinguish them from explanatory text in mixed case. It does not matter whether upper or lower case or combinations of both are used. The use of upper case also distinguishes macro commands from the mixed case entries in menus, as we shall show later.

We have met the tilde key ~ which is always used in place of Enter. We have also encountered the typing equivalent of the Home key and some of the pointer movement keys. Figure 8.4 shows the macro writing equivalents for the other pointer movement and Function keys.

Macro Key	Description
~	RETURN (referred to as tilde)
{DOWN}	DOWN
{UP}	UP
{LEFT}	LEFT
{RIGHT}	RIGHT
{HOME}	HOME
{END}	END
{PGUP}	PAGE UP
{PGDN}	PAGE DOWN
{BIGLEFT}	BIG LEFT (move left one screen)
{BIGRIGHT}	BIG RIGHT (move right one screen)
{EDIT}	EDIT
{NAME}	NAME
{ABS}	ABS
{GOTO}	GOTO
{WINDOW}	WINDOW
{QUERY}	QUERY
{TABLE}	TABLE
{CALC}	CALC
{GRAPH}	GRAPH
{ESCAPE} or {ESC}	ESCAPE
{BACKSPACE} or {BS}	BACKSPACE
{DELETE} or {DEL}	DELETE (use only EDIT mode)
{~}	to have tilde appear as ~
{{} and {}}	to have braces appear as { and }

Figure 8.4   Macro equivalents for special keys

8.5   Automail—A semi-automatic letterwritter

A more realistic example of a model using macros, AUTOMAIL, writes a standard letter to customers selected from a database of names and addresses. Conditions can be set to restrict the customers to, say, those with addresses in London or whatever. Thus the macros are constructed on the back of 1-2-3's Data Query facilities. (If you know nothing about the Data Query facilities in 1-2-3, you may wish to refer to the 1-2-3 Reference Manual about this topic. Alternatively, you could consult Chapter 6 of the author's *Creative Modelling*.)

The automatic letter writer has two main parts:

1) A data selection operation in which the 'criterion' for selecting customer records is set up (say the TOWN must be London) and the relevant records selected and copied into an 'output' range.
2) The procedures for getting names and addresses out of the output range and correctly positioned in the letter and the letter writing itself.

Figure 8.5 shows the various parts of the AUTOMAIL worksheet. The standard letter is in columns A to G and the database of names and addresses in columns I to N. The worksheet has been set up for Data Query Extract. The Criterion range (simply the TOWN fieldname and the cell beneath) is the cell range P1..P2 and the Output range for the Data Query Extract is the row of fieldnames in the cell range P4..U4. The ranges used in the Data Query (named using the Range Name Create command) are as follows:

RANGE		NAME
Criterion range	P1..P2	CR
Output range	P4..U4	OUT
Input range, i.e. Database	I1..N40	N&ADD

Figure 8.6 shows three macros positioned in column X in the worksheet. Their names S, Q and P, for Select, Query and Print, have been entered in the left-hand column W adjacent to the first cell of each macro:

Macro S This handles the *Selection* of a town. The standard letter will be sent to all customers whose addresses are in Leeds, say. The user enters the Town chosen (Leeds) at the pointer position reached after invoking Macro S (in fact in the Criterion range cell P2).

Macro Q This handles the *Query* itself. The details of all customers who satisfy the selection criterion are copied into the Output range. When this is complete, the pointer is positioned over the first NAME entry (Jones in this case) under the Output range.

Macro P This macro takes details from a selected record under the Output range and transfers them to the letter. When *Printing* has finished, the pointer is back in the NAME column (over Jones again) waiting to be moved down to the next row. Once this has happened, the next letter (to Wright) is printed by invoking Macro P again. This process is repeated until the end of the list.

The macros have been named in one operation using the Range Name Labels command. That is, point at cell W3 and type:

	A					G
1	Quantum Leapers,					
2	14/22, The Boulevard,					
3	Leeds					
4	L22 6TY					
5						
6	attention:	Mr. T.E. Jones				13-Nov-87
7						
8	Dear Sir,					
9						
10	I was extremely disappointed to see that once again your account is in					
11	arrears. If you do not pay within 6 days, I regret we shall be unable					
12	to continue to supply you.					
13						
14	Yours sincerely,					
15						
16	J.Jolly					

	I	J	K	L	M	N
1	NAME	INITS	COMPANY	NO/STREET	TOWN	POSTCODE
2	Barratt	F.A.	Rightway Ltd.	234, Button Hook Lane,	Wakefield,	WA3 7UP
3	Brown	R.W	Yarn Spinners Ltd.	Yarn House, Oxford Road	Nottingham	N05 6WE
4	Jones	T E	Quantum Leapers	14/22, The Boulevard,	Leeds	L22 6TY
5	Proctor	B.S.	B F P O plc.	21, Archer Street,	London	SW2 9TT
6	Smith	R.S.	Latepay Ltd.	23, The Ringway,	London	NW3 4FG
7	Wright	P.S.	The Loop Group plc.	45, Beech Street,	Leeds	L34 7YU
8	Uptight	f.St	Crashproof Investmen	Yupp's Brow	Basingstoke	BAS X57
9	Veenal	E.E.	Eete Rite	Currie Mews	Leeds	L57 7TY
10	Zinker	K.K.	Black Monday Club	1, Threadneedle Street	London	EC2 4US

	P	Q	R	S	T	U
1	TOWN					
2	Leeds					
3						
4	NAME	INITS	COMPANY	NO/STREET	TOWN	POSTCODE
5	Jones	T.E.	Quantum Leapers,	14/22 The Boulevard,	Leeds	L22 6TY
6	Wright	P.S.	The Loop Group plc.	45, Beech Street,	Leeds	L34 7YU
7	Veenal	E.E.	Eete Rite	Currie Mews	Leeds	L57 7TY

Figure 8.5   Parts of AUTOMAIL worksheet

```
        W              X              Y         Z
 1 M Names   Macros                    Documentation
 2
 3 '\S       {GOTO}CR~{DOWN}           Pointer to Crit Range
 4
 5 '\Q       {QUERY}{GOTO}OUT~{DOWN}   Query on settings saved in WS
 6
 7 '\P       {RIGHT 2}                 Point to Company name
 8           '/C~A1~                   Copy to letterhead
 9           {RIGHT}                   Point to street
10           '/C~A2~                   Copy to letterhead
11           {RIGHT}                   Point to town
12           '/C~A3~                   Copy to letterhead
13           {RIGHT}                   Point to Postcade
14           '/C~A4~                   Copy to letterhead
15           {LEFT 4}                  Point to initials
16           '/C~B6~                   Copy
17           {LEFT}                    Point to name
18           '/C~C6~                   Copy
19           '/PPRA1.G17~AGQ           Print letter
```

Figure 8.6   AUTOMAIL's three macros

/ Range Name Labels Right W3..W7   to name all three macros.

To try out AUTOMAIL, after retrieving the datafile, make sure that your printer is switched on.

To run AUTOMAIL, activate Macro S (Selection) which causes the pointer to jump to cell P2 in the Criterion range. Enter the town chosen (say London) and then invoke Macro Q (Query). When Macro Q has finished, there should be a list of names and addresses in the Output area and the pointer should be over the first name. Invoke Macro P (Print). When the first letter has been printed, the pointer is over the first name again. Move the pointer down to the next name and invoke Macro P again. Repeat until all the letters are printed. Figure 8.7 shows the resulting letters for London.

As mentioned earlier, the AUTOMAIL file contains pre-set Range Names. These can be displayed in a convenient empty part of the worksheet using the sequence: / Range Name Table. Also the settings for the Data Query have been saved with the AUTOMAIL file. These can be investigated from READY mode by going to the Data Query menu with the sequence:

/ Data Query

and looking at the Input, Criterion and Output ranges in turn.

```
B F P O plc
21, Archer Street,
SW2 9TT
                                                    13-Nov-87

attention:       Mr. B.S. Proctor


Dear Sir,


I was extremely disappointed to see that once again your account is in
arrears.  If you do not pay within 6 days, I regret we shall be unable
to continue to supply you.


Yours sincerely,


J.Jolly


Latepay Ltd.
23, The Ringway,
London
NW3 '4FG
                                                    13 Nov-87


attention:       Mr. R.S. Smith


Dear Sir,


I was extremely disappointed to see that once again your account is in
arrears.  If you do not pay within 6 days, I regret we shall be unable
to continue to supply you.


Yours sincerely,


J.Jolly
```

Figure 8.7   Letters which result from selecting London

Lastly, explore the macros in column X which 'drive' AUTOMAIL. Macro S merely positions the pointer under the TOWN fieldname in the Criterion range. Macro Q is particularly simple. The settings for the Data Query Extract have been pre-set, so it is sufficient to use the Query key (denoted {Query}) to output the records of customers matching the selection criterion. Macro P is rather longer. Most of its instructions concern the positioning of customer details on the letter screen, the last one carrying out the printing of the customized letter. (Incidentally, if you add new customer records to the database, make certain that you fill in all the cells up to and including the POSTCODE cell. If cells are left blank, the Print Macro will not function properly.)

Notice in Macros S and Q the use of Range Names (CR and OUT) rather than cell addresses. Macros built in this way will need far less updating and editing if the spreadsheet layout is subsequently altered. When named cell ranges are moved around the worksheet, 1-2-3 adjusts its store of Range Names and cell addresses to reflect the new addresses. Thus macros that use the Names will still work after layout changes whereas those with cell addresses will probably need to be edited.

This, then, is a semi-automatic letter writing procedure, controlled by just three macros. In normal 1-2-3 working, lengthy sequences of commands would be required to achieve the same results. The AUTOMAIL type of model (particularly the automated querying of a database with a routine printout) is a practical proposition for general use in an office environment. With the addition of a few instructions on the worksheet to remind the user which keys to press, it could be used effectively by someone who knew little about the workings of 1-2-3.

8.6 A macro for consolidation

Macros are especially useful for automating repeated file handling although great care is needed to ensure that data does not become scrambled in the process. In this section, a macro is built for consolidating sales figures held in different files. A second macro is introduced for plotting the aggregated results. Any procedure in which several similar spreadsheets are to be aggregated gains from being handled via macros.

The basic layout of the summary sheet (contained in file SUMMARY) is shown in Figure 8.8. Sales results for the Northern sales region and the Southern sales region are set out in similarly structured files called NORTH and SOUTH respectively. The results for North and South are to be consolidated into one summary worksheet. To look at the separate results, retrieve each of the spreadsheets called NORTH and SOUTH in turn to examine them. They contain weekly sales figures for the three months. The SUMMARY file contains only formulae for monthly and weekly sales (in column F and row 10 respectively).

In building the macros, the first step is to work through the procedure manually, noting down *all* the keystrokes. Therefore, first load the summary worksheet using:

/ File Combine Copy Entire-File SUMMARY   to load the SUMMARY File

The summary file is 'combined' because it is copied into the empty worksheet which will in due course contain the various macro routes.

Leaving the pointer on A1, next bring in the sales results for the North using File Combine, that is:

/ File Combine Add Entire-File NORTH

which adds all the numerical entries in the NORTH file to the corresponding cells in the SUMMARY file. Similarly, the results for the South are aggregated to those for the North (already entered in the cells of the SUMMARY file) by typing:

/ File Combine Add Entire-File SOUTH

```
        A       B        C        D        E        F        G        H
  1            FOURTH QUARTER REPORT
  2            NORTH & SOUTH REGIONS SALES
  3
  4
  5            WEEK 1   WEEK 2   WEEK 3   WEEK 4    TOTAL
  6  OCT                                              0
  7  NOV                                              0
  8  DEC                                              0
  9
 10  TOTAL        0        0        0        0        0
 11
 12
 13
 14
 15
 16
```

```
            FOURTH QUARTER REPORT:NORTHERN REGION


                 WEEK 1   WEEK 2   WEEK 3   WEEK 4
        OCT       1,020    1,423    1,522    1,843
        NOV       1,833    1,428    1,593    1,499
        DEC       1,279   15,683    1,633    2,760
```

Figure 8.8   SUMMARY worksheet

This adds all the numerical entries in the SOUTH file to the corresponding cells in the SUMMARY file.

Figure 8.9 shows the results after consolidating the sales figures for the two regions. Having performed the steps manually, we can write the Consolidation Macro (C):

1. Start with an empty worksheet. Enter the macro shown in column M of Figure 8.10 (cells M3 to M6) and enter its name C as a label (that is ' C) in cell L3.
2. To name the macro, point at L3 and use Range Name Label Right to name the macro starting in M3.
3. Activate the macro to check that it works.

Once again it is useful to have an Erase Macro during the building stage, so:

4. Add macro E in row 18 as shown in Figure 8.10. Name the macro E and use it.

Once you are satisfied that both Macros C and E work:

5. Use the Erase Macro to blank out the first 'page' of the worksheet. Then Save the worksheet containing the macros.

	A	B	C	D	E	F	G
1		FOURTH QUARTER REPORT					
2		NORTH & SOUTH REGIONS SALES					
3							
4							
5		WEEK 1	WEEK 2	WEEK 3	WEEK 4	TOTAL	
6	OCT	3,140	3,846	3,544	3,831	14,361	
7	NOV	3,803	3,384	3,265	3,363	13,815	
8	DEC	3,555	17,251	3,266	5,520	29,592	
9							
10	TOTAL	10,498	24,481	10,075	12,714	57,768	
11							
12							
13							
14							
15							
16							

Figure 8.9   Results for NORTH and SOUTH consolidated

	L	M	N	O	P	Q
1	M Name	Macro				Description
2						
3	'\C	{HOME}				Consolidation
4		'/FCCESUMMARY~				Combine summary
5		'/FCAENORTH~				Combine north
6		'/FCAESOUTH~				Combine south to consolidate
7						
8						
9	'\G	'/GTBXA6.A10~AF6.F10~VQ				Graphs totals in Col F
10						
11						
12						
13						
14						
15						
16						
17						
18	'\E	{HOME}/REA1.H20~				Erase first page
19						

Figure 8.10   Macros C, G and E for Consolidation, Graph and Erase

This file with macros but no sales statistics will be referred to as CONSOL hereafter.

To extend the application, we will add a macro to produce a graph of the Total Sales figures after consolidation. The Totals are positioned in column F.

6. Start by using Macro C to carry out the consolidation and hence obtain the monthly sales in column F of the worksheet.
7. Next work out the procedure required to graph Total Sales (cells F6 to F10) as a Bar-chart against the labels OCT, NOV, etc., in column A. Now write the associated macro for producing the graph.

One possible sequence for this operation is shown in M9 of Figure 8.10. When you are satisfied that the Graph Macro works, use the Erase Macro to erase the consolidated results and File Save your worksheet CONSOL containing the three macros.

8.7 Adding a menu

In carrying out the consolidation exercise, it would be helpful if the different operations—Consolidate, Graph and Quit—could be handled by a menu similar to 1-2-3's familiar command menu. Instead of calling the macros associated with letter keys one by one, it should be possible to choose them from a menu on the control panel. To illustrate the process, the previous consolidation example will be extended to include a menu.

Suppose the choices in the menu are to be:

OPTIONS   Consolidate   Quit   Graph

EXPLANATIONS Consolidate for quarter Graph quarter totals Leave menu

To maintain the normal style of 1-2-3 menus, we want the options to appear on the second row of the control panel and the explanations on the third row when the menu appears. The macro command:

{MENUBRANCH location}

tells 1-2-3 to look to the specified location and treat the entries as part of this type of menu.

Retrieve the CONSOL file and point to cell L12 below the Consolidation Macro. Start building the Menu Macro as follows:

1. In cell L12, enter the label ' M.
2. In the adjacent cell M12, key in the instruction:

{MENUBRANCH M14}

which tells 1-2-3 to branch to a menu starting in cell M14.
3. Type in the three options on the menu, namely:

Consolidate   Graph   Quit

into the three cells M14, N14 and O14 respectively.

4. Underneath, in cells M15, N15 and O15, key in the explanations of each option shown above. Each explanation should be positioned in the cell immediately below the option it describes.

The layout is shown in Figure 8.11. Since the columnwidth is currently only nine characters, most of the explanations will be hidden in the spreadsheet display.

```
          L         M          N         O        P       Q
     1 M Name    Macro                                   Description
     2
     3 '\C       {HOME}                                  Consolidation
     4           '/FCCESUMMARY~                          Combine summary
     5           '/FCAENORTH~                            Combine north
     6           '/FCAESOUTH~                            Combine south to consolidate
     7
     8
     9 '\G       '/GTBXA6.A10~AF6.F10~VQ                 Graphs totals in Col F
    10
    11
    12 '\M       {MENUBRANCH M14}
    13
    14           Consolidate Graph      Quit            Main Menu
    15           Consolidate Graph FirstEnd use of this menu
    16           {BRANCH \C} {BRANCH \G}{QUIT}           Action
    17
    18 '\E       {HOME}/REA1.H20~                        Erase first page
    19
```

Figure 8.11   Adding a menu Macro M

5. To name the Menu Macro M, point to cell L3 and use Range Name Labels Right on the range L3..L18 to name all the macros.

When Macro M is activated, the command {MENUBRANCH M14} is read. This tells 1-2-3 to branch to a menu that starts in cell M14.

6. Check that the menu appears when Macro M is invoked. To jump out of the macro, use **BREAK** (the Control key plus Break). The menu will not work properly until the actions to be taken for each option are entered.

To specify which macro is to be used when Consolidate (or Graph) is chosen from the menu, the macro command {BRANCH location} is used. The program branches to the specified location when this instruction is read. The location can be a cell address or a range name, in which case the top left-hand cell of the range is used. A special command {QUIT} takes care of the third option on the menu.

The 'branch' commands are entered on the third row of the menu range underneath the appropriate option. The steps are:

7. Point to M16 and enter:

{BRANCH C}   to branch to the Consolidate Macro C

8. Point to N16 and enter:

{BRANCH G}   to branch to the Graph Macro G

9. Point to O16 and enter:

{QUIT}   to Quit from the Macro.

The full worksheet entries for the menu are shown in Figure 8.11, cells L12 to O16. It is important to leave cells P14 to P16 blank, so that 1-2-3 knows that the menu stops in column O. Otherwise, entries in column P will be drawn into the menu inadvertantly with bizarre results! (Even the label prefix ' left in cell P14 will cause the menu to malfunction.)

After keying in the options, explanations and actions on the menu:

10. Save the file (CONSOL), then invoke Macro M and check that the menu works.

The commands {BRANCH} and {MENUBRANCH} are much used in macro building. To recap and stress their difference, a {BRANCH location} command when read as part of a macro tells 1-2-3 to branch to the specified location and continue processing commands at that location. A {MENUBRANCH location} command indicates that the entries at the specified location are to be treated as a menu.

In complex macros, it often helps to give menus names, particularly when several different menus are involved. Instead of specifying the cell address M14 for the menu, it could be named MAIN say. To use this procedure, carry out the following steps:

1) Edit the entry in M12 to read {MENUBRANCH MAIN}.
2) Go down to cell L14 and key in the name of the menu, MAIN.
3) Pointing at cell L14, name the range to the right of the label cell MAIN by using:

/ Range Name Label Right MAIN (R)   to Name the Range
                                                    starting in M14 MAIN

When 1-2-3 reads cell M12 in the course of executing Macro M, this command says there is a menu to be processed starting at the cell named MAIN. This is illustrated in Figure 8.12.

In passing, we note that our model now consists of the main Menu Macro M which is called by pressing the Alt and M keys. The Consolidate and Graph routines are called from Macro M; that is, it is no longer necessary to call the Graph routine (say) directly by using the Alt and G keys together. The names of the Macros could therefore be replaced by more suitable names, which are more suggestive of content. For example, the Graph routine could be called DISPLAY. As with the naming of menus, the name DISPLAY would be attached to the first cell of the Macro using Range Name. In place of the instruction {BRANCH G} under the MAIN menu, we write {DISPLAY}

```
          L         M            N        O      P      Q
 1 M Name    Macro                                Description
 2
 3 '\C       {HOME}                                Consolidation
 4           '/FCCESUMMARY~                        Combine summary
 5           '/FCAENORTH~                          Combine north
 6           '/FCAESOUTH~                          Combine south to consolidate
 7
 8
 9 '\G       '/GTBXA6.A10~AF6.F10~VQ               Graphs totals in Col F
10
11
12 '\M       {MENUBRANCH MAIN}
13
14 MAIN      Consolidate Graph       Quit          Main Menu
15           Consolidate Graph FirstEnd use of this menu
16           {BRANCH \C} {BRANCH \G}{QUIT}        Action
17
18 '\E       {HOME}/REA1.H20~                      Erase first page
19
20
21
```

Figure 8.12   Naming the menu MAIN

to call the Graph Macro or 'subroutine'. Similarly, the Name   C for the Consolidation routine could become CONSOLIDATE, say, and the routine be called thereafter by the command {CONSOLIDATE}. (Note that it is important to avoid using GRAPH as the name for the Graph routine, because {GRAPH} is the Macro equivalent of pressing the F10 Graph key.)

To tidy up the application, the flow of control will be modified to return to the MAIN menu after each option has been chosen. To do this:

1. Point to cell M7 and enter:

   {MENUBRANCH MAIN}   to return to the MAIN menu

   at the conclusion of the consolidation routine.
2. Copy the above entry into cell M10 as well so that the user is returned to the MAIN menu when the graph is complete.

   Figure 8.13 shows the macros after these amendments.

3. Check that the Menu Macro still works (Alt and M together) and test out each of the options.

```
          L         M           N       O      P       Q
  1 M Name    Macro                                  Description
  2
  3 '\C       {HOME}                                 Consolidation
  4           '/FCCESUMMARY~                         Combine summary
  5           '/FCAENORTH~                           Combine north
  6           '/FCAESOUTH~                           Combine south to consolidate
  7           {MENUBRANCH MAIN}                      Goto Main Menu
  8
  9 '\G       '/GTBXA6.A10~AF6.F10~VQ                Graphs totals in Col F
 10           {MENUBRANCH MAIN}                      Goto Main Menu
 11
 12 '\M       {MENUBRANCH MAIN}
 13
 14 MAIN      Consolidate Graph      Quit           Main Menu
 15           Consolidate Graph FirstEnd use of this menu
 16           {BRANCH \C} {BRANCH \G}{QUIT}          Action
 17
 18 '\E       {HOME}/REA1.H20~                       Erase first page
 19
 20
 21
```

Figure 8.13   All macros lead back to MAIN

4. Clear out the consolidation cells using the Erase Macro. Then Save the CONSOL
   file with its set of macros.

8.8   Automatic execution of macros

In some applications, it is desirable that a Macro operates automatically when a particular worksheet file is retrieved. To achieve this, it is simply necessary to name the
Macro 0 (zero). In addition, it is possible to force 1-2-3 to retrieve a particular worksheet from a disc each time 1-2-3 is itself loaded into memory. The chosen worksheet
must be saved under the filename AUTO123. To illustrate these features, we will make
1-2-3 automatically load the file CONSOL and go straight into the Menu Macro.

1. With the latest version of CONSOL in memory, name Macro M 0, that is point to
   M12 and type:

   / Range Name Create 0   to attach the special Name 0 to the
                                              Macro starting in cell M12.

2. Next Save the current worksheet in a file called AUTO123, that is type:

   / File Save AUTO123

Switch off the PC and when you switch on and reload 1-2-3, the Consolidation spreadsheet should be retrieved automatically and the menu with choices Consolidate/Graph/Quit should appear. Note that AUTO123 must be on the *same disc* as the SUMMARY, NORTH and SOUTH files for proper functioning.

8.9   Advanced macro commands

As well as the familiar commands that appear on the control panel when the slash key is pressed, 1-2-3 has some 'advanced macro commands'. These are special macro keywords like {BRANCH} and {MENUBRANCH} which have no equivalents on the 1-2-3 command menu. These commands can only be used within macros. Together with the extensive range of special @ functions, they provide a fuller programming language for building 1-2-3 applications. These commands are available in Release 2 of 1-2-3 but not in the earlier version.

The macro commands fall into several groups: for example commands for controlling the screen such as {WINDOWSOFF} and {PANELOFF}; for allowing keyboard interaction, {GETNUMBER} and {MENUBRANCH}; and for controlling program flow, {BRANCH}, {FOR} and {QUIT}. The commands cited above form only a small subset and the reader is referred to the 1-2-3 Reference Manual for further details. The simulation models in the next chapter illustrate the use of a few more of the important macro commands.

Previous versions of 1-2-3 had a set of programming commands (the /X commands). They have been retained in Release 2, so that earlier applications written with /X instructions can be used with Release 2. However, the /X commands have been superseded by the macro keyword commands in terms of ease of programming.

Datafiles MAC1.DAT and MAC2.DAT on your ASM disc show the developed macros for the examples discussed in Sections 8.3 and 8.6 and 8.7 of this chapter.

CHAPTER 9

Simulation Models

9.1 Simulation in sensitivity analysis

The financial planning models considered earlier in the book (for example Skywalker Video and Glowworm Lamps) were deterministic ones. That is to say, all the relationships in the SKY and GLOW models were assumed to be known exactly and the input data was treated as certain. Thus in Skywalker, demand was assumed to be at a constant level (one play per week on average for every tape). Similarly in Glowworm, sales were assumed to increase by a constant percentage (in fact, 15 per cent) each year.

The essence of spreadsheet modelling is experimenting with assumptions. This most often takes the form of trying other values for assumptions, for example changing the sales increase in Glowworm to 10 per cent or 14 per cent or 16 per cent per annum. However, there is no provision for varying the increase in sales from year to year in a probabilistic way. Thus rather than a constant 15 per cent sales increase each year for Glowworm, the percentage figures could easily turn out to be more like:

15 per cent, 14 per cent, 15.4 per cent, 14.2 per cent, 16.5 per cent,...

If so, how much difference would these more variable increases in sales make to the cashflow and the ensuing profitability?

In discussing sensitivity analysis for Skywalker, one approach was to contrast the results obtained for the 'most likely' set of assumptions with an 'optimistic' and a 'pessimistic scenario'. However, in the real world, it is rarely the case that all variables take their best (or worst) values simultaneously. This method tells us about the profitability in extreme cases, but does not provide information about the range of intermediate situations, one of which is more likely to materialize in practice.

A more thorough approach is to establish appropriate probability distributions for uncertain variables and evaluate the profitability of the project by using simulation. Simulation involves building a probabilistic model of a situation and subjecting the model to sampling 'trials'. When simulation is used to evaluate the Net Present Value (NPV) or Internal Rate of Return (IRR) of an investment proposal, it is often referred to as 'risk analysis'.

The approach is illustrated by two examples: Alexsville, where the profitability of a sales promotion campaign is being analysed, and Novaduct, in which a new product proposal is being considered. The concepts of random sampling probability distributions and conducting simulations are explained briefly in the context of the Alexsville example, before details of the 1-2-3 implementation are described. The discussion shows the development of sensitivity analysis progressing from single-point estimates through 'best' and 'worst' scenarios to simulation trials with repeated random sampling of assessed probability distributions.

9.2   Example: Alexsville

The Alexsville Products Company is debating whether to spend £1 million on a one-year promotional campaign to boost sales. First estimates suggest that the most likely value for sales volume next year is 2 million units and the most likely increase in sales resulting from the campaign will be a 25 per cent increase.

One shift capacity is currently 2400000 units per annum. Below one shift capacity, fixed costs are estimated to be £5 million (not including the costs of the promotional campaign) and variable costs are £7 per unit. Above one shift capacity, fixed costs would increase by £500000 and variable costs by £1 per unit. Since the item is semi-perishable, no finished goods are held in stock from one year to the next. The selling price of each unit is expected to be £10.

Using the above figures, the most likely sales level is 2 million units without promotion and 2.5 million units with promotion. Calculations for the likely profits to Alexsville are set out in Table 9.1.

Table 9.1   Calculation of profits with and without promotion

Estimate	Profit (in £ millions)	
	No promotion	Promotion
Most likely	2*(10-7)-5 = 1	2.4*(10-7)+0.1*(10-8)-6.5 = 0.9

Thus, on the basis of most likely estimates, the promotion appears to lead to lower profits. The difference in profits is £0.1 million (a negative quantity deducting the 'No Promotion' result from the 'Promotion' result). However, we must ask how likely it is that both the 'unknowns' (that is Sales and Percentage Increase due to promotion) will take their most likely values. Also, how sensitive is the profit difference to changes in the expected Sales figure or the Percentage Increase in sales figure?

An improvement might be to obtain optimistic and pessimistic estimates as well as most likely estimates to get a feel for the best and worst scenarios. Suppose further discussion about sales suggests that without the campaign the expected sales level will be between 1 and 3 million. Similarly, the promotion will result in a sales increase of between 20 per cent and 33 per cent. The resulting profits in each case are shown in Table 9.2.

Table 9.2 Profit calculations for pessimistic and optimistic scenarios

Estimate	Profit (£millions) No promotion	Promotion	Difference (£millions)
Pessimistic	1*3 - 5 = -2	1.2*3 -6 = -2.4	–0.4
Most likely	2*3-5 = 1	2.4*3+0.1*2-6.5 = 0.9	–0.1
Optimistic	2.4*3+0.6*2-5.5 =8.4-5.5 = 2.9	2.4*3+1.6*2-5.5-1 =10.4 - 6.5 = 3.9	1.0

Therefore the difference in profitability ranges from about $-£400000$ to $+£1$ million. With the pesssimistic estimates, Alexsville would be best off without the promotion; with the most likely values, they would also be better off without the promotion, although there is not much to choose between promoting or not promoting. With the optimistic estimates they should promote sales. However, how likely is it that all the worse assumptions would hold or, alternatively, all the optimistic assumptions?

Management usually have some feel for the relative likelihood of various outcomes. If this can be formalized into 'an assessed probability distribution', the analysis can be developed further.

9.3 Assessed probability distributions for unknown variables

Suppose that further discussions with Alexsville indicate that without promotion the median (or 50–50) level for sales is assesed at 2 million (identical to the most likely value). Also it is estimated that there is a 1 in 4 chance that sales will exceed 2200000 units and likewise a 1 in 4 chance that they will be 1800000 units or less.

Similarly, although the immediate effect of the promotion on sales is expected to be an increase of between 20 per cent and 33 per cent, the median increase is assessed as 26 per cent. Also it is estimated that there is a 1 in 4 chance of the increase being 25 per cent or less, and likewise a 1 in 4 chance of the increase being 28 per cent or more. These figures apply to next year's sales increase. Future years' sales are believed to be unlikely to be affected by the campaign.

Figure 9.1 shows rough sketches of the assessed probability distributions for Sales and sales Percentage Increase. The distributions are shown as 'cumulative probability distributions' (or CDFs as explained below). Interpreting the first graph showing the probability of different levels of Sales, the vertical height shows the probability of Sales being as great as the value on the horizontal axis. For example, there is a 0.25 probability (1 in 4) of Sales of up to 1.8 million. This is written:

P(Sales less than or equal to 1800000) = 0.25

Similarly, interpreting the cumulative probability distribution for sales Percentage Increase, there is a 0.5 probability of the Increase due to the promotion being 26 per cent or less. This is written:

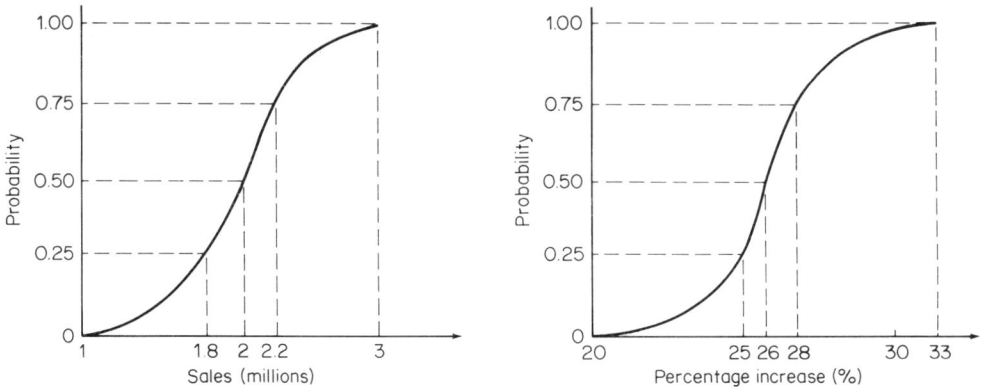

Figure 9.1   Sketch of cumulative probability distribution of Sales and Percentage Increase (%)

P(Percentage Increase less than or equal to 26 per cent) $=0.5$

Notice that it follows that there is an equal 0.5 chance of the Increase being greater than 26 per cent. In other words, 26 per cent is the 'evens' value for the Increase, it being equally likely to be above or below this value.

9.4   Simulation approach

The simulation approach is to take random samples from the two assessed distributions and evaluate the profits. If the samples are random and if sufficient samples are selected, a variety of different cases will be evaluated. 'Good' and 'bad' scenarios will crop up in the random sampling with roughly the right frequency. The result will be a distribution of expected profit results rather than a single value or a triple of optimistic, pessimistic and most likely profits.

However, to select a random sample from each of the distributions, we need a sequence of random numbers uniformly distributed on the range of values from zero to one. This can be written as the range (0,1). Restricting our interest to two decimal place numbers such as 0.56, say, we require a sequence of numbers between 0.00 and 0.99 such that all hundred numbers are roughly equally frequent and the order in which they occur is unsystematic or random. Hereafter, numbers behaving in this manner will be referred to as random numbers. Every programming language has a random number generator that provides a sequence of such numbers. Alternatively, random numbers can be read out of special purpose tables.

Next, we need a way of converting these random numbers into a sequence of random values drawn from each distribution. The cumulative probability curve (or cumulative distribution function, CDF, as it is sometimes called) is the conversion mechanism. Its use is illustrated below for the distribution of Sales.

Consider random numbers with two decimal places in the range (0,1) and suppose the first number selected is 0.15. Then, as shown in Figure 9.2, we read off (for 0.15 on the vertical scale) the corresponding sales level on the horizontal scale—about 1.68 million in this case. Repeat this procedure for each random number and so generate a random sample of sales levels.

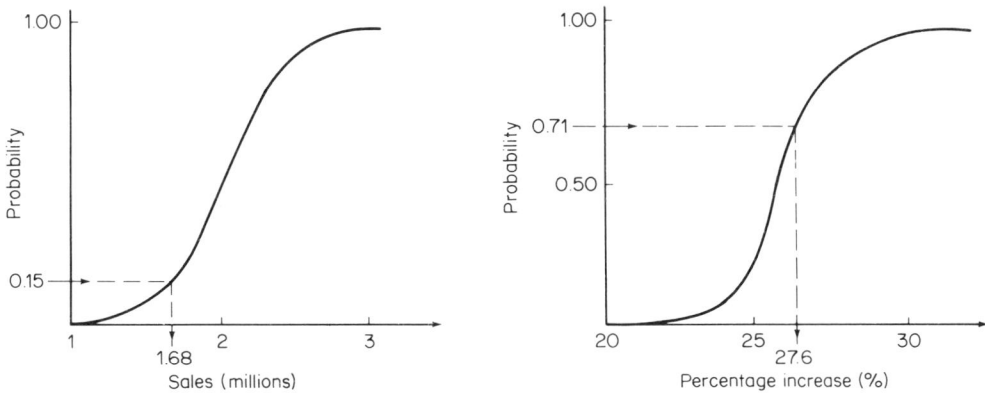

Figure 9.2   Converting random numbers into random sample

A moment's reflection will reveal the justification for this approach. For example, random numbers in the range (0,0.25) have an overall probability of 0.25 of turning up in a sequence of random numbers. These in turn give rise to sales levels in the range 1 million to 1.8 million with an overall probability of 0.25. Within this range, sales levels at the upper end have a higher probability of selection than those at the bottom end, because the cumulative probability curve increases in steepness.

Figure 9.2 illustrates how a pair of random numbers, 0.15 and 0.71, lead to the first scenario (or simulation trial):

Sales level next year   1.68 million units
Percentage Increase from the promotion   27.6 per cent

Given this one randomly selected scenario, we can calculate the profits both without and with the promotion, as we did in the earlier optimistic and pessimistic cases. The results are given in Table 9.3.

Table 9.3   Profit calculations for first scenario (simulation trial)

Estimate	Profit (£millions)		Difference (£millions)
	No promotion	Promotion	
Sales 1.68 million	1.68*3-5=0.040		0.392
Percentage Increase (2.144 million)	27.6%	2.144*3−6.0=0.432	

Thus, for this simulation trial, the profit increase due to the promotion is £392000. A second randomly selected scenario would lead to a different result. Repeating the random sampling many times would result in a range of profit figures from which the average or expected profit increase could be obtained.

The advantage of carrying out a simulation to assess the sensitivity of profit measures (here profit difference) is that the distribution of results is obtained in addition to the expected (or average) profit difference. The probability distribution of profit difference contains more information than a single-point estimate. It gives the anticipated ranges in profits together with corresponding probabilities. It gives the probability of a loss and an estimate of expected size of a loss. An aversion to risk might lead some decision-makers to reject a project with a positive expected profit because they are aware of the downside risk of a loss.

We now show how to implement the simulation discussed for Alexsville using the facilities in Lotus 1-2-3.

9.5 Lotus 1-2-3 implementation of Alexsville simulation model

Modelling Alexsville consists of three stages: first, the random sampling of the Sales and Percentage Increase distributions; second, the calculation of profits; and last, the simulation itself together with the presentation of results. Figure 9.3 shows the overall layout of the spreadsheet model with 'pages' devoted to random sampling and profit calculations and storage areas for simulation results. The 'program' that drives the simulation is a sequence of macros also set out in the spreadsheet.

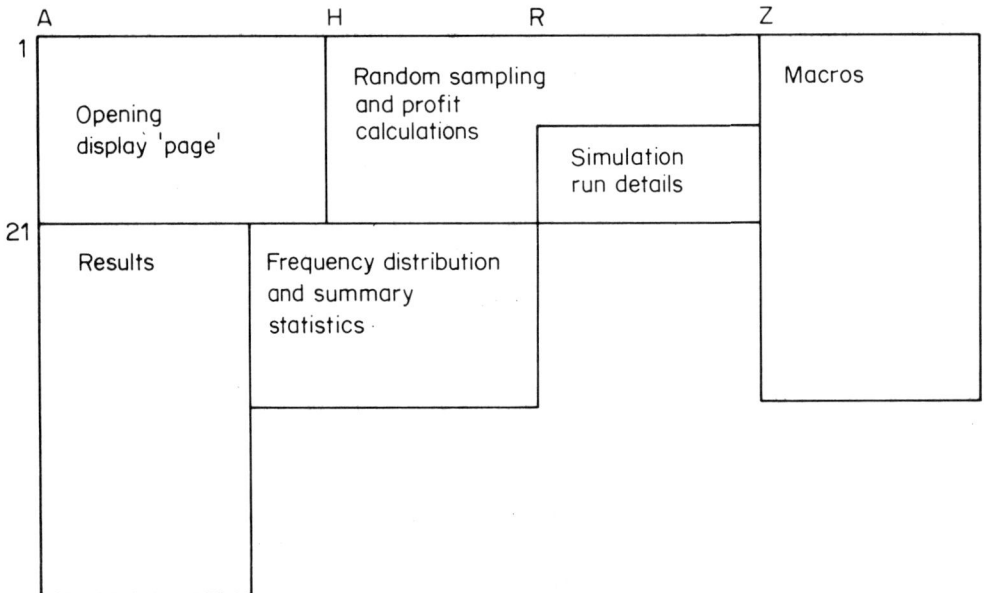

Figure 9.3   Layout of worksheet for Alexsville simulation

The following paragraphs describe how the model for Alexsville is built up. It may be helpful to Retrieve File ALEX from the ASM disc and explore the model as its construction is described. As a precaution, it would be advisable to work with a copy of the ALEX file in case any of the settings are inadvertently changed in the process of exploration.

The file ALEX contains some ranges that have already been named and there are others that are named as the simulation proceeds. A listing of the preset ranges and their names can be obtained from the command sequence / Range Name Table. To use this, first point to an empty part of the worksheet, for example column V; then issue the command to see the Table of pre-set Range Names.

Stage 1. Random sampling the assessed distributions

Summary: A 'piecewise linear' approximation for each of the assessed cumulative probability distributions (CDFs) is obtained by calculating suitable slopes and constants. The @RAND special function gives random numbers in the range 0 to 1. The @VLOOKUP special function allows random numbers to be converted into random samples from the Sales and Percentage Increase in sales distributions.

Linear approximations for the cumulative probability curves   The probability distributions and random sampling operations are set out in columns J through to T, in the top eleven rows. The cumulative probability distributions for Sales and sales Percentage Increase are set out in two tables headed SALES CDF and % INCREASE CDF. Figure 9.4 shows the layout in columns J and K, and P and Q of the spreadsheet. Two cells, K3 and Q3, contain the special function @RAND which gives random numbers for use in the sampling.

	J	K	L	M	N	O	P	Q
1	ALEXSVILLE	SIMULATION	–	RANDOM	SAMPLING			
2	SALES CDF					!	% INCREASE	CDF
3	Rn No.	0.44				!	Rn No.	0.79
4	PROB	SALES				.!	PROB	%INCR
5	0	1				!	0	20
6	0.05	1.5				!	0.05	22.5
7	0.25	1.8				!	0.25	25
8	0.5	2				!	0.5	26
9	0.75	2.2				!	0.75	28
10	0.95	2.5				!	0.95	30
11	1	3				!	1	33

(@RAND)

Figure 9.4   Probability distributions for random sampling

Graphs of the two distributions have been 'named' G1 and G2 and saved within the ALEX model. These can be viewed using / Graph Name Use. Figure 9.5 shows the 1-2-3 graph named G1 which displays the probability values (as the A range) against the Sales (as the X range) in an *XY* type of graph (a scatter plot). A similar *XY* graph of the Percentage Increase distribution, named G2, is also shown. To smoothe out the tails of the distribution, sales values have been interpolated for the 5 per cent and 95 per cent probabilities, and similarly for the Percentage Increase CDF. (A third named graph called GVALS is also included in file ALEX. This is incomplete until the simulation has been run.)

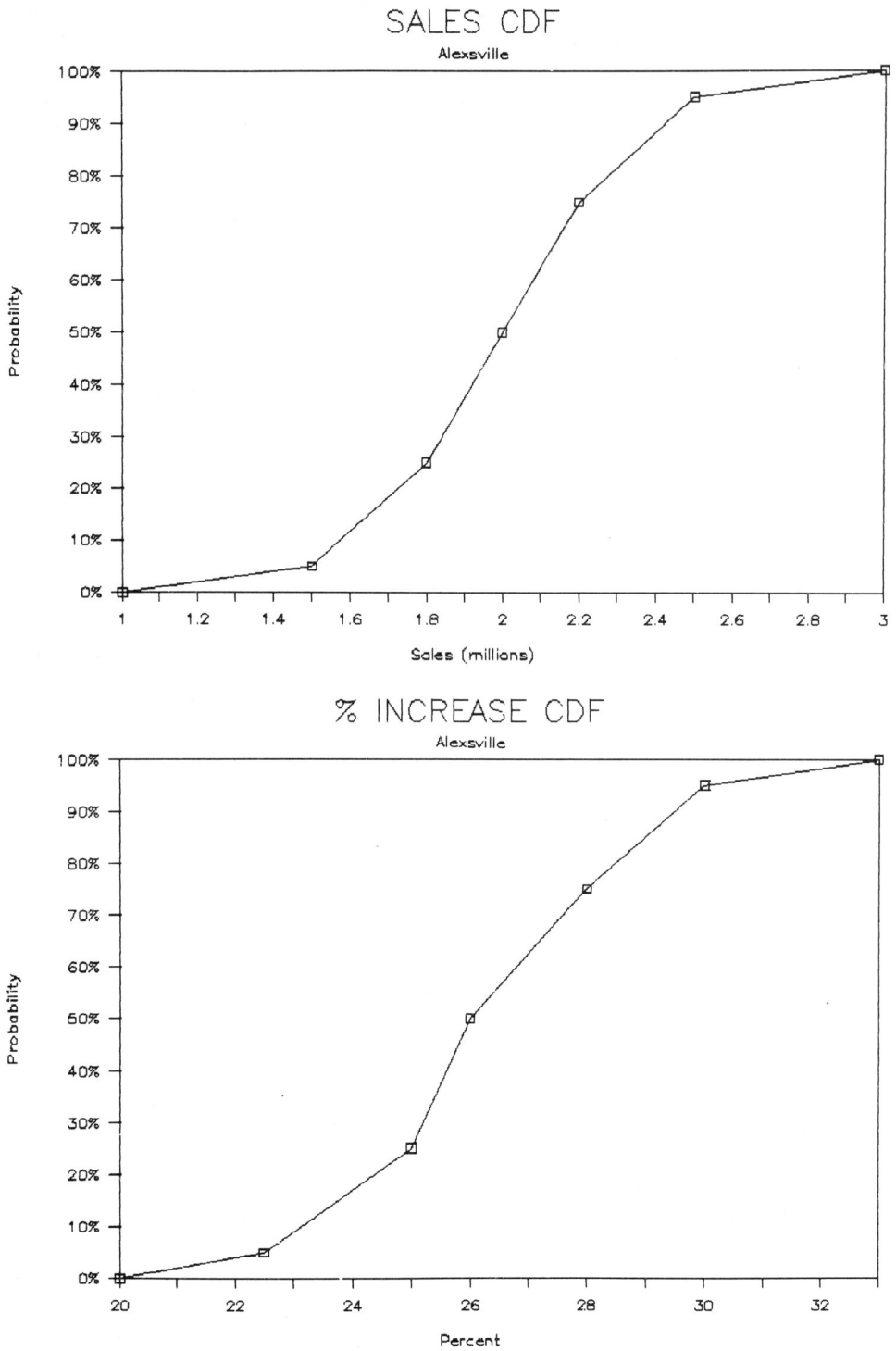

Figure 9.5   Lotus 1-2-3 graphs of Sales and Percentage Increase

The objective is to program the transformation of a random number, represented by height on the vertical (Y) axis into a sales value on the horizontal (X) axis. This requires us to identify the point of intersection on the probability curve of a horizontal line whose intercept on the Y axis is equal to the random number. As we shall see, the crucial 1-2-3 tool in implementing the transformation process is the Lookup Table and the associated @VLOOKUP function.

Because discrete values have been plotted, what we see on screen (with graph G1, say) is a linearized approximation to the underlying assessed distribution. In programming the transformation procedure, it is conventional to work with this linear approximation to the curve. Hence slopes and constants for each linear segment of the graphs are calculated in the spreadsheet. (See columns M, N and S, T of Figure 9.6). Since the objective is to decide the horizontal (or X value) given the vertical reading (or Y value), the slopes, m, and constants, c, are calculated for a line of form: $X = mY + c$. The label 'Rn No' is shorthand for Random Number (between 0 and 1), 'RnS' means Random Sample and 'RnS Sales' means a Random Sample from the Sales distribution. For example, the first line joining the 0.05 probability value to 0 has the equation:

RnS Sales $= 10*$ (Rn No) $+ 1.00$

where slope $10 = \dfrac{(1.5 - 1)}{(0.05 - 0)}$ and constant $1.00 = 1.5 -$ slope*0.05

	J	K	L	M	N	P	Q	R	S	T
1	ALEXSVILLE SIMULATION			- RANDOM SAMPLING				ALEXSVILLE SIMULATION		
2	SALES CDF					! % INCREASE CDF				
3	Rn No.		0.44	RnS Sales	1.95	! Rn No.	0.79	RnS %	28.40	
4	PROB	SALES	RnS Sales	Slope	Constant !	PROB	%INCR	RnS %	Slope	Constant
5	0	1	5.40	10.00	1.00 !	0	20	59.50	50.00	20.00
6	0.05	1.5	2.09	1.50	1.43 !	0.05	22.5	31.75	12.50	21.88
7	0.25	1.8	1.95	0.80	1.60 !	0.25	25	27.16	4.00	24.00
8	0.5	2	1.95	0.80	1.60 !	0.5	26	28.32	8.00	22.00
9	0.75	2.2	1.74	1.50	1.08 !	0.75	28	28.40	10.00	20.50
10	0.95	2.5	-2.60	10.00	-7.00 !	0.95	30	20.40	60.00	-27.00
			(K6-K5)/(J6-J5)		+K6-(M5*J6)		(Q6-Q5)/(P6-P5)			+Q6-(S5*P6)

Figure 9.6 Calculating slopes and constants for linear approximations

Notice that the slope and constant values for this line are set out adjacent to the 0 Probability value (row 5), in fact in cells M5 and N5.

Thus, for a given Y (Random Number) in the range 0.00 to 0.05, the value of X (Random Sample of Sales) is determined by the above equation.

For any given Y (Random Number), the value of sales can be calculated for each of the six lines. These values are given in the spreadsheet in column L (cells L5 to L10). However, only one value is appropriate: namely the value calculated on the basis of the relevant line segment. 1-2-3's VLOOKUP function takes care of the choice of the correct line segment. For Sales, the Lookup Table is the range J5..L10 named SALESCDF: for Percentage Increase, the Lookup Table is P5..R10 named INCRCDF, as shown in Figure 9.7. (These named ranges can be checked in the ALEX model with the command sequence / Range Name Create.)

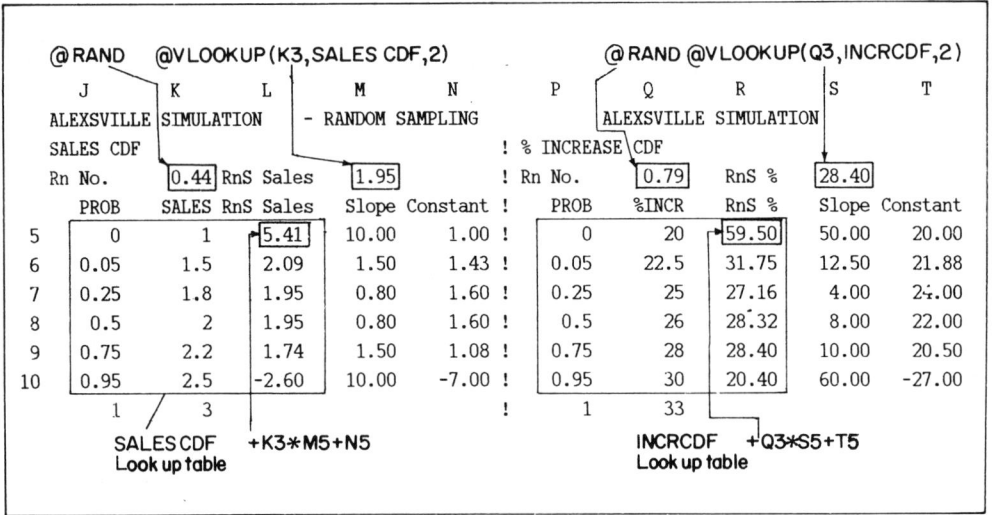

```
 @RAND   @VLOOKUP(K3,SALES CDF,2)                @RAND @VLOOKUP(Q3,INCRCDF,2)

     J       K     L        M       N        P     Q       R      S       T
  ALEXSVILLE SIMULATION  - RANDOM SAMPLING        ALEXSVILLE SIMULATION
  SALES CDF                                ! % INCREASE CDF
  Rn No.  |0.44| RnS Sales |1.95|        ! Rn No. |0.79| RnS %  |28.40|
          PROB  SALES RnS Sales  Slope Constant !   PROB  %INCR  RnS %   Slope Constant
  5        0     1    | 5.41|     10.00  1.00  !    0     20   | 59.50|  50.00  20.00
  6       0.05  1.5   | 2.09|      1.50  1.43  !   0.05  22.5  | 31.75|  12.50  21.88
  7       0.25  1.8   | 1.95|      0.80  1.60  !   0.25   25   | 27.16|   4.00  24.00
  8        0.5   2    | 1.95|      0.80  1.60  !    0.5   26   | 28.32|   8.00  22.00
  9       0.75  2.2   | 1.74|      1.50  1.08  !   0.75   28   | 28.40|  10.00  20.50
  10      0.95  2.5   |-2.60|     10.00 -7.00  !   0.95   30   | 20.40|  60.00 -27.00
           1     3                            !    1     33
       SALES CDF    +K3*M5+N5                      INCRCDF    +Q3*S5+T5
       Look up table                              Look up table
```

Figure 9.7   Adding equations for random samples of Sales and Percentage Increase

For example, suppose the random number function @RAND in cell K3 gives number 0.44 as shown in Figure 9.7. This value lies between probability 0.25 and 0.5, so the line approximating to the assessed distribution has:

slope=0.80   and constant=1.60   (see row 7, cells M7 and N7)

and equation:

RnS Sales = 0.80*(Rn No)+1.60

Substituting Rn No =0.44 gives:

RnS Sales=0.80*0.44+1.60=1.95   (1.95 million)

This value is shown in cell L7 and also in M3.

Thus, the formula for RnS Sales in cell M3 is:

@VLOOKUP(K3,SALESCDF,2)   or   @VLOOKUP(K3,J5..L10,2)

This instructs 1-2-3 to enter the VLOOKUP Table in range J5..L10 with the random number in cell K3 and read off the appropriate value two columns over in the Table (column L). Hence the value in cell M3 given by the LOOKUP formula is identical to that in cell L7 for the random number 0.44.

Stage 2. Calculation of profits

The profits for any scenario depend on the level of sales (whether above or below 2400000 units) and whether the promotion campaign costs are to be included. If Sales are below 2400000 (2.4 million), Fixed Costs (FC) amount to £5 million and Contribution per unit is £3. If Promotional activity is undertaken, Fixed Costs go up to £6 million. If Sales are greater than 2.4 million, Fixed Costs increase to £5.5 million and Contribution per unit comes down to £2. With the Promotion, Fixed Costs go up to £6.5 million. The calculations to get profits in each case are set out in Figure 9.4.

Table 9.4.   Expressions for calculating profit in terms of sales

Sales estimate	Profit (£millions)	
	No promotion	Promotion
2.4 million or less	Sales*3–5	Sales*2–6
More than 2.4 million	2.4*3 + (Sales-2.4)*2–5.5 = Sales*2–3.1	2.4*3+(Sales-2.4)*2–6.5 =Sales*2–4.1

Each expression can be thought of as (Sales*Contribution—Fixed Costs) (after allowing for the slightly different interpretation of 'Fixed Costs'). Setting out the 'Fixed Costs' figures and the 'Contribution' figures for Sales below and above 2.4 million in adjacent columns, the Profit figures can be calculated via a vertical Lookup Table. The ALEX model contains this cost information in the range K15..N16, which has been given the range name COSTS (see the inset diagram in Figure 9.8). Notice that column L (cell L15 and 16) contains 'Fixed Costs' when there is No Promotion and column N contains the figures that apply if there is a Promotion.

The profit figures are evaluated from the COSTS Lookup Table as follows. If Sales are below 2.4 million, the contribution and cost figures in the first row of the table are used. If Sales are 2.4 million or more, the second row is used. Thus for Sales of 1.95 million, Profit is given by the elements of the first row of the Lookup Table, that is 5 and 3, so that:

Profits = -5+3*Sales = 0.85 million   in cell K19

The formula in cell K19 involving the Lookup Table COSTS in range K15..N16 is:

+K18*@VLOOKUP(K18,COSTS,2)-@VLOOKUP(K18,COSTS,1)

where K18 contains the Sales value and 'column numbers' 2 and 1 give the appropriate Contribution and Fixed Cost figures for No Promotion from the Lookup Table COSTS.

A similar expression is stored in cell L19 to give the Profit from the Sales increased by the Promotion (in cell M18).

	J	K	L	M	N	P	Q	R	S	T
1	ALEXSVILLE SIMULATION		- RANDOM SAMPLING			!	ALEXSVILLE SIMULATION			
2	SALES CDF					! % INCREASE CDF				
3	Rn No.	0.44	RnS Sales	1.95		! Rn No.	0.79	RnS %	28.40	
4	PROB	SALES	RnS Sales	Slope	Constant	! PROB	%INCR	RnS %	Slope	Constant
	0	1	5.40	10.00	1.00	! 0	20	59.50	50.00	20.00
	0.05	1.5	2.09	1.50	1.43	! 0.05	22.5	31.75	12.50	21.88
	0.25	1.8	1.95	0.80	1.60	! 0.25	25	27.16	4.00	24.00
	0.5	2	1.95	0.80	1.60	! 0.5	26	28.32	8.00	22.00
	0.75	2.2	1.74	1.50	1.08	! 0.75	28	28.40	10.00	20.50
	0.95	2.5	-2.60	10.00	-7.00	! 0.95	30	20.40	60.00	-27.00
	1	3				! 1	33			

		No Promotion		Prom		SIMULATION
	Sales		FC	Contrib	FC	DETAILS:
15 COSTS	0		5	3	6	No.RUNS
	2.4		3.1	2	4.1	COUNTER
						STOP -1
18 SalesNP	1.95	SalesP	2.50			
19 RESULTS	0.85	0.91	0.06 Profits			
20	NP	P	Diff			

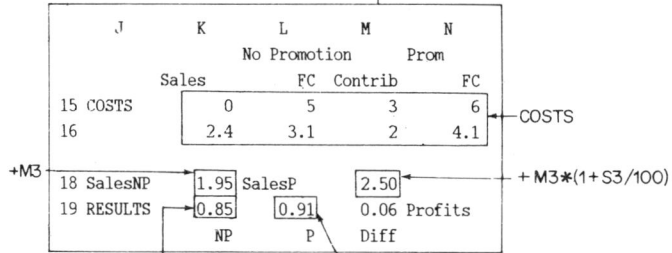

Figure 9.8   Calculating profits from COSTS Lookup Table

Continuing the example shown in Figure 9.8, Sales rise to 2.50 million with the Promotion (in cell M18), giving:

Profits = -4.1+2*Sales = 0.91 million   in cell L19

and the Difference in Profits = 0.06 million   in cell M19

The range of cells holding the Profits results, K19..M19, is 'named' TRIAL (using the Range Name Create sequence). This set of values (Profits without and with Promotion and the Difference in Profits) will be saved for each random scenario in the simulation.

You may wish to check that the range names COSTS and TRIAL in the ALEX model do tie up with this description and that you understand how the profit results for each scenario are calculated. One approach might be to print out the range J1..T20 and work through from the random numbers in cells K3 and Q3 to the RESULTS in cells K19..M19. A printout is preferable to pointing to the screen as the random numbers change with every recalculation of the worksheet.

The TRIAL set of results can be regarded as coming from one scenario. To carry out a simulation, further trials with different random samplings from the assessed distributions must be undertaken. This procedure is described in Stage 3.

Stage 3. Repeating the sampling

The easist way of repeating the random sampling is to write a suitable set of macros. Figure 9.9 shows the simple flowchart for a sequence of routines including two menus, MAIN and DISPLAY. It shows the main stages of the simulation. The MAIN menu allows the user to choose to SIMULATE, to arrange the simulation results into a DISTRIBUTION or to QUIT (leave the simulation model). The DISPLAY menu controls choices within the DISTRIBUTION part of the program. The macros are detailed in Figure 9.10.

If the user chooses SIMULATE from the MAIN menu, the program flow passes to the initialization subroutine (INITIAL). This consists of clearing out old results and naming some ranges. START is the name given to the cell where the results from each trial are stored. At the end of the INITIAL subroutine, the program flow returns to the instruction immediately below {INITIAL}, namely:

{BRANCH SIMULATE}

whereupon, the program branches to the SIMULATE subroutine.

The SIMULATE routine asks the user for the Number of simulation 'Runs' which influences how many times the SIMTRIAL routine is carried out. The 'looping' instruction is:

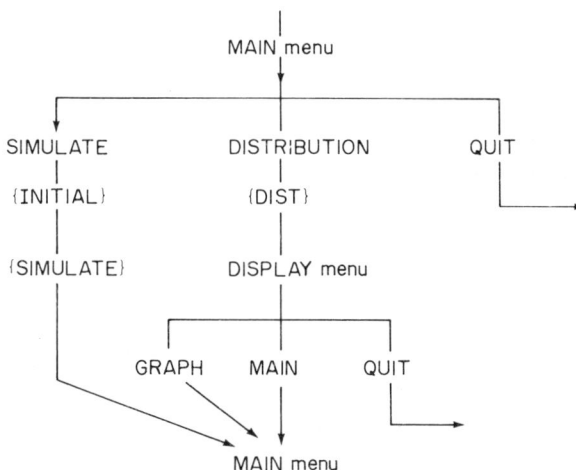

Figure 9.9   Flowchart for Alexsville simulation

```
ALEXSVILLE SIMULATION
M Name   Macro                                      Description
\M       {GOTO}SHOW~{WINDOWSOFF}                     Display window SHOW:A1
         {MENUBRANCH MAIN}
                                                     Main Menu
MAIN     SIMULATE        DISTRIBUTION  QUIT
         choose          choose        choose
         {INITIAL}       {DIST}        {QUIT}
         {BRANCH SIMULATE}{MENUCALL DISPLAY}

SIMULATE {GETNUMBER "Enter No. of Runs ? ",R15}     No of Runs in R15
         {GOTO}START~                                Results area
         {FOR COUNTER,0,STOP,1,SIMTRIAL}             Sim trial loop
         {GOTO}START~
         /RNCNO_PROM~{BS}.{end}{down}~               Name 1st results NO_PROM
         {RIGHT}/RNCPROM~{BS}.{END}{DOWN}~           Name 2nd results PROM
         {RIGHT}/RNCDIFF~{BS}.{END}{DOWN}~           Name 3rd results DIFF
         {GOTO}START~{BRANCH \M}

SIMTRIAL /RVTRIAL~~{DOWN}                            Copy trial result down

INITIAL  {GOTO}B23~/RNCSTART~~                       START is B23
         /RNCTRIAL~K19.M19~                          TRIAL is K19..M19
         /REB23.D8192~                               Clear previous results

DIST     {GOTO}BIN~                                  BIN starts in E23
         /DDDIFF~BIN~                                Distribution of DIFF
                                                     Display Menu
DISPLAY  GRAPH           MAIN MENU     QUIT
         See Graph       Start Again   Finish
         {GOTO}SHOW~     {BRANCH \M}   {QUIT}        Display pre-set graph GVALS
         {WINDOWSON}                                 or Return to Main Menu
         /GNUGVALS~Q
         {BRANCH \M}
```

Figure 9.10   Macros for Alexsville simulation

{FOR COUNTER, 0,STOP,1,SIMTRIAL}

A COUNTER cell is set up with the value 0 and increments by one each time the SIMTRIAL routine is carried out, stopping when the COUNTER exceeds the STOP value. The formula in the cell named STOP, cell R17, links the STOP value to the number of simulation Runs specified by the user. SIMTRIAL merely copies the values of the present simulation trial (temporarily stored in range TRIAL) down to the 'results' area which begins in the START cell (B23 in this case).

Next, in the SIMULATE part of the program, the column of results is named—here the results from No Promotion are called NO_PROM, from Promotion PROM and the differences between pairs of results DIFF. Then control passes back to the MAIN menu.

If DISTRIBUTION is chosen, processing jumps to the DIST subroutine. Intervals for the distribution have been pre-set starting in cell E23, the column of interval ranges being called BIN. To get the distribution, DIST uses the Data Distribution command on the results of the simulation stored in the cell range called DIFF (profit differences). Control passes back to the MAIN menu.

The next instruction after returning to the DISTRIBUTION branch of the MAIN menu is a MENUCALL (or MENUBRANCH) to the DISPLAY menu. If the user chooses GRAPH, a graph named GVALS using previously organized settings is displayed. It is a cumulative frequency distribution graph of the simulation trials just completed. When the user has inspected the graph, the program returns to the MAIN menu.

The ALEX simulation model is driven into action by invoking the Macro attached to the M key. The first instruction in this routine contains the command {WINDOWSOFF} which stops the screen changing as the simulation calculations are carried out. Notice that the {WINDOWSON} command in the GRAPH routine ensures that the 'current pointer' screen does return so that the graph named GVALS is seen.

9.6 Simulation results using the ALEX model

The datafile ALEX on your ASM disc contains the model described in the previous sections for simulating Alexsville's future sales with and without the promotional campaign. If you have not already done so in the previous sections, retrieve the model from disc, and explore the layout and the macros. The following paragraphs describe one way of carrying out a simulation with the ALEX model:

1. Activate the macro sequence in ALEX by pressing the Alt and the M keys together.
2. Choose the SIMULATE option.
3. Choose a reasonable number of runs, say 50 or 100, which will take a few minutes to process. The results of trials build up in cells B23 and below.
4. Choose DISTRIBUTION then GRAPH. You should be presented with a cumulative probability curve for the Difference in Profits with and without Promotion.

Figure 9.11 shows one such distribution based on 100 runs. To get a printout of the graph, one method is to QUIT from the simulation model, use the Graph key to get the graph on screen and then press the PrintScreen key on your keyboard. You may also like to print out the summary statistics for the DIFF distribution which are stored in cells J25 to J29.

After running the simulation, the worksheet also contains the values for Profits with No Promotion (in and below C23) and for Profits with Promotion (in and below D23). Distributions of these results can be constructed (with the Data Distribution command) and the values displayed graphically. When the Profits with No Promotion and with Promotion are graphed together with the Difference in Profits, cumulative distribution curves like those in Figure 9.12 result.

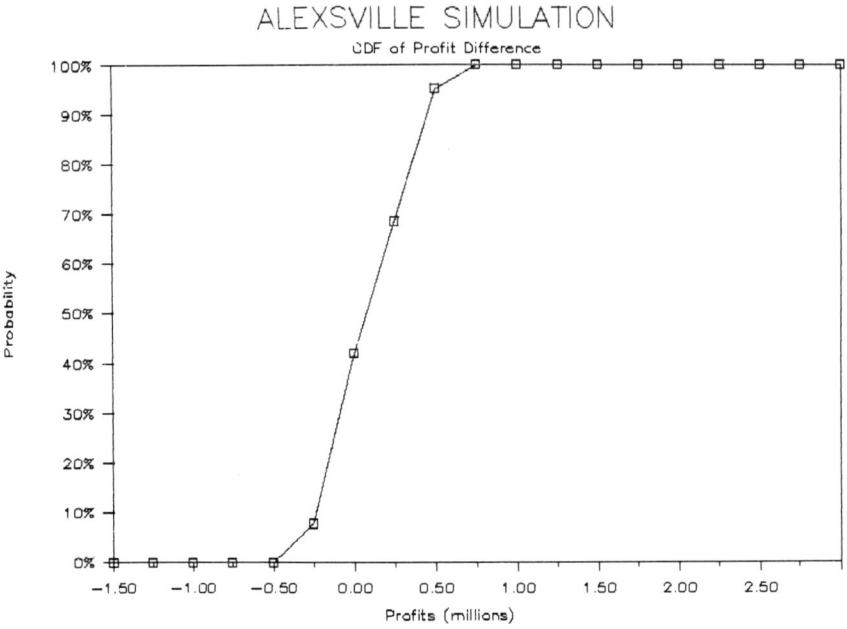

Figure 9.11 Difference in Profits distribution (results from 100 simulation trials)

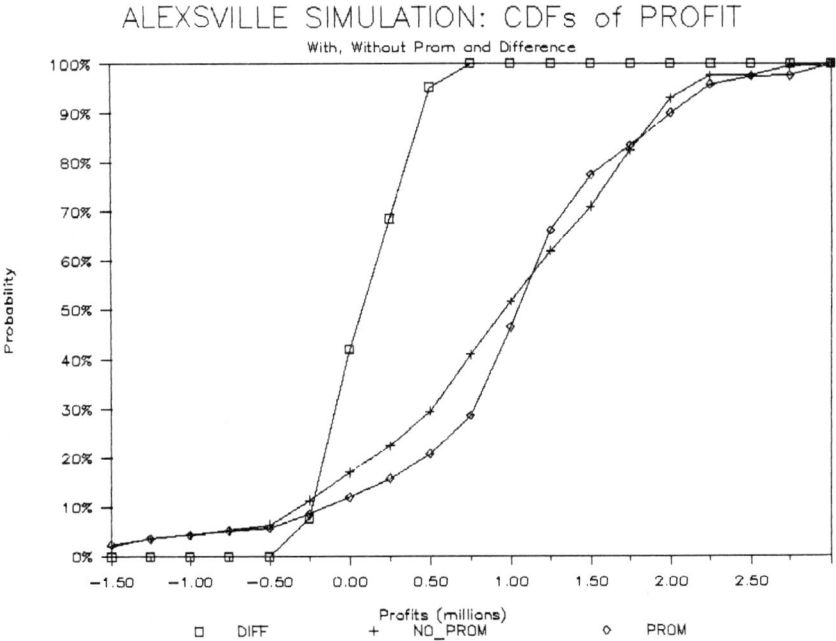

Figure 9.12 Distribution of Profits with No Promotion, and the Difference in Profits (results from 100 simulation trials)

Thus the simulation approach results in a complete picture of the sensitivity of results to assessed uncertainty about assumptions. For the simulation trials shown summarized in Figure 9.11, the mean of the 100 values of the difference in profits using @AVG is £93400; that is the expected difference in profits is positive, so profits with the promotion are expected to be better than without. However, Figure 9.11 shows that there is a 40 per cent chance that profits are worse with the promotion, and the difference (relative loss) could be as large as −£400000.

9.7 Example: Novaduct new product

The second model, Novaduct, attempts to simulate uncertainty about market share and market share growth for a new product by random sampling from probability distributions. In contrast to Alexsville, theoretical distributions are used (as opposed to empirical distributions). This means that there are equations for transforming random numbers into random samples. It is therefore not necessary to use Lookup Tables and the associated interpolation.

Management are trying to decide whether or not to launch a 'novelty' product which is expected to have a market for the next five years. The following information about the product has been gathered:

1. The expected market size is 8000000 units in the first year with 3 per cent growth per year thereafter.
2. A 15 per cent market share is anticipated in the first year, growing linearly by 0.5 per cent per annum afterwards.
3. In the first year, the price is likely to be £7, growing by 6 per cent annually thereafter.
4. The expected variable cost per unit is £5, increasing by 3 per cent per annum. Fixed costs are expected to start at £2000000 and to grow annually at 3 per cent as well.
5. An initial investment of £2500000 is planned.
6. A discount rate of 15 per cent is usually taken in calculating the Net Present Value for projects of this kind.

These estimates represent the 'single-figure estimates' for the project's prospects in a growing market. Management require two measures of profitability for the venture—the present value of the cashflows and the rate of return.

It is easy to produce a spreadsheet solution such as that shown in Figure 9.13. The analysis has been carried out in units of thousands of pounds. The assumptions are set out below the computations. (The spreadsheet logic is explained in more detail later in the chapter.) 1-2-3's financial functions for NPV and IRR are employed on the cashflow (row 9) to give the required financial measures of profitability.

Here, if the market and market share grow exactly as predicted, the Net Present Value will be £1387000 (in M12) and the Internal Rate of Return (before tax) will be 31 per cent (in N12) for this investment. However, the question is: how sensitive is profitability to variation in these estimates?

Further discussion about some of the assumptions in the estimates persuades management that more explicit modelling of uncertainty is required for market growth and market share growth. Let us assume that further heart-searching about the future reveals the following.

162

H	I	J	K	L	M	N
NOVADUCT SPREADSHEET FOR FIVE YEARS						
		1	2	3	4	5
3 MARKET		8000	8240	8487	8742	9004
4 PRICE		7.0	7.4	7.9	8.3	8.8
5 V COST		5.0	5.2	5.3	5.5	5.6
6 SALES (MS)		1200	1277	1316	1355	1396
7 NET REVENUE		2400	2899	3369	3894	4480
8 FIXED COSTS		-2000	-2060	-2122	-2185	-2251
9 CASHFLOW	-2500	400	839	1247	1708	2229
			RESULTS		NPV	IRR
12 ASSUMPTIONS			Base Case		1387	31%
13 Discount	0.15					
14 Prod Cost	5	103.0%				
15 Price	7	106.0%				
16 Market Sh	15%					
17 MS Incr	0.5%					
18 Mkt Growt	103.0%					

Figure 9.13   Five-year spreadsheet for Novaduct project

Firstly, market growth is most likely to be a 2 per cent increase but could range from a 10 per cent decrease to an 8 per cent increase following a roughly triangular distribution. (A triangular probability distribution is one for which the probability density function takes a triangular shape. The lowest and highest values determine the base of the triangle; the modal or most likely value determines the highest point of the triangle.) This form of distribution is quite plausible: the most likely values are around 2 per cent but values as extreme as −10 per cent and +8 per cent are possible but not so likely to occur.

Secondly, market share growth can be assumed to be uniformly distributed between −0.2 per cent and 0.8 per cent (in contrast to the 0.3 per cent figure assumed before). This means that growth is equally likely to take any value in the range −0.2 per cent to 0.8 per cent.

Armed with these probability distributions the spreadsheet model of Figure 9.13 needs to be expanded to include random sampling of the distributions. The next sections describe these stages in modelling Novaduct.

9.8   Lotus 1-2-3 Implementation of Novaduct simulation model

Figure 9.14 shows the worksheet layout for the entire Novaduct model. It may be helpful to retrieve the Novaduct model called NOVA from the ASM disc. You can explore the layout and construction of the NOVA model as the various stages are described.

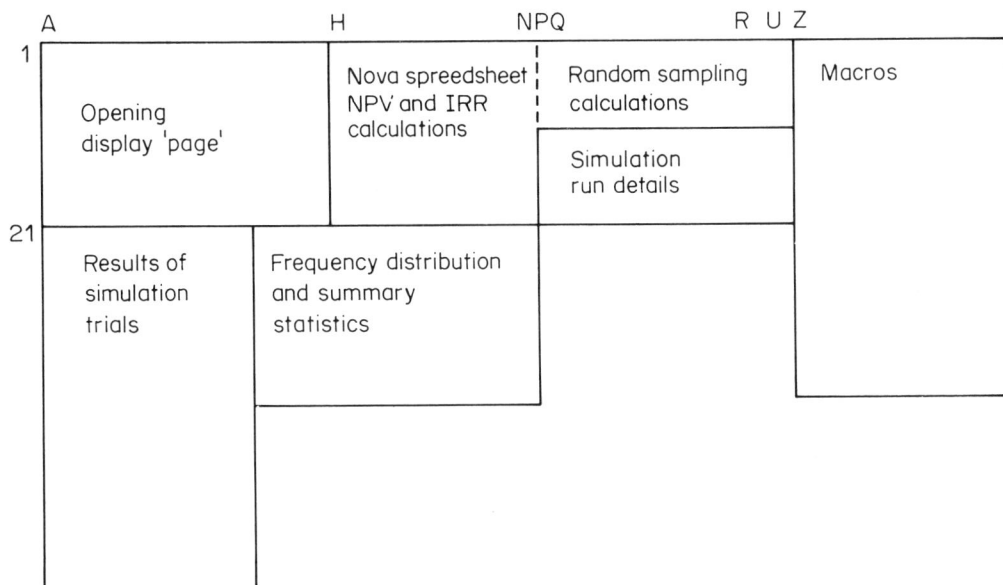

Figure 9.14   Layout in worksheet of Novaduct simulation

The cashflow calculations, already viewed in Figure 9.13, are in the range H1..N20. The random sampling operations are in the range Q1..U12. The counters for the simulation trials are in R15..R18. The simulation macros start in column AA. Results build up below B23 and distributions below E23. The overall layout and structure of the worksheet are similar to that for Alexsville.

In this example, a conventional spreadsheet layout for Novaduct's cashflow is required to calculate the Net Present Value and Internal Rate of Return. However, the assumed values for the Market Growth and Market Share Growth are random samples from the specified triangular and uniform distributions.

As with the Alexsville simulation, there are three stages in building the simulation model: first, the mechanism for generating random samples from the uniform and triangular distributions; second, the cashflow calculations giving the Net Present Value and Internal Rate of Return for one scenario; and third, repeating the sampling many times to obtain many randomly selected scenarios and get a distribution of profitability measures.

Stage 1. Random sampling the distributions

Since algebraic expressions are available for the uniform and triangular distributions, equations can be set up to transform 1-2-3's random numbers into random samples from these two distributions. Although straightforward, the mathematics is somewhat beyond the scope of this book and therefore must be taken on trust. The random sampling operation is carried out in columns Q to U in the spreadsheet. See Figure 9.15 for the detailed layout. The uniform distribution is described first as it is the simplest.

@RAND

	Q	R	S	T	U
1 !	NOVADUCT	SIMULATION: RANDOM SAMPLING			!
2 !	MKT GWTH	Tri	0.9	1.02	1.08 !
3 !	Rn No	0.43 RnS MGth	1.00		!
4 !	PROB	MGth			!
5 !	0.00	1.00	TRIRAND		!
6 !	0.67	1.00			!
7 !					!
8 !					!
9 !	MKT SH GRWTH	Uniform	-0.002	0.008	!
10 !	RnNo	0.67 RnS MShG	0.005		!
11 !	PROB	MShG			!
12 !	0.67	0.005 + T9+(U9-T9)*R10			
!					
!					
15 !	RUNS	7			
16 !	COUNTER	7			
17 !	STOP	6			

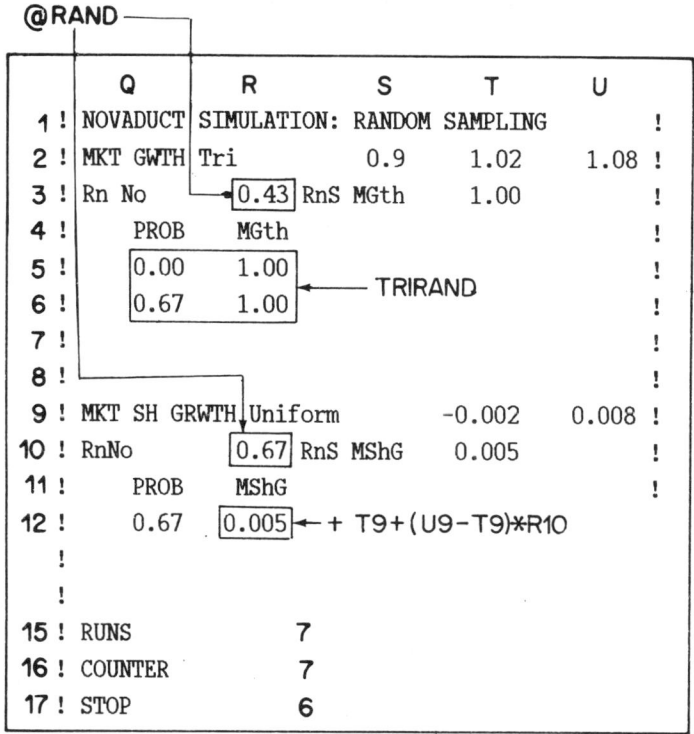

Figure 9.15 Random sampling uniform and triangular distributions

Uniform Distribution The arithmetic of scaling suggests that uniformly distributed random numbers on a (0,1) scale are converted into their equivalents on a (-0.002,0.008) scale by the equation:

RnS MShG = -0.002+(0.008-(-0.002))*Rn No.

where RnS MShG is the label for a Random Sample from the Market Share Growth distribution and Rn No is the random number given by function @RAND. The random number is in cell R10 and the resulting Market Share Growth figure is in cell R12. For example, if the random number in cell R10 is 0.67, then the corresponding Market Share Growth in cell T10 is 0.0047 or 0.5 per cent after rounding.

Triangular distribution The probability characteristics of the triangular distribution depend on its three parameters, here 0.9, 1.02 and 1.08. For random sampling, different expressions are required according to whether the Market Growth figure is above or below the modal value of 1.02. The cumulative probability of a value below 1.02 is 0.67, derived from the geometry of triangles as:

$$\frac{(1.02 - 0.9)}{(1.08 - 0.9)} = 0.67$$

The two expressions for Market Growth are in cells R5 and R6. The formulae are not immediately obvious and their derivation needs to be taken as given. For example, the expression in cell R5 is:

+S2+@SQRT(R3*(T2-S2)*(U2-S2))

where R3 holds the random number, and S2, T2 and U2 hold the three defining parameters of the triangular distribution. @ SQRT calculates the square root of the expression within its brackets.

The range Q5..R6 containing the random sampling expressions and the cumulative probability values is named TRIRAND see Figure 9.15. TRIRAND forms a vertical Lookup Table giving the random sample value for Market Growth.

The random sampling operates as follows: a random number is generated by the RAND special function in cell R3. The two expressions in R5 and R6 which depend on the value of R3 are evaluated. From the Lookup Table based on range TRIRAND, the appropriate expression is selected according to whether it corresponds with values below or above the mode. The resultant value of Market Growth is located in cell T3 which contains the Lookup expression:

@VLOOKUP(R3,TRIRAND,1)

It is labelled 'RnS MGth', which indicates a Random Sample of Market Growth.

For example, suppose the random number in cell R3 is 0.43. This is below 0.67 (in cell Q6) so that the first of the two expressions is appropriate. The @VLOOKUP function will give the expression in cell R5 (as opposed to R6) which has the value 1.00 for Market Growth (in fact 0.996 or -0.4 per cent decline). For convenience this is copied into cell T3.

Stage 2. Cashflow calculations

It is straightforward to set up a spreadsheet for this problem and evaluate the Net Present Value and the Internal Rate of Return for a variety of assumptions. Figure 9.13, which has already been mentioned, shows the conventional layout with calculations for Cashflow over the five years. The assumptions in the model are set out below the annual cashflow figures. Notice in particular the per cent Increase in Market Share in cell I17 (0.5 per cent) and the Market Share Growth in cell I18 (103 per cent), the original single-point estimates.

In Figure 9.16, the aforementioned cells are linked to the results of the random sampling; that is, in cell I17, the value 0.005 is replaced by +T10, and in cell I18, the value 1.03 is replaced by +T3. Figure 9.16 shows the results of the random sampling in those cells: namely 0.5 per cent (or 0.005) for Increase in Market Share and 99.6 per cent (or 0.996) for Market Growth. The lower values for this one random scenario lead to lower values for NPV (£669000) and IRR (24 per cent). Figure 9.16 shows the 'trial' values for this scenario and also the original single-point values (called the Base Case) for easy comparison.

As in Alexsville, the range of cells holding the results, M13..N13, is named TRIAL. In the simulation described in the next section, each set of trial values is saved. The values for NPV and IRR change each time the random number generator is recalculated, which in turn occurs when the worksheet as a whole is recalculated.

	H	I	J	K	L	M	N
	NOVADUCT SPREADSHEET FOR FIVE YEARS						
			1	2	3	4	5
3	MARKET		8000	7971	7942	7913	7885
4	PRICE		7.0	7.4	7.9	8.3	8.8
5	V COST		5.0	5.2	5.3	_ 5.5	5.6
6	SALES (MS)		1200	1233	1229	1224	1220
7	NET REVENUE		2400	2799	3146	3518	3915
8	FIXED COSTS		-2000	-2060	-2122	-2185	-2251
9	CASHFLOW	-2500	400	739	1024	1332	1664
10							
11					RESULTS	NPV	IRR
12	ASSUMPTIONS				Base Case	1387	31%
13	Discount	0.15			TRIAL	669	24%
14	Prod Cost	5	103.0%					+ T10
15	Price	7	106.0%					+T3
16	Market Sh	15%			BaseCase	Pess	ML	Opt
17	MS Incr	0.5%Uniform	T10		0.5%	-0.2%	0.3%	0.8%
18	MktGrowth	99.6%Triangle	T3		103.0%	90.0%	102.0%	108.0%

Figure 9.16   Spreadsheet with random sampled inputs

Stage 3. Repeating the sampling

The macros which control the repeated random sampling and save and analyse the trial results are detailed in Figure 9.17. As can be seen, the routines are almost identical to those for the Alexsville simulation. The only differences are in the position of the TRIAL range of results and in the names given to the resulting distributions—here they are named NPV and IRR.

The macro routines in both simulations are deliberately simple so that the logic and program flow is easy to follow. The aim is to help those new to macro writing to see what can be achieved with relatively little complexity.

9.9   Simulation results using the NOVA model

If you have not already done so, retrieve the NOVA file which is on your ASM disc. This contains the random sampling procedures and macros for the simulation of Novaduct's new product proposal. The file NOVA contains some ranges which have already been named. To examine these, point to an empty part of the worksheet (for example column V) and use the command Range Name Table to produce a listing of the pre-set range names. (Note that some other ranges are named in the course of the simulation.)

Having explored the NOVA model, the simulation can be carried out as follows:

```
NOVADUCT SIMULATION
M Name   Macro                                      Description
\M       /RNCSHOW~{BS}H1~                           Window SHOW starts H1
         {GOTO}SHOW~{WINDOWSOFF}                    Freeze screen
         {MENUBRANCH MAIN}                          Main Menu


MAIN     SIMULATE        DISTRIBUTION  QUIT
         choose          choose        choose
         {INITIAL}       {DIST}        {QUIT}
         {BRANCH SIMULATE}{MENUCALL DISPLAY}        Goto SIMULATE/DISPLAY


SIMULATE {GETNUMBER "Enter No. of Runs ? ",RUNS} No of Runs in R15
         {GOTO}START~                               Results area
         {FOR COUNTER,0,STOP,1,SIMTRIAL}            Sim trial loop
         {GOTO}START~                               End of loop, back to top
         /RNCNPV~{BS}.{END}{DOWN}~{RIGHT}           Name 1st results NPV
         /RNCIRR~{BS}.{END}{DOWN}~{LEFT}            Name 2nd results IRR
         /RNCSTART~{BS}~{BRANCH \M}


SIMTRIAL /RVTRIAL~~{DOWN}                           Copy trial result down


INITIAL  {GOTO}B23~/RNCSTART~~                      Name ranges: START B23
         /RNCTRIAL~M13.N13~                         TRIAL M13..N13
         /RNCRUNS~R15~                              RUNS R15
         /REB23..DC192~                             Clear previous results


DIST     {GOTO}BIN~                                 BIN starts in E23
         /DDNPV~BIN~                                Distribution of NPV


DISPLAY                                             Display Menu

         GRAPH           MAIN MENU     QUIT
         See Graph       Start Again   Finish
         {GOTO}SHOW~     {BRANCH \M}   {QUIT}       Unfreeze windows
         {WINDOWSON}                                Display pre-set graph
         /GNUGVALS~Q                                GVALS, or Return to
         {BRANCH \M}                                Main Menu
```

Figure 9.17   Macros for Novaduct simulation

1. Activate the macro sequence by pressing the Alt and M keys together.
2. Choose the SIMULATE option from the menu.
3. Choose a reasonable number of runs, say 50 or 100, and wait for the processing to finish. The results build up below cells B23 and C23.
4. Choose DISTRIBUTION then GRAPH. You should be presented with a cumulative probability curve of the Net Present Value for the venture.

Figure 9.18 shows one such NPV distribution based on the pooled results of 100 simulation trials. As with Alexsville, if you want a printout of your NPV graph, the best approach is to QUIT from the simulation model, press the Graph key (f10) to get the graph on screen and then press PrintScreen. You may also wish to print out the summary statistics for the NPV distribution which are stored in cells I24 to I29.

After the simulation, the worksheet also contains the values for the Internal Rate of Return for each trial. The IRR values are stored in cells C23 and below. They have been 'named' IRR within the simulation. Their summary statistics such as mean and standard deviation have been evaluated (in cells O24 and below). A layout for working out their distribution exists in the worksheet in the area below K21..P21. Column K contains the 'bin values', that is the bounds of the intervals or 'bins' into which all the IRR values are to be allocated and counted. These counts, one for each bin, make up the frequency distribution.

To get the frequency distribution and hence a graph of the cumulative probability distribution for the IRR values, do as follows:

5. Point to cell K23, which is at the head of the 'bin range' for the IRR distribution.
6. Get the frequency distribution of the IRR values with:

/ Data Distribution

Specify the 'values range' as IRR and the 'bin range' as K23..K38.

This command sequence gives the frequency distribution of IRR values in column L and the cumulative frequencies in column M.

7. View the graph of IRR values by using a previously named graph called GVALSIRR, with the commands:

/ Graph Name Use GVALSIRR

Figure 9.19 shows the graph of IRR values taken from the same 100 run simulation whose results on NPV were shown in Figure 9.18.

The graphs show that the probability of a positive Net Present Value (and also an IRR that exceeds 15 per cent) is greater than 70 per cent. The expected NPV and IRR values are estimated to be £650000 and 22 per cent, respectively. The estimates (based on the 100 simulation runs) come from the Summary Statistics stored in columns I and O, one page down in the worksheet. These NPV and IRR results are not quite as good as the measures based on single-point estimates. Modelling the uncertainty in the market for Novaduct has given management a more comprehensive picture of possible outcomes and a measure of the sensitivity of the NPV and IRR to this uncertainty.

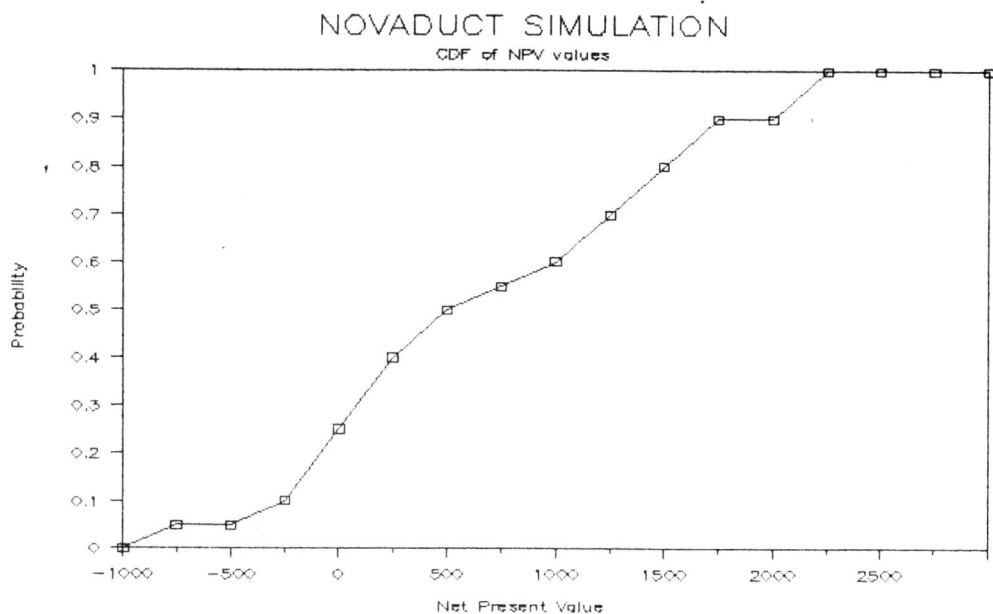

Figure 9.18   Distribution of Net Present Value (results from 100 simulation trials)

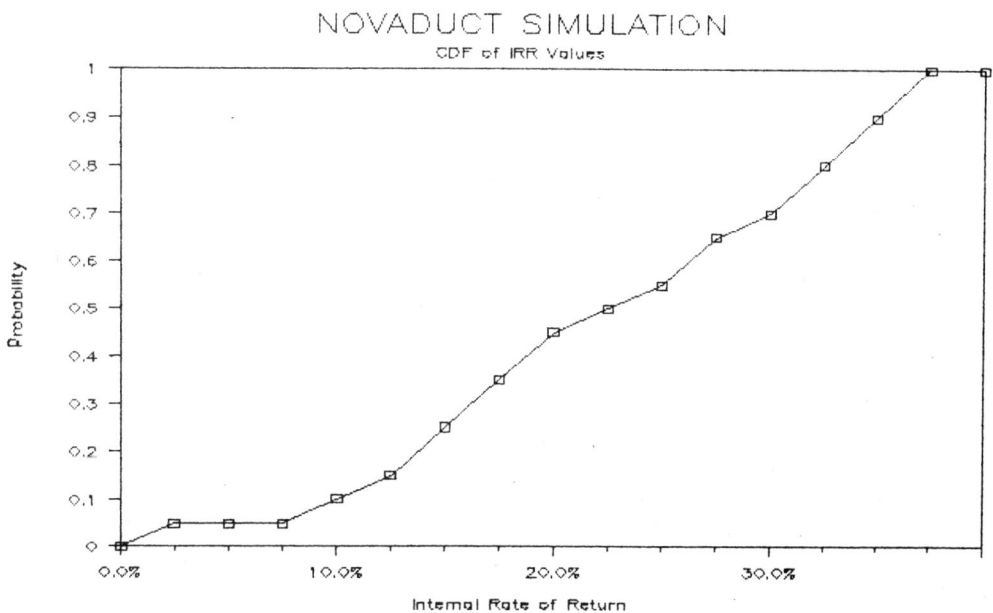

Figure 9.19   Distribution of Internal Rate of Return (results from 100 simulation trials)

Appendix

Lotus 1-2-3 (Release 2): Main Command Menu

Worksheet commands(/W)

Global   Sets overall spreadsheet settings such as formats, column width, protection and printing setups for size of page and type of printer.

Insert   Inserts a column or (row) to left (or above) current pointer position.

Delete   Deletes one or more rows or columns.

Column width   Sets the column width for an individual column.

Erase   Erases the entire worksheet and its global settings.

Titles   Freezes selected rows and or columns on the display screen so that they will always be on the screen.

Window   Displays two sections of the spreadsheet.

Status   Displays the global settings of the spreadsheet.

Range commands(/R)

Format   Format cells within a specified range. Formats include a fixed number of decimals, scientific format and various currencies.

Erase   Erase a specified range of cells.

Name   Name a specified range of cells. Any useful name can be provided such as Sales or Profits.

Protect   Protect a specified range of cells from being written over.

Value   Copies a range of entries converting formulas to values.

Copy command(/C)

Copies cell entries to new locations. This is useful for replicating formulas such as a January closing cash to months February through to December.

Move command(/M)

Moves a block of one or more cells to a new location.

File commands(/F)

Retrieve   Loads a spreadsheet into the computer's memory from a disc.

Save   Stores spreadsheet currently in computer memory to disc.

Combine   Loads a part of a spreadsheet from disc into the spreadsheet currently in the computer's memory. This is useful for combining reports from a variety of sources such as salespersons in different territories. (Equivalently, **Xtract** stores part of a spreadsheet to disc.)

Erase   Erase one or more spreadsheets stored on a datadisc.

Print commands(/P)

Printer or File Specify if output is to be directed to the printer or to a disc file for printing later, or use with another program.

Range   Specify the portion of the spreadsheet to be printed.

Options   Set printer options for margins, headers and footers, page length and printer control characters for compressed print.

Go   Actually print the specified range.

Graph commands(/G)

Type Select the type of graph: pie, bar, stacked bar, line or XY.

X A B C D E F Select one of these seven letters to specify location ranges for up to seven sets of data on the spreadsheet (the X range corresponding to labels or values for the horizontal axis).

Options Set graph options including titles, legends for data sets, graph title and colours.

View Display the graph.

Save Save the graph on a datadisc for use with the PrintGraph option in the Lotus 1-2-3 Access System. These graphs can be printed on a printer or plotter.

Name Keep the graph settings for different graphs.

Data commands (/D)

Sort Arranges a range of rows in ascending or descending order based on the order in a 'primary-key' column and an optional 'secondary-key' column.

Query Selects specific records in the spreadsheet satisfying a stated criterian; for example select records for specific salespersons or customers.

Regression Carry out regression analysis.

Distribution Calculate a frequency distribution.

System command(/S)

Exit temporarily to DOS the disc operating system.

Quit command(/Q)

Ends 1-2-3 session.

Index

175